KERRVILLE MOUNTAIN SUN

and

KERRVILLE ADVANCE

T E X A S

Obituary and Death Notice Index

1898–1965

Compiled by

Gloria Clifton Dozier

HERITAGE BOOKS
2015

HERITAGE BOOKS

AN IMPRINT OF HERITAGE BOOKS, INC.

Books, CDs, and more—Worldwide

For our listing of thousands of titles see our website
at
www.HeritageBooks.com

Published 2015 by
HERITAGE BOOKS, INC.
Publishing Division
5810 Ruatan Street
Berwyn Heights, Md. 20740

Heritage Books by the author:
Kerr County, Texas Birth Records
Kerr County, Texas Death Records, 1903–1960
Kerr County, Texas Divorce Records, 1856–1990
Kerr County, Texas Land Records, 1837–1927, Volume 1, A-K
Kerr County, Texas Land Records, 1837–1927, Volume 2, L-Z
Kerr County, Texas Probate Records, 1856–2002
Kerrville Daily Times *Obituary Books, 1986–2000, Master Index*
Kerrville Daily Times *Obituary Index, 1925–April 30, 1979*
Kerrville Mountain Sun *and* Kerrville Advance
Obituary and Death Notice Index, 1898–1965

International Standard Book Numbers
Paperbound: 978-0-7884-0898-4
Clothbound: 978-0-7884-6124-8

Foreword

The first section of this book is the 1898-1929 obituaries from the KERRVILLE MOUNTAIN SUN AND THE KERRVILLE ADVANCE. The ADVANCE went out of business by 1920 leaving the MOUNTAIN SUN as the only local paper for a number of years.

I am always suspicious of any of these early papers that are over 8 pages in length. There may have been two weeks' papers put together as one during the filming. This is especially true before 1920.

The 1929 papers start with January 17th issue.

There are only three 1921 papers.

1923 starts with June 21st paper.

The second section of the book is made up of notices and obituaries from the MOUNTAIN SUN. This section covers the period from 1930 through 1985. Each year is done separately and the names are in alphabetical order. At times the spelling of the names in the paper was rather creative!

Symbols used:

PG--Page number
FL--Film number
/ --Indicates the word AND, i.e. 4/8 means found on page 4 and page 8 OR
          if under Section, it means it is found in both section 4 and section 8.
S + number --Section of paper
Sec.--Section of paper

March 1997   Gloria Clifton Dozier

INDEX

NAME	DATE			PG	FM
Abell, A. C.	Jun 13	1929		3	13
Acree, Mrs. A. Z.	May 15	1924		1	10
Adams, Flora	Apr 21	1927		3	12
Adams, John	Apr 21	1927		3	12
Adams, T. J.	Feb 3	1927		2	12
Adams, Tom	Feb 3	1927		8	12
Adams, Mrs. Walter	Apr 14	1927		1	12
Adams, Mrs. Walter	Apr 21	1927		3	12
Adams, son of Mrs. Walter	Apr 14	1927		1	12
Adanson, John Hughs	Mar 5	1926		1	11
Adden, Alice Lockitt	Jun 1	1915		1	3
Ahr, Mrs. Joe (Rosa Sophie Wolcken)	Sep 6	1928		7	12
Albe, Frank	Apr 24	1915		1	63*
*Old front page in February 3, 1982 issue of Mt. Sun.					
Albrecht, Paul	Nov 26	1925		6	11
Alby, Frank	Apr 22	1915		1	3
Alderman, Mrs. John H.	Feb 28	1924		3	10
Alexander, Bertie	Jul 15	1926		7	11
Alexander, Della	Feb 13	1913		1	3
Alexander, child of Lum	Jul 29	1926		11	11
Alexander, Mary	Mar 15	1928		1	12
Alexander, R. C. (Ben)	Apr 1	1926		11	11
Alexander, W. J. D. (Dr.)	Mar 17	1927		8	12
Allen, Carl F.	Dec 27	1923		1	10
Allen, W. W.	Sep 25	1913		1	3
Allen, W. W.	Sep 27	1913		1	9
Allerkamp, Henry	Jan 14	1899		1	1
Allstrom, Mrs. Oliver	Dec 19	1908		3	4
Allstrom, Mrs. Oliver	Dec 19	1908		5	7
Altgelt, George Conrad	Nov 27	1924		8	10
Anaya, Teresita	Mar 7	1914		1	62*
*Old front page in October 3, 1981 issue of Mt. Sun.					
Anderson, Mrs. Arthur	Mar 19	1920		2	9
Anderson, daughter of Bud	Jun 2	1922		8	10
Anderson, Everett L.	Jun 16	1909		1	2/6
Anderson, Everett L.	Jun 19	1909		1	7
Anderson, Mrs. J. H.	Jun 25	1925		10	11
Anderson, James	Jun 5	1909		7	7
Anderson, Mrs. M. O.	Sep 6	1917		1	3
Anderson, Marguerite	Nov 13	1924		5	10

NAME	DATE		PG	FM
Anderson, Ottie	Mar 6	1909	7	4
Anderson, Ottie	Mar 6	1909	3	7
Anderson, Richard	Oct 8	1904	4	4
Anderson, W. C.	Oct 30	1909	1	5/7
Anderson, Mrs. W. C.	Dec 30	1921	6/7	10
Andrews, Edde	Jun 25	1925	10	11
Andrews, Louis	Jan 13	1927	3	12
Andrews, Samuel G.	Sep 12	1929	1	13
Angel, Mrs. M. A.	Nov 3	1927	5	12
Archer, Mrs. W. T.	Feb 12	1925	7	11
Armstron, Carrie Belde	Feb 4	1926	10	11
Armstrong, George R.	Nov 25	1905	3	4
Arnett, George	Oct 10	1908	6	5/7
Arnold, Grant H.	Jul 31	1909	1	5/7
Aronsohn, Miss	Apr 29	1899	1	1
Arreola, Aleaido	May 5	1927	7	12
Arreola, Alejandro	Aug 2	1913	2/5	9
Arreola, Roque	Oct 24	1918	8	3
Arriola, Alex (Jr.)	Jul 31	1913	1	3
Arriola, Georgia C.	May 5	1927	3	12
Ashburn, Mrs. Louis (Josephine)	Aug 2	1928	1	12
Ashcroft, L. J. (Thanks)	Jan 17	1914	2	9
Ashworth, Arthur	Jan 10	1924	5	10
Atkison, G. F.	Aug 9	1923	3	10
Aubey, Mrs. Horace	Apr 7	1922	3	10
Auld, Mrs. A. K. (Susan Lowrance)	Dec 31	1925	1	11
Autry, J. H.	Mar 18	1926	3	11
Autry, Lela Mc Elroy	Oct 24	1918	1	3
Ayala, Beatrice	Jul 4	1929	5	13
Ayala, Daniel	Nov 7	1929	7	13
Ayala, Mrs. Hippolite (Juanita Lopez)	Oct 14	1926	7	11
Ayala, Jennie M.	Dec 6	1928	1	12
Ayala, John Gregory (Estate)	Aug 27	1925	9	11
Ayala, Mrs. Luis	Aug 12	1926	7	11
Babb, Burnet	Apr 21	1927	3	12
Babb, Burnett	Apr 14	1927	1	12
Babineaux, Annie R.	May 23	1929	1	13
Babineaux, Mrs. Edwin	Jan 19	1928	5	12
Babineaux, Wilson	Mar 8	1929	1	12

NAME	DATE		PG	FM
Babineaux, Wilson	Mar 15	1928	7	12
Bacon, C. P.	Oct 6	1906	2	4
Baccus, Miss Pinckney	Aug 9	1902	4	4
Bailey, J. T.	Dec 6	1928	6	12
Bailey, Mrs. L. J. (Thanks)	Apr 1	1926	7	11
Bailey, W. T. (Dr.)	Apr 26	1928	1	12
Baker, Bill	Oct 15	1914	1	8
Baker, Cad	Nov 11	1915	1	3
Baker, Mrs. Cad	Nov 11	1915	1	3
Baker, Caleb W.	May 14	1925	3	11
Baker, Charles	Apr 14	1927	1	12
Baker, Charles	Apr 21	1927	3	12
Baker, Nolan	Oct 30	1909	9	5/7
Baker, Myrtle Carruthers	Mar 5	1925	4	11
Baker, Pit--child of	Apr 10	1913	1	3
Baker, Sarah L.	Jan 23	1909	5	4/7
Baker, Sidney	Nov 14	1918	1	3
Baker, T. O.--baby of	Mar 1	1917	9	3
Baker, Mrs. Walter	Nov 4	1926	2	11
Baldwin, Arbie	Nov 1	1923	1	10
Baldwin, Grandma (Eleanor)	Feb 15	1917	6	3
Baldwin, H. M.	Aug 4	1927	1	12
Baldwin, H. Maxwell	Jul 28	1927	1/9	12
Baldwin, Lettie Olivia	Jun 19	1913	1	3
Baldwin, Oliva	Jun 21	1913	9	9
Baldwin, Peter	Jan 14	1915	1	3
Baldwin, Mrs. T. S.	Aug 5	1926	9	11
Ballard, J. W.	Mar 13	1909	3	4/7
Banning, Marvin	Mar 14	1929	1	13
Banties, child of Dave	Oct 24	1908	2	5/7
Barez, J. B. (Rev.)	Jan 23	1920	3	9
Barnes, Billy	Jan 14	1926	2	11
Barnes, Billy	Jan 21	1926	3	11
Barnes, G. A.	Feb 28	1909	3	5/7
Barnes, G. A. (Thanks)	Apr 3	1909	5	7
Barnes, George A. (Exec.'s Note)	Apr 21	1909	5	6
Barnes, George A. (Exec.'s Note)	Apr 23	1909	5	2
Barnes, son of Henry	Sep 13	1917	4	3
Barnes, Mrs. W. I.	Jun 24	1926	2	11
Barry, Eugene	May 9	1929	1	13

3

NAME	DATE		PG	FM
Barry, Mary Therese (Mrs. Jim)	Dec 20	1928	5	12
Bartel, Adolph	Sep 16	1916	1	62*
*Printed in September 5, 1981 issue of the Mountain Sun.				
Bartles, J. H.	Jan 25	1908	5	5
Bartley, J. T.	Aug 4	1927	1	12
Barton, Gretna	Jul 22	1905	4	4
Barton, Jesse	Sep 20	1902	2	4
Barton, Mrs. S. M.	Dec 11	1909	1	5
Barton, Mrs. S. M.	Dec 18	1909	4	5
Basse, Udo	Jan 28	1899	1	1
Bassett, Mrs. -- Haralson (Thanks)	Apr 27	1907	8	4
Bassett, J. A.	Dec 23	1926	8	11
Bate, Lois	Apr 6	1907	4	4
Bates, Lutie L.	Aug 14	1914	1	3
Bauer, Joe	Feb 18	1926	7	11
Bauman, Mrs. Edmund	Apr 16	1920	5	9
Bausch, Aleen Cecilia	Nov 17	1927	6	12
Bean, Tilford (Sr.)	Jan 31	1918	1	3
Bear, Joseph F.	Oct 9	1909	1	7
Beard, Christine B.	Dec 12	1929	1	13
Beard, Mrs. J. C.	Dec 3	1920	1	9
Beard, son of Mr/Mrs Lon Beard	Apr 2	1920	5	9
Bearden, father of F. E.	Mar 19	1925	3	11
Beasley, Kennon	Jun 11	1920	4	9
Beasley, Leslie (Sr.)	Jun 16	1927	1	12
Beastead, Liza	May 30	1929	1	13
Beauchamp, Delemeaty	Dec 5	1929	1	13
Beckman, Ferdinand	Jul 1	1916	3	9
Beckmann, Henry	Nov 26	1914	1	3
Beitel, Annie	Mar 4	1926	5	11
Beitel, Charles F.	Sep 24	1925	1	11
Belder, Peter	Dec 16	1905	2	4
Beller, Mrs. J. P.	Jan 19	1928	5	12
Bellinger, E. C.	May 6	1899	1	1
Bellinger, E. C.	May 13	1899	4	1
Below, Paul	Apr 26	1902	4	2
Below, Sr., Otto	May 19	1909	5	6/7
Below, Sr., Otto	May 22	1909	5	5/7
Benedick, Jerome	Oct 4	1928	7	12
Bennett, Estelle	Jul 14	1922	6	10

4

KERRVILLE MOUNTAIN SUN AND KERRVILLE ADVANCE
1898-1929

NAME	DATE	PG	FM
Bennett, Nellie M.	Nov 24 1922	5	10
Benson, Bill	Jul 4 1929	1	13
Benson, Ira	Aug 2 1923	7	10
Benson, Minnie Mae	Mar 31 1927	4	12
Benson, Mrs. Noah J.	Mar 22 1902	4	4
Benson, Naoh J.	Jan 9 1913	1	3
Benedick, Jerome	Oct 4 1928	7	12
Benton, A.	Sep 20 1928	1	12
Benton, Ab.	Sep 27 1928	3	12
Benton, W. C. (Thanks)	Oct 13 1922	3	10
Benton, William Counts	Nov 10 1922	5	10
Berger, Mrs. W. C.	May 25 1916	1	3
Berger, Willie Raymond	Sep 29 1927	15	12
Bernhardt, Chester John	May 13 1910	1	7
Biehler, C. L.	Dec 13 1917	1	3
Bien, Mrs. M. A.	May 9 1913	1	3
Bierschwale, Andrew J.	Nov 14 1908	4	7
Bierschwale, Conrad	Dec 20 1928	6	12
Bierschwale, Ella Delavan	May 14 1914	1	8
Bierschwale, Mrs. H. W.	Mar 15 1917	1	3
Bietorio, Francisco	Nov 3 1922	2	10
Biles, Clyde M.	Nov 7 1918	1	3
Billings, Carra W.	May 29 1928	3	12
Billings, Etta Jane	Apr 21 1927	3	12
Billings, Mrs. S. E.	Nov 13 1924	6	10
Billings, Sybil	Apr 14 1927	1	12
Billings, Sybil	Apr 21 1927	3	12
Billingsly, Brother	Jan 23 1909	2	5/7
Bingham, Mrs. L. K.	Feb 9 1907	4	4
Bird, Rosa	Mar 9 1907	7/8	4
Black, A. B.	Jan 17 1929	2	13
Blair, Thomas	Apr 2 1910	1	7
Blanchard, Hugo	Oct 25 1918	1	9
Blackburn, Aime	Apr 23 1925	1	11
Blackburn, Louis	Oct 1 1925	6	11
Blackburn, Mrs. Louis	Oct 1 1925	6	11
Blackwell, John G.	Oct 18 1928	1	12
Blanks, Eugene	Jul 29 1899	1	1
Blaschke, Willie	Jul 16 1920	3	9
Blevins, Mrs. Gluthe Stidhorne	Apr 15 1926	3	11

NAME	DATE		PG	FM
Blum, Katie Ruth Peterson	Dec 15	1922	1/3	10
Boatwright, Jesse	Mar 1	1902	5	4
Boatwright, Jesse	Mar 8	1902	2	4
Bobbitt, Eric B.	Mar 22	1928	6	12
Bode, Esther (Thanks)	Oct 3	1918	1	3
Boeckmann, Jim	Jan 13	1922	6	10
Boelhauwe, Jennie Wahrmund	Sep 22	1922	2	10
Boerner, William	Feb 12	1925	8	11
Bohnert, A.	Jan 17	1903	2	4
Bolen, Will M.	Jan 19	1928	1/9	12
Bond, Mary Alice	Feb 8	1902	10*	4

*This woman died January 1903, but the issues of the
January 31, 1903 and the February 8, 1902 papers have
been mixed together when photo-copying so it appears
that the notice is on page 10 of the February 1902 paper

NAME	DATE		PG	FM
Bonnell, Charlotte F.	Jan 16	1919	1	3
Bonnell, Mrs. F. S.	Jan 10	1919	5	9
Boon, J. A.	Jun 9	1922	6	10
Booth, C. W.	Feb 19	1925	1	11
Booth, Charles Whitney	Feb 19	1925	3	11
Bossy, Coleman	Oct 20	1906	3	4
Bossy, Mrs. L. R.	Apr 20	1907	1	4
Bosquez, Amadeo	Apr 24	1924	5	10
Boudreaux, Willis	Oct 1	1920	3	9
Boulware, infant of Toni	Jun 19	1913	5	3
Bourland, Jim	Apr 21	1927	3	12
Bowers, Giles L.	Sep 30	1915	1	3
Bowers, Mrs. N. C. (Thanks)	Apr 3	1924	5	10
Bowker, Erwin	Feb 16	1907	5	4
Bowman, William D.	Oct 8	1925	4	11
Braden, A. B.	May 3	1928	1	12
Bradwell, T. M.	May 14	1920	8	9
Braeutigam, August	Aug 17	1916	1	3
Brambella, Ernest	Dec 17	1914	1	3
Brandon, J. B.	Mar 10	1922	1	10
Brandon, Claud	Dec 25	1913	4	8
Brantley, Dr. J. H.	Oct 20	1906	5	4
Brazeal, J. W.	May 7	1914	1	8
Breeding, Mrs. C. T.	Aug 23	1902	5	4
Breeding, D. S.	Aug 23	1902	5	4

NAME	DATE		PG	FM
Breihan, Bertha E.	Jan 10	1935	1	16
Bridge, Captain C. Z.	Dec 1	1913	1	8
Brice, Mrs. William	May 12	1922	3	10
(Mabel Ainsworth)				
Bridges, Joe	Aug 29	1929	7	13
Briggs, Thomas A.	Jul 15	1915	5	9
Brightwell, Lee	Sep 26	1914	4	9
Britt, W. D.	Jan 24	1929	8	13
Britton, John	May 13	1915	1	3
Broussard, D. L.	Oct 6	1927	3	12
Brown, Charles	Mar 21	1908	5	5/7
Brown, Charles B.	Jan 20	1922	5	10
Brown, Charles Douglas	Dec 13	1928	5	12
Brown, Mrs. Charles E.	Mar 8	1928	1	12
Brown, Elmer	Mar 29	1928	10	12
Brown, F. A.	Dec 23	1921	6	10
Brown, Georgia	Oct 11	1917	3	3
Brown, John Willis (Thanks)	Feb 21	1924	10	10
Brown, Nick	Feb 16	1907	2	4
Brown, Thomas	Jun 17	1926	8	11
Brown, Mrs. W. S. (Maggie E.)	Jul 23	1925	3	11
Browne, Helen	Jun 20	1929	5	13
Bruff, Gladys	Oct 13	1906	7	4
Buck, Arthur	Jan 30	1920	6	9
Buckelew, L.B.C.	Jan 28	1923	4	10
Buckner, R. E. (Robert Emmett)	Oct 24	1918	4	3
Buckner, Robert Emmett	Oct 31	1918	1	3
Bullard, C. C.	May 29	1909	1	7
Bullard, Mrs. Jesse B	Jul 3	1924	5	10
Burdick, Charles	Sep 27	1902	5	4
Burch, Mrs. Laurance	Apr 9	1925	5	11
Burge, Mrs.	Nov 24	1906	2	4
Burge, Mrs. A. E.	Apr 5	1928	1	12
Burgess, John E.	Jan 17	1929	6	13
Burhans, Mrs. B. M.	Dec 26	1929	1	13
Burke, Erma L.	Sep 13	1923	6	10
Burkett, George	Jun 16	1909	1	2/6
Burkett, R. S.	Jul 8	1905	4	4
Burkhalter, Mrs. F. J.	Jan 23	1919	1	3

NAME	DATE			PG	FM
Burks, J. J.	Sep 6	1898		6	10*
*Found in May 5, 1922 Mt. Sun					
Burks, John	Feb 25	1899		1	1
Burks, John J.	Mar 11	1899		1	1
Burks, Mrs. Willie	Apr 16	1910		1	7
Burleson, Ed	Oct 3	1913		1	3
Burleson, William Eddie	Oct 4	1918		1	9
Burnett, Dixie	Aug 27	1909		1	5/7
Burnett, Elwood	Jul 17	1913		1	3
Burnett, James R.	May 3	1917		1	3
Burnett, Mrs. Julia	Aug 29	1929		12	13
Burnett, W. W.	Sep 15	1922		2	10
Burney, H. M.	Apr 29	1915		1	3
Burney, Hance Mc Cain	Apr 24	1915		1	63*
*Found in February 3 1982 of Mt Sun on old front page.					
Burney, Mrs. Lee	Jul 23	1920		4	9
Burney, Mc Cain	Sep 6	1917		1	3
Burney, Mary A.	May 21	1925		1	11
Burney, Percy Clitus	Sep 9	1915		1	3
Burney, Mattie Prather (Mrs. R. H.)	Mar 19	1914		1	8
Burney, Mattie Prather	Mar 2 ?	1914		6	9
Burney, Mrs. R. H.	Dec 30	1905		2	4
Burney, Robert H.	Apr 8	1926		1	11
Burney, Robert L.	Aug 23	1928		1	12
Burns, Mrs.	Feb 13	1909		5	5/7
Burris, Miss C-----na	Jul 15	1899		1	1
Burriss, Willaim	Sep 2	1899		4	1
Burton, Mrs. A. B.	Sep 10	1920		3/4	9
Burton, Mrs. Alice L.	Oct 8	1920		12	9
Busch,Sr., F. L.	Aug 14	1909		5	5/7
Busch,Sr., F. L.	Aug 14	1909		4	7
Busby, J. W.	May 27	1905		5	4
Bushong, Dottie	Mar 25	1915		1	3
Butler, Mrs. C. H.	Dec 12	1929		1	13
Butler, M. F.	Sep 11	1909		1	5/7
Butt, C. C. (Sr.)	Mar 13	1915		1	9
Butt, Charles C.	Mar 11	1915		4	3
Butt, Charles C.	Apr 1	1926		1	11
Buttimer, Mrs.	Jul 15	1915		2	9
Byas, Joseph	Apr 30	1925		12	11

NAME	DATE		PG	FM
Byas, Leonard	May 6	1926	10	11
Byrd, Sampson	Apr 14	1927	11	12
Byron, Annie Cardine	Oct 18	1918	1	9
Byrum, Mrs. A. C.	Oct 17	1918	1	3
Cabazos, Salvador	Aug 11	1927	7	12
Caddel, Mart	Jul 1	1905	2	4
Cadell, Russell	May 30	1929	1	13
Caldana, Victor	Apr 21	1927	3	12
Cain, Marvin Victor	Mar 29	1928	1	12
Calderon, I.	Apr 29	1926	5	11
Caldwell, Mrs. W. R.	Feb 14	1918	1	3
Callahan, Andrew Jackson	Jan 19	1928	1	12
Calley, father of J. S.	Mar 8	1928	2	12
Campa, Adolph	Mar 1	1928	8	12
Campbell, J. C.	Nov 11	1899	4	1
Campbell, T. T.	Mar 5	1925	1	11
Campos, Martin	Feb 27	1920	1	9
Canafax, John Taylor (Estate)	Oct 23	1924	7	10
Cannon, Ada	Feb 24	1922	6	10
Canfield, J. E.	Nov 20	1924	2	10
Canfield, King	Jul 5	1928	1	12
Cantwell, son of Earl	Jan 14	1926	9	11
Cantwell, son of Earl	Jan 21	1926	9	11
Cantwell, Lou Ella	Mar 5	1914	1	8
Cantu, Esther	Jan 21	1926	5	11
Cararnza, Marguerite	May 7	1925	5	11
Carlisle, H.J.	Apr 28	1927	1	12
Carmack, S. V. (Samuel V.)	Oct 27	1927	1	12
Carmichael, Loss L.	Jul 15	1915	1	3
Carpenter, Effie	Nov 15	1902	4	4
Carpenter, F. W.	Oct 22	1914	1	3
Carpenter, H. L.	Sep 25	1924	1	10
Carpenter, Wheeler G.	May 23	1929	1	13
Carr, Ella	Feb 16	1907	7	4
Carr, Ella (Thanks)	Feb 23	1907	8	4
Carr, Eleanore Margaret	Dec 31	1914	1	3
Carr, James M.	Mar 24	1927	1	12
Carr, Mary	Apr 4	1918	1	3
Carrico, Mae Ama	Jul 5	1923	5	10
Carrico, Marcellus W.	Jul 12	1923	5	10

NAME	DATE		PG	FM
Carrington, C. T.	Oct 13	1927	2	12
Carson, Ima Alleen	Aug 9	1928	4	12
Carson, Jim	Dec 27	1928	1	13
Case, Roy A.	Aug 8	1929	11	13
Casey, Walter	Jan 2	1913	1	3
Castello, Frank J.	Nov 6	1898	6	10*
*Found in May 5, 1922 Mt. Sun				
Castillo, Emrique	Oct 16	1924	5	10
Castillo, Paul	May 5	1927	1	12
Castillo, Teresa	May 14	1925	5	11
Castillo, Teresa	May 21	1925	5	11
Caton, Ed	Oct 29	1920	6	9
Caton, Leonard	Oct 20	1922	2	10
Cavitt, Mrs. J. F.	Jan 10	1918	1	3
Cavitt, Texana	Feb 7	1918	3	3
Chamber, L. A.	Jun 28	1928	11	12
Chapman, Curtis L.	Aug 13	1927	1	12
Chapman, Rinda C. (Estate Notice)	Apr 11	1903	2	4
Charcon, Carlos	Feb 25	1910	3	7
Charles, Victor	Feb 2	1928	1	12
Childs, Myra Gene	Nov 15	1928	1	12
Childs, Elmira Branch	Jan 2	1920	3	9
Chilton, Mrs. Carl	Oct 29	1925	10	11
Ching, William Charles	Jan 12	1928	7	12
Christian, C.B. (Thanks)	May 4	1916	1	3
Ciomperich, Mr.-----	Oct 14	1926	7	11
Clapp, Rev. H. B.	Jan 15	1914	1	8
Clapp, Rev. H. B.	Jan 17	1914	5	9
Clark, Amasa	Feb 3	1927	8	12
Clark, C. Lloyd	Oct 11	1928	7	12
Clark, Helene	Jul 12	1928	7	12
Clark, J. B.	Dec 30	1926	1	11
Clark, mother of J. M.	Oct 11	1928	11	12
Clark, Janie	Dec 26	1929	1	13
Clark, Loyd	Jan 30	1909	2	5/7
Clark, Loyd (Thanks)	Feb 13	1909	3	5
Clark, Robert	Aug 2	1923	7	10
Clayton, H. C.	May 3	1918	4	3
Clayton, H. C.	May 3	1918	1	9
Clayton, Mrs. J. W.	Mar 30	1907	8	4

NAME	DATE		PG	FM
Clements, W. C.	Aug 30	1928	1	12
Clemmons, Howell	Jul 11	1929	7	13
Click, Mrs. Cecil May (Thanks)	Mar 26	1920	5	9
Cloudt, Mrs. Frank	Dec 2	1915	1	3
Cluck, Hollis B.	Nov 8	1928	4	12
Coats, Agnes	May 13	1926	11	11
Cobb, George	Jun 3	1926	7	11
Cobb, Lomax	Aug 6	1914	1	8
Cobb, Mrs S. B.	Jan 20	1916	5	3
Cochran, Martin Bruce	Jul 21	1922	1	10
Cocke, Mrs. Turley	Mar 12	1914	1	8
Codrington, Thomas O.	Dec 1	1927	5	12
Codrington, Tom	Dec 15	1927	5	12
Coffee, John L.	Nov 7	1929	8	13
Cohron, R. A. (Rev.)	Feb 7	1918	1	3
Coke, Mrs.	Apr 17	1909	7	5/7
Colbath, infant son of A. J.	Apr 12	1928	9	12
Colbath, mother of Moulton	May 17	1928	11	12
Coldwell, Emeline Moore	Mar 31	1906	8	4
Coldwell, Neal	Nov 12	1925	6	11
Coleman, son of B. J.	Jul 1	1926	1	S2 11
Coleman, David	Jan 24	1929	1	13
Coleman, Francis Henderson	Jul 12	1917	1	3
Coleman, Frank R.	Aug 11	1927	1	12
Coleman, Mrs. Green	Feby 16	1907	8	4
Coleman, Green H.	May 20	1915	1	3
Coleman, Jesse	Mar 25	1915	3	3
Coleman, Milton	Oct 6	1927	1	12
Coleman, Sallie	Mar 20	1909	2	5/7
Coleman, Sallie	Mar 27	1909	7	5
Coleman, Sallie	Mar 27	1909	9	7
Comparette, Mrs. D. H.(Lula Hankins)	Jul 23	1925	1	11
Comparette, T. Louis (Dr.)	Jul 21	1922	2	10
Compton, Mrs. M. A.	Apr 9	1925	6	11
Conn, Thomas (Thanks)	Mar 16	1907	4	4
Consolata, Sister M.	May 21	1920	3	9
Conwill, Luther	Jul 9	1914	1	8
Cook, Mrs. J. R.	Nov 12	1925	6	11
Cook, Martha	Aug 7	1913	1	3
Cook, Martha	Aug 9	1913	1	9

NAME	DATE		PG	FM
Cooksey, Jeff	Aug 7	1924	8	10
Cooksey, Mahala (Estate)	Jan 15	1925	8	11
Cooney, Will	Aug 21	1924	5	10
Cooper, H. C.	Dec 23	1926	1	11
Cooper, Mrs. H. M.	Mar 17	1922	7	10
Cooper, J. M.	Aug 8	1929	1	13
Copenhaven, Robert Samuel	Dec 3	1925	8	11
Copple, Loren	Dec 4	1924	1	10
Corkill, Ed (Sr.)	Oct 7	1915	1	3
Corkill, Ed	Oct 16	1915	1	66*
*Found in the October 1, 1983 Mt. Sun.				
Corlyle, G. W.	May 2	1918	4	3
Cortez, Leoniday	May 10	1928	7	12
Cortez, Valenetina	May 31	1928	5	12
Cottle, Floyd	Nov 20	1909	1	5/7
Cottle, J. T.	Jun 15	1912	5	9
Cotton, J. A.	Aug 23	1928	1/7	12
Couch, A. G.	May 27	1926	5/6	11
Council, Leah Florence	Aug 19	1915	1	3
Council, Leah	Sep 18	1915	5	9
Council, Roxie Anna	Jan 3	1918	1	3
Council, William De Estrange	Jul 4	1908	5	5/7
Courand, Mrs. Poe	Feb 12	1925	5	11
Cowardine, R. C.	Jan 18	1908	2	5/7
Cowden, Jay	Jan 24	1918	1	3
Cowden, baby of Tolbert	Apr 14	1927	1	12
Cowden, Tolbert	Apr 14	1927	1	12
Cowden, Tolbert	Apr 21	1927	3	12
Cowden, Mrs. Tolbert	Apr 14	1927	1	12
Cowden, Mrs. Tolbert	Apr 21	1927	3	12
Cowen, Louis	Apr 25	1903	4	4
Cowsert, Mrs. Ed	Apr 17	1924	7	10
Cox, D. C.	Mar 11	1905	4	4
Cox, Mrs. D. C.	Dec 3	1920	6/7	9
Cox, Mrs. Fred	Jul 3	1925	3	11
Cox, Mrs. J. A.	Apr 22	1899	1	1
Cox, J. T.	Jan 15	1914	1	8
Cox, J. T.	Jan 17	1914	5	9
Cox, Mrs. W. Fred	Jul 9	1925	2	11
Craig, Charles	Dec 20	1923	7	10

NAME	DATE		PG	FM
Craig, Thomas	Dec 20	1923	7	10
Crausbay, T. H.	Jan 14	1915	1	3
Cravey, Ben	Oct 17	1918	1	3
Cravey, Johnnie	Jul 8	1905	5	4
Crawford, Mose	Dec 26	1929	1	13
Creagh, Emily	Mar 7	1908	8	5/7
Crenshaw, Mrs. Carey	Mar 7	1908	8	5
Crenshaw, Nathan---son of	Jun 25	1910	1	7
Crenshaw, Nathan G.	Jan 23	1919	8	3
Crider, Frank Edgar	Aug 18	1927	5	12
Crider, Joe	May 20	1926	11	11
Crider, Milton	Apr 7	1927	5	12
Crider, Milton Claude	Aug 18	1927	7	12
Crider, Walter H. (Jr.)	Jul 30	1920	3	9
Crockett, E. B.	Mar 22	1902	2	4
Crockett, Lavenia M.	Mar 8	1902	5	4
Crofford, Melvina Henrietta	Jan 14	1915	1	3
Crook, R. L.	Nov 27	1924	5	10
Crotty, A. E. (Bert)	Jan 2	1913	1	3
Crotty, James (Estate Notice)	Jul 19	1923	4	10
Crowder, W. H.	Sep 10	1920	1	9
Crowfoot, ---	Apr 11	1918	8	3
Cruce, Mabel Lowrance	Oct 27	1927	1	12
Cuhlek, Pvt. Carl L.	May 28	1920	7	9
Cummings, M.	Jun 5	1909	1	5/7
Cunningham, J.H.	Nov 27	1909	2	5/7
Curtis, son of Louis	Jun 3	1926	7	11
Dacy, Emilye	Sep 12	1908	4	5/7
Dacy, Emilye (Thanks)	Sep 12	1908	1	5/7
Dallahite, Mattie	Apr 14	1927	1	12
Dallahite, Mattie	Apr 21	1927	3	12
Dallahite, R.	Apr 14	1927	1	12
Dallahite, R.	Apr 21	1927	3	12
Darby, J. D.	Nov 26	1920	1	9
Davenport, John	Oct 9	1913	1	3
Davey, Mrs. Ben A. (Martha Miranda)	Jun 19	1924	1	10
Davies, W. P.	Jan 14	1899	1	1
Davis, Blake	Oct 17	1913	4	3
Davis, Elvira	Jul 30	1914	1	8
Davis, J. H.	Aug 8	1908	7	5

NAME	DATE		PG	FM
Davis, J. H.	Aug 8	1908	5	7
Davis, J. H.	Aug 15	1908	7	5
Davis, Nat F.	Feb 24	1906	14	4
Davis, Mrs. N.S.	Dec 23	1905	8	4
Davis, Randolph	Jul 2	1920	1	9
Davis, Ruth Evitt	Oct 7	1926	12	11
Day, Hugo F.	Nov 21	1929	1	13
Dayries, Leonel	Dec 1	1927	5	12
Dean, son of Dale	Apr 28	1922	7	10
Deciur, A. J.	Dec 2	1915	1	3
Decker, Mrs. R. J.	May 19	1922	7	10
Deering, John T.	Apr 28	1927	1	12
Deinger, Elsie	Feb 25	1910	5	7
Delaney, Joe H. (Dr.)	Mar 13	1926	2	11
Demaline, Joseph	Feb 13	1909	7	7
de Martinez, Dolores Medina	Oct 11	1923	5	10
De Montel, Charles	Jun 28	1928	10	12
de Sandoval, Juana Gracia	Nov 10	1927	1	12
Denman, Dr. A. N.	Oct 3	1908	8	5
Dennis, Mrs. mother of J. M.	Mar 10	1927	11	12
Denny, B. F.	Apr 2	1910	1	7
Denton, Leonard	Apr 18	1913	1	3
Denton, Leonard	Apr 26	1918	1	9
Denton, Nora (Thanks)	Jan 22	1914	1	8
Derr, J. M.	Aug 1	1908	8	5
De Vore, Erline	Jan 5	1928	6	12
Dewees, Charles T.	Dec 12	1929	1	13
Dewees, J. E.	Oct 10	1918	8	3
Dewees, Kate H.	May 15	1924	10	10
Dewees, Nellie	Nov 10	1927	1	12
Dewees, Oscar S.	Jul 19	1928	1	12
De Woody, Lydia	Mar 26	1920	8	9
Dial, Otis L. (Thanks)	Jun 27	1929	4	5
Dickey, Charles	Feb 17	1927	5	12
Dickey, Dovie	Feb 14	1918	5	3
Dickey, Mrs. L. A.	May 17	1928	11	12
Dickey, Mrs. W. P.	Aug 8	1929	1	13
Dickinson, Mr.	Jun 3	1915	1	3 2nd
Dies, Martin	Jul 21	1922	1	10
Dies, Tom S.	Jul 4	1929	10	13

NAME	DATE		PG	FM
Dietert, Annie	Feb 1	1908	10	5
Dietert, Annie	Feb 1	1908	8	7
Dietert, Christian	May 31	1902	2	4
Dietert, Fred	Feb 14	1924	3	10
Dietert, Mrs. Fredericke Karger	Aug 27	1925	8	11
Dietert, Lloyd Elvin	Jul 1	1899	1	1
Dietert, Rosalie	Apr 11	1929	1	13
Dietrich, Edgar	Jan 21	1926	6	11
Dietrich, Hugo	Jan 21	1926	6	11
Dillard, Dr. W. J.	Oct 28	1905	2	4
Dille, Alvin	Jun 25	1920	1	9
Dillon, H. L.	Sep 1	1922	1	10
Dimaline, Joseph	Feb 13	1909	7	5
Dobbs, W. N.	Mar 28	1903	4	4
Dobson, J. W. (Walter)	Jul 16	1914	1	8
Dobson, Walter	Feb 4	1915	1	3
Doebbler, Louis	Sep 22	1922	7	10
Doebbler, Mrs. Richard	Dec 1	1922	5	10
Dolan, Robert	Jan 1	1926	5	11
Domingues, Didier J.	Aug 19	1926	2/7	11
Doty, Mrs. J. M.	Jul 31	1913	1	3
Doty, Mrs. J. M. (Thanks)	Aug 2	1913	1	9
Dowda, Celia A.	May 9	1918	1	3
Dowda, Laura	Aug 31	1916	1	3
Dowda, Russell Erwin	Oct 17	1918	1	3
Dowda, Russell Erwin	Oct 11	1918	1	9
Dowdy, Lee	Sep 18	1909	1	5/7
Dowdy, Louella	Nov 11	1915	1	3
Dowdy, Susan C.	Jul 19	1913	1	3
Dowdy, infant of Tarleton	Dec 3	1914	1	3
Dowdy, Mrs. Tarleton	Oct 28	1915	1	3
Doyle, P. H.	Jun 23	1927	1	12
Dozier, Edwill	Dec 10	1925	5	11
Dozier, P. H.	Jan 1	1918	1	3
Dozier, P. H.	Jan 10	1918	4	3
Dragoo, Ben	Feb 28	1929	8	13
Drake, Rev. S. J.	Dec 31	1914	1	3
Dress, Mrs. A. K.	Mar 19	1925	3	11
Drew, Pierce William	Jun 28	1917	1	3

NAME	DATE		PG	FM
Drummond, Mrs. James	Jul 10	1909	7	5/7
Drummond, Mrs. Jean S.	Jul 7	1909	8	2/6
Dryden, Alice	Oct 26	1926	1	11
Dryden, Alice	Nov 4	1926	7	11
Du Bose, Burl	Sep 20	1902	2	4
Du Bose, Mrs. Will	Mar 3	1927	11	12
Dubose, Dent	Aug 13	1925	9	11
Dubose, John H.	Sep 10	1910	5	7
Duderstadt, Henrietta Kennille	Jun 25	1914	1	8
Dudley, J. C.	Sep 2	1915	4	3
Dugan, John	Jan 6	1927	5	12
Dulitz, E.	May 5	1909	1	6
Dunn, Anna	Oct 9	1909	2	5/7
Dunn, Lewis	Jun 30	1908	1	2
Dunn, Patrick	Jun 30	1920	3	9
Dunbar, Robert A.	Jul 16	1920	1	9
Duran, Esmeralda	Apr 21	1927	3	12
Durfee, Edward Dewey (Rev.)	Jul 12	1923	5	10
Durham, Jane	Mar 14	1914	1	8
Durrin, H. S.	May 15	1924	2	10
Durrin, Ruby Freeman	Feb 28	1918	1	3
Durst, ——— (Rev.)	Sep 4	1924	9	10
Dykes, Katie	Oct 10	1908	5	5/7
Dykes, Katie (Thanks)	Oct 10	1908	2	5/7
Eager, William M.	Feb 3	1927	4	12
Eagleton, Dr. D. F.	Jun 15	1916	1	3
Eby, Lester F.	Feb 17	1922	3	10
Eckstein, Amelia Elizabeth	Feb 18	1926	7	11
Eckstein, Mrs. Barbara	Mar 1	1902	5	4
Edens, Hugh B.	Feb 12	1925	2	11
Edens, Carrolee Williams (Mrs. N.B.)	Nov 28	1918	8	3
Eddins, Carlton	Feb 2	1928	1	12
Eddins, J. S. (Dr.)	Mar 14	1924	9	10
Eddins, Lucinda G.	Jul 11	1929	8	13
Edkins, John A.	Sep 19	1929	1	13
Edmund, ———	Oct 9	1924	9	10
Edmunds, Nellie	Jan 18	1917	1	3
Eivet, daughter of Leonard	Jul 4	1918	8	3
Elder, Robert Fallon	Aug 2	1928	1/7	12
Ellebracht, Emma	May 19	1928	11	12

NAME	DATE		PG	FM
Elledge, J. M.	Mar 23	1907	3	4
Elliott, Mrs. L. A.	Sep 2	1899	1	1
Ellis, Hiram L.	Jun 24	1926	8	11
Ellison, C. D.	Mar 15	1928	5	12
Ellison, Mrs. F. A.	Feb 28	1924	3	10
Ellison, Robert	Mar 18	1916	1	9
Ellzey, B. G.	Dec 30	1926	5	11
Ely, D. W.	Mar 11	1926	9	11
Ely, Grace Francis	Oct 11	1923	5	10
Englebert, Ernest	Aug 14	1909	4	7
Ernst, Anton	Jul 26	1928	1	12
Ernst, Ferninand	Dec 29	1927	1	12
Ernst, Herbert L.	Feb 11	1926	1	11
Espinosa, Doniciano	Jan 8	1914	1	8
Estes, Howard	Feb 7	1929	11	13
Estrada, Joe	Aug 11	1927	7	12
Evans, A. D.	Nov 24	1922	1	10
Evans, Fannie	Oct 8	1920	12	9
Evans, Flora	Aug 15	1908	6	5
Evans, Flora	Aug 15	1908	4	7
Evans, H. C. (Rev.)	Apr 10	1913	5	3
Evans, H. C. (Rev.) (Thanks)	Apr 12	1913	1	9
Evans, H. C. (Rev.)	Apr 17	1913	1	3
Evans, Mrs. H. W.	Jul 23	1920	6	9
Evans, infant of Rufus	Dec 25	1913	1	8
Evans, John Wesley	Apr 15	1926	10	11
Evers, Clara	Mar 2	1914	6	9
Evers, Henry	Jul 7	1927	1	12
Evers, Walter	Jul 11	1908	1	5/7
Evertson, Joseph C.	Jun 13	1929	1	13
Fairchild, Mrs. H. W.	Aug 16	1929	2	13
Fairchild, daughter of J. C.	Dec 12	1929	11	13
Fairchilds, baby girl	Mar 14	1903	4	4
Fairman, H. P.	Jun 19	1924	1	10
Faltin, August (Sr.)	Jun 17	1905	4	4
Farlow, John	Nov 3	1922	1	10
Farnsworth, Sarah Downer	Oct 1	1926	1	11
Farr, Jefferson B.	Mar 26	1920	1	9
Faubion, Ida	Oct 9	1909	7	5/7
Fawcett, Claude	Apr 2	1910	1	7

17

NAME	DATE		PG	FM
Fawcett, Clifton	Dec 21	1912	5	9
Faust, August	Jul 28	1922	3	10
Feller, Albert	Jan 13	1922	5	10
Fellows, C. W.	Jul 17	1913	8	3
Felts, Mrs. William	Apr 21	1927	3	12
Ferguson, Mary Jane	Feb 2	1928	6	12
Ferris, Mr. ---	Apr 14	1927	1	12
Ferris, Mrs.---	Apr 14	1927	1	12
Ferris, Mrs. ---	Apr 21	1927	3	12
Ferris, H. C.	Jun 11	1925	11	11
Ferris, John F.	Oct 24	1908	1	5/7
Ferris, Kohn F.	Dec 12	1908	2	5/7
Ferris, Riley	Apr 21	1927	3	12
Ferris, William	Jul 3	1913	1	3
Fessenden, Mrs. W. F.	Nov 19	1920	1	9
Fifer, Lee	Jul 29	1926	2	11
Field, George B.	Sep 4	1909	5	5
Field, George B.	Sep 4	1909	3	7
Field, J. C.	Jan 14	1915	1	3
Fisher, Mrs Calthea C.	Aug 21	1909	5	5
Fisher, Mrs. T. D.	Feb 18	1899	1	1
Fisher, Mrs. T. D. (Re-internment)	Dec 6	1899	8	1
Fitzgerald, Mrs. W. H.	Feb 18	1926	8	11
Fitz Simon, John	Jul 3	1924	5	10
Flach, Ernst	Jun 30	1927	9	12
Flach, Frank	Dec 13	1923	1	10
Flach, Matilda (Mrs. Frank)	Jul 11	1918	1	3
Flanagan, Mrs. James	May 14	1920	3	9
Fleming, Ed	Jun 16	1922	1	10
Fleming, Ellen V.	May 20	1929	7	13
Flemming, Dottie	Apr 21	1927	3	12
Fleshman, Arthur	Jul 5	1928	1	12
Fletcher, Charley	Mar 12	1914	1	8
Flores, Masimo	Oct 4	1928	7	7
Floyd, Louie	Oct 17	1918	4	3
Floyd, Louie	Oct 18	1918	1	9
Floyd, Thomas Walter	Mar 30	1916	1	3
Fluitt, C. B.	Jul 15	1926	2	11
Fly, Jeff	Apr 7	1927	1	12
Flye, Annie Laurie	Jun 17	1926	7	11

NAME	DATE			PG	FM
Flynn, Francis Milton	Oct 11	1923		5	10
(Charley O'Connor)					
Flynn, Joseph	Jan 14	1915		1	3
Forbes, Mrs. G. W. (Lillian Benson)	Oct 15	1925		10	11
Fordtran, Francis Lalliek	Feb 5	1910		2	7
Fordtran, Portia	Jan 15	1925		3	11
Foster, A. C.	May 22	1913		5	3
Foster, Elizabeth	Oct 10	1929		1	13
Foster, Lillian Lawson	Nov 25	1926		2	11
Foster, W. P.	Jul 12	1902		4	4
Foyt, Mrs. Joseph	Jul 15	1915		2	9
Franco, Jose	Nov 25	1926		7	11
Frayer, Nannie	Sep 27	1928		1	12
Frayne, Thomas	Nov 28	1929		1	13
Freeman, G. W.	Aug 20	1925		7	11
Freeman, O. L.	Jul 14	1922		1	10
Friar, James	May 28	1914		1	8
Friar, Joe	Nov 13	1913		1	3
Friar, Joe	Nov 27	1913		1	8
Fritz, George	Oct 23	1924		5	10
Fuentes, Benito	Apr 21	1927		3	12
Fuentes, Delfina	Apr 21	1927		3	12
Fuentes, Gloria	Apr 21	1927		3	12
Fuentes, Maria	Apr 21	1927		3	12
Fuentes, Pedro	Apr 21	1927		3	12
Fuentes, Rosa De La	Apr 21	1927		3	12
Furguson, J. L.	Mar 12	1914		1	8
Futch, J. A.	Apr 26	1928		5	12
Galbraith, Mrs. R. (EmmaJane Barnes)	Feb 11	1926		1	11
Galbraith, Mrs. R. (Emma)	Mar 11	1926		4	11
Galbraith, Rev. Richard	May 25	1912		1	9
Galinda, Clelo	Jan 2	1920		3	9
Gallagher, John	May 2	1918		4	3
Gallagher, John	May 3	1918		6	9
Galloway, J. H.	Oct 10	1929		1	13
Gammon, Sallie	Jan 2	1913		6	3
Garcia, Modesto (Estate notice)	Jan 22	1923		5	10
Gardner, Buck	Aug 11	1922		1	10
Garduno, Ninfo	Nov 15	1928		7	12
Garrett, Earl	Nov 28	1918		1	3

NAME	DATE			PG	FM
Garrett, Mrs. F. E.	Oct 26	1926		2	11
Garrett, Mrs. George H.	Jun 16	1927		7	12
Garrett, daughter of I. H.	Nov 27	1909		8	5/7
Garrett, William M.	Oct 10	1929		8	13
Garza, Juanita	Jun 15	1917		6	9
Garza, Simona	Oct 16	1924		5	10
Gay, E. K.	Aug 23	1928		8	12
Gedney, H. E.	Feb 24	1906		11	4
George, Calvin	Dec 28	1916		3	3
George, Calvin	Jan 4	1917		1	3
George, I. M.	May 19	1922		7	10
George, Mamie Lou	May 3	1928		8	12
George, Rosa	Nov 26	1920		3	9
Gerdes, Ed B.	Jun 3	1905		4**	4

**This is the second June 3, 1905 paper. Have found that the editor forgot to change date and is actually June 10, 1905 paper.

NAME	DATE			PG	FM
Gibbens, Andrew Jackson	Oct 3	1929		1/8	13
Gibbens, baby	Jul 29	1915		1	3
Gibbens, Ida	Jul 21	1909		1	2/6
Gibbens, Ida	Jul 21	1909		2	2/6
Gibbens, Mrs. J. A.	Jul 29	1915		1	3
Gibbons, Rachel	Sep 13	1917		4	3
Gibbons, Ida	Jul 24	1909		1	5/7
Gibbons, Ida	Jul 31	1909		7	5/7
Gibbons, John F.	Aug 19	1926		6	11
Gibbs, Mrs. C. E.	Dec 27	1928		1	12
Gilbert, L. L.	Jan 20	1916		4	3
Gillespie, D. W.	Nov 21	1908		1	5
Gillespie, George H.	May 9	1913		1	3
Gilmer, Airs	Nov 25	1899		3	1
Glause, Mrs. F.	Apr 15	1926		3	11
Glause, Mrs. F.	Apr 29	1926		5	11
Glause, Fred	May 20	1915		1	3
Glenn, Mary Rosa May	May 12	1922		3	10
Glenn, Rosa Mae	May 19	1922		2	10
Glenn, W. J.	Aug 13	1925		9	11
Glidden, Effie	Mar 14	1903		2	4
Gold, Eugene	Apr 21	1906		8	4
Gold, William	May 26	1922		2	10

NAME	DATE		PG	FM
Golinda, Cleto	Jan 2	1920	3	9
Gonzales,————	Nov 8	1902	4	4
Gonzalez, Maria Lucia	Aug 16	1928	7	12
Gonzalez, Regino	Nov 10	1927	7	12
Gonzales, daughter of Steven	Jul 23	1925	5	11
Goodhue, J. Forrest	Jan 17	1929	1	13
Goodman, Leon	Jun 27	1908	3	5/7
Goodman, R. W.	Aug 27	1898	6	10*
*Found in May 5, 1922 Mt. Sun				
Gore, Frank H.	Jun 6	1929	1	13
Gore, Hugh	Jan 15	1925	5	11
Goss, J. B.	Oct 25	1928	1	12
Goss, J. Lee	Jan 4	1908	3	7
Goss, Maggie	May 19	1927	11	12
Gowan, George A.	Mar 18	1916	5	9
Graham, C.	Nov 15	1928	1	12
Graham, O. C.	Nov 12	1920	3	9
Graham, Mrs. Orville (Zora Moos)	Mar 17	1927	11	12
Graham, Otis C.	Dec 3	1920	1	9
Graham, Ruff	Jan 13	1917	4	9
Graham, Zora Moos	Mar 31	1927	11	12
Granville, George Ellis	Aug 14	1909	1	5/7
Granville, Hulda	Feb 29	1908	5/8	7
Graven, Addie Lee	Apr 13	1916	1	3
Graven, H. C. (Jack)	Nov 3	1922	7	10
Graven, Milton	Nov 8	1902	2	4
Gray, Estelle Collins	Mar 28	1918	1	3
Gray, O.	Oct 28	1905	8	4
Gray, Will A.	Jan 27	1927	1	12
Greathouse, Garland	Aug 27	1925	3	11
Green, Mrs. Ed	Dec 26	1929	1	13
Green, Minnie Van Emmon	Mar 14	1903	4	4
Green, Nora	May 5	1927	1	12
Green, William E.	Apr 2	1920	1/5	9
Greenwood, Mrs. Mattie	Mar 22	1902	8	4
Greer, Mrs. John	Jan 22	1914	1	8
Gregory, Leon	Sep 11	1924	5	10
Grey, O Dola	Oct 28	1905	8	4
Grider, John P.	Jul 11	1929	1	13
Grider, Mrs. J. P.	May 2	1918	1	3

NAME	DATE		PG	FM
Grider, Mrs. John P	May 3	1918	8	9
Grider, Thomas	Sep 27	1902	2	4
Griffin, infant of Walter	Apr 1	1926	11	11
Griffin, W. O. (Obie)	Apr 19	1928	1	12
Griffin, Mrs. W. O. (Seba Childress)	Apr 19	1928	1	12
Griffin, Walter P.	Mar 13	1909	5	5/7
Griffith, H. B.	Apr 14	1927	1	12
Griffith, Mrs. Kate	Dec 3	1920	7	9
Griffith, Mona	Apr 14	1927	1	12
Grona, Walter	Jan 23	1909	2	5/7
Grona, Mrs. William	Apr 11	1935	1	16
Gronemann, Otto	Feb 7	1903	2	4
Grounds, Gladys	Dec 24	1925	6	11
Grunage, Austin	Novr 27	1916	1	9
Guardiola, Feliciana	Jan 6	1927	1/5	12
Guerrerro, Eutinio	Jan 31	1929	7	13
Guinn, H. C.	Apr 9	1914	1	8
Guldberg, Oscar E.	Oct 10	1929	2	13
Haag, Leon August	Feb 12	1910	2	7
Haag, P. J.--son of	Feb 14	1910	5	7
Habecker, Freda	Oct 6	1906	5	4
Habermann, Mrs. mother of Mary	Mar 19	1925	5	11
Haddock, Rosetta	Mar 2	1916	1	3
Hagens, A. P. (Pete)	May 12	1927	1	12
Hagens, Mrs. Tom W. (Eva Robinson)	Mar 26	1925	10	11
Hahn, son of Ben F. (Thanks)	Jun 10	1926	8	11
Hahn, Louisa D. M.	Apr 2	1920	8	9
Hairston, Mary A. (Thanks)	Aug 15	1918	5	3
Haley, Ernest E.	Oct 10	1929	1	13
Halker, Edward	Aug 6	1920	5	9
Halker, Edward	Sep 10	1920	1	9
Hall, A. M.	Feb 29	1908	5	7
Hall, Mrs. Albert Lee	Nov 28	1929	5	13
Hall, Mrs. C. E.	Nov 8	1923	1	10
Hall, Mrs. C. E. (Grandma)	Nov 15	1923	7	10
Hall, William Spaulding	Sep 24	1920	3	9
Halpin, Louis (Tige)	Sep 13	1923	6/9	10
Hamblen, Henry	Jul 10	1909	1	5/7
Hamilton, Ann	Nov 22	1917	3	3
Hamilton, Emmett	Feb 12	1914	1	8

NAME	DATE		PG	FM
Hamilton, Emmet	Feb 7	1914	4	9
Hamilton, Grubb	Jan 3	1903	2	4
Hamilton, John E.	Apr 4	1913	1	3
Hamilton, Hilary	Feb 15	1902	7	4
Hamlyn, boy	Mar 7	1908	8	5
Hamlyn, Harold	Feb 29	1908	5	7
Hammons, Mrs. Zelphian	Dec 23	1921	3	10
Hammond, Fred	Aug 1	1913	1	3
Hampil, C. W.	Jan 28	1926	5	11
Hampton, Tucker	Feb 12	1925	8	11
Hankins, Eli C.	Aug 20	1925	10	11
Hankins, Glendora	Nov 17	1932	1	68*
*November 7 Mt. Sun				
Hankinson, T. W.	Apr 26	1902	2	4
Hardwick, J. V.	Feb 24	1906	4	4
Hardwick, Lola E.	Dec 4	1913	4	8
Hardwick, Mrs. Mark	Nov 27	1913	1	8
Hardy, Grandma	Apr 10	1909	8	5/7
Harkrider, Robert	Jan 24	1929	7	13
Harper, Bruce L.	Mar 14	1929	1	13
Harper, Frank	Apr 8	1926	7	11
Harper, John H.	May 9	1929	1	13
Harper, Lee H.	Oct 14	1915	1	3
Harper, Mrs. S.	Jun 19	1924	7	10
Harris, Mrs. G. F.	Oct 2	1913	1	3
Harris, Dr. G. N.	Jan 8	1914	1	8
Harris, daughter of John A.	Jan 29	1925	3	11
Harris, Mary Lee	May 10	1928	7	12
Harris, Sarah Elizabeth	May 30	1908	8	5/7
Harrison, Mrs. Frank	May 17	1928	11	12
Harrison, George A.	Nov 21	1908	7	5/7
Harrison, Henry C.	Jun 13	1929	6	13
Hart, Thomas P.	May 30	1918	1	3
Hartwell, Elizabeth (Gypsy)	Feb 27	1920	8	9
Harvey, Willie E.	May 27	1915	1	3
Haskell, Murray G.	Aug 13	1925	1	11
Hastings, Dorris	Mar 30	1916	1	3
Hatch, Mary C.	Feb 28	1918	1	3
Hatch, R. L. (Lee)	Dec 11	1924	1/9	10
Haufler, Louis	Mar 24	1922	4	10

NAME	DATE		PG	FM
Hayes, R. H.	Oct 22	1920	6	9
Head, J. H.	Feb 18	1899	1	1
Heard, Virginia V.	Oct 31	1929	1	13
Hebe, Paul	Oct 25	1913	1	9
Hedick, Mrs. (Thanks)	Feb 5	1914	4	8
Hedick, Elsa	Jan 31	1914	1	9
Heichen, John Frederick	Mar 22	1902	2	4
Heil, Lenard Allen	Oct 29	1925	5	11
Heimann, William	Feb 28	1924	7	10
Hein, William	Jul 23	1914	5	8
Heinen, Charles	Nov 11	1926	1	11
Heinen, J. P. (Sr.)	Dec 8	1922	7	10
Heise, Johanna Mary Lidwina	Jan 20	1922	3	10
Helton, Edward O.	May 31	1928	1	12
Hencerling, A. F. (??)	Apr 19	1928	5	12
Hencerling, Dan J.	Apr 19	1928	7	12
Henderson, Annie	Dec 22	1922	7	10
Henderson, Gus	Apr 14	1927	1	12
Henderson, Mrs, Gus	Apr 14	1927	1	12
Henderson, child of Gus	Apr 14	1927	1	12
Henderson, child of Gus	Apr 14	1927	1	12
Henderson, Howard	Nov 21	1908	8	5/7
Henderson, Mrs. J. W.	Jul 3	1915	1	3
Henderson, Mrs. L. K	Nov 5	1910	1	7
Henderson, Margaret	Jan 29	1916	1	9
Henderson, Paul	Nov 10	1922	6	10
Hendricks, Emma	Jan 2	1909	6	5
Hendricks, Emma	Jan 2	1909	2	7
Hendricks, Emma	Jan 9	1909	7	5/7
Hendricks, Peter	Jun 21	1928	1/5	12
Hendrixson, Robert	Sep 26	1929	8	13
Henke, Amelia	Apr 12	1902	8	4
Henke, Lena	Feb 8	1908	2/8	5/7
Henke, William	Mar 4	1926	8	11
Hennessy, Will	Feb 14	1929	7	13
Henry, Mrs. S. A.	Apr 14	1927	1	12
Henry, Mrs. S. A.	Apr 21	1927	3	12
Hensley, ------	Aug 14	1924	8	10
Herbst, Charles	Feb 11	1905	4	4
Herrera, Mrs. Rafael	Jan 10	1919	3	9

KERRVILLE MOUNTAIN SUN AND KERRVILLE ADVANCE
1898-1929

NAME	DATE		PG	FM
Herrera, Jose M.	Nov 21	1929	7	13
Hersey, William A.	May 30	1929	7	13
Hicks, Mrs. Fannie	Feb 18	1905	5	4
Hicks, Harry M.	Dec 12	1929	1	13
Higgins, L. J.	Jan 4	1917	1	3
Higgins, Lawrence	Jan 13	1917	1	9
Hightower, James I.	Oct 13	1927	2	12
Hill, Edward	Apr 19	1928	10	12
Hill, Grizella Q.	Jul 10	1924	7	10
Hill, Mrs H. T.	Feb 25	1905	4	4
Hill, Mrs. Sam B.	Jun 27	1902	2	4
Hill, Mrs. Vicy	Mar 15	1902	2	4
Hill, father of W. T.	Oct 27	1927	11	12
Hilliard, H. G.	Nov 8	1928	5	12
Hitchcock, Annie	Dec 5	1929	8	13
Hixson, Mrs. B. M.	Mar 30	1907	8	4
Hixson, Mrs.	Apr 13	1907	1	4
Hobby, Edwin	Nov 24	1927	1	12
Hocker, Tom	Jul 18	1903	4	4
Hodge, Mary J.	Mar 28	1935	1	16
Hodges,-- (Thanks)	Aug 23	1902	4	4
Hodges, Joe Box	Jul 25	1929	1	13
Hodges, J. N.	Oct 14	1915	5	3
Hodges, Mrs. J. R.	Jan 26	1928	1	12
Hoke, Walter S.	May 9	1908	5	5/7
Holdyke, Raymond	Sep 10	1920	1	9
Holekamp, Betty Wilhelmina	Nov 15	1902	8	4
Holland, W. W. (Thanks)	Jan 31	1924	5	10
Hollimon, Ernest	Jul 18	1929	1	13
Hollimon, Mrs. Phereby	Mar 18	1899	4	1
Holloman, Grover	Jul 23	1920	1	9
Holloman, Grover Kile	Dec 12	1918	1	3
Hollomon, Grover	Jul 23	1920	1	9
Holloway, Pharabee (Probate)	Nov 19	1904	6	4
Holman, B. C.	Jul 11	1929	1	13
Holman, Calvin E.	Sep 20	1928	1	12
Holst, L. R.	Jan 5	1928	1	12
Holt, Eloise	Mar 16	1907	3	4
Holt, Rex	Nov 3	1927	5	12
Honse, W. J.	Mar 15	1928	1	12

25

KERRVILLE MOUNTAIN SUN AND KERRVILLE ADVANCE
1898-1929

NAME	DATE		PG	FM
Hood, Laura	Nov 13	1913	1	3
Hood, W. P.	Jan 28	1923	9	10
Hope, Ace	Sep 9	1915	1	3
Hope, Mrs. John	Feb 17	1927	1	12
Hope, Mrs. John (Maggie Pugh)	Feb 24	1927	11	12
Hopf, Fred (Probate)	Oct 27	1922	6	10
Hopkins, Ellen	Feb 7	1929	11	13
Hopping, A.	Jan 30	1909	2	5/7
Howard, Maude L.	Aug 23	1923	2	10
Howard, Silas F.	Aug 12	1915	1	3
Howard, Silas P.	Aug 14	1915	2	9
Howard, Silas F.	Aug 19	1915	1	3
Howard, Silas F. (Thanks)	Aug 19	1915	1	3
Howard, Tony	Jan 5	1928	2	12
Howe, Mrs. Ara	Nov 13	1924	3	10
Howell, Alton	Mar 20	1913	1	3
Howell, Mrs. Earl (Edith Switzer)	Apr 21	1927	11	12
Howell, Matilda	Nov 22	1917	3	3
Howell, Sarah	Apr 5	1928	5/11	12
Howell, William	May 22	1913	5	3
Howell, William	Jun 12	1913	1	3
Howland, C. W.	Jun 27	1918	1	3
Hubble, Garland	Dec 6	1917	4	3
Hubble, Mary Anna	Jan 15	1925	5	11
Hubble, William H.	Mar 13	1909	3	5/7
Hudson, Hortense	Dec 19	1929	12	13
Hudson, John B. (Dr.)	Jan 31	1929	1	13
Hudspeth, infant of Eldred	Nov 12	1920	3	9
Hudspeth, Henry Street	Sep 2	1926	7	11
Hudspeth, J. A.	Sep 10	1920	1	9
Hudspeth, Lillie	Oct 17	1918	4	3
Hudspeth, Mary E.	Jul 12	1923	3	10
Hudspeth, Mary E.	Jul 19	1923	5/7	10
Hudspeth, Street	Dec 22	1927	10	12
Huffman, infant	Feb 8	1908	5	5/7
Hughes, Amanda	Jul 19	1917	13	3
Hughes, Josie	Aug 14	1913	1	3
Hughes, Mrs. M. E.	Jun 25	1898	6	10*
*Found in May 5, 1922 Mt. Sun				
Hughes, son of Ollie	Jan 20	1927	9	12

NAME	DATE		PG	FM
Hughs, Elizabeth Stansell	May 28	1920	1	9
Hughs, George W. (Thanks)	Oct 6	1906	5	4
Hughs, Mrs. G. W.	May 28	1920	1	9
Hunt, Elbert	Jun 9	1927	1	12
Hunt, R. F.	Sep 1	1927	5	12
Hunt, Robert F.	Aug 25	1927	1	12
Hunt, W. M.	Nov 24	1906	6	4
Huntington, Fannie (Frances H.)	Apr 5	1928	1/5	12
Hunter, Mary E. (Thanks)	Mar 29	1928	7	12
Hurlock, Eula	Dec 6	1928	1	12
Hurt, Elbridge I.	Jun 20	1929	1	13
Husbands, Martha Myrtle	Nov 15	1928	1	12
Huse, N. P. (Thanks)	Oct 26	1917	3	9
Hutchinson, Mamie	Dec 9	1898	6	10*
*Found in May 5, 1922 Mt. Sun				
Hutchinson, W. H.	Apr 4	1908	4	5
Hutchinson, W. H.	Apr 4	1908	6	7
Huth, Emilie	Apr 21	1927	5	12
Hyde, Ben J.	Oct 7	1915	1	3
Hyde, daughter J. B.	Nov 14	1918	8	3
Hyde, Guy (Thanks)	Aug 16	1929	2	13
Ichner, Charles	Mar 7	1929	2	13
Icke, Walter	Sep 14	1924	10	10
Ingenhuett, Hubert	Jul 24	1924	1	10
Ingenhuett, Peter	Nov 1	1923	1	10
Ingenhuett, Thomas (Letter of Ad.)	Aug 30	1902	5	4
Insall, Mrs. T. M.	Dec 19	1929	1	13
Inscore, Adolph	Jul 29	1926	1	11
Jack, Verna Hewlett	Nov 7	1908	5	5
Jack, Verna Hewlett	Nov 7	1908	4	7
Jackson, J. D.	Apr 27	1916	1	3
Jackson, Joseph	Sep 25	1909	4	5/7
James, Anna Margaret (Mrs. D. W.)	Nov 4	1926	5	11
James, Byrd (Estate)	Sep 11	1924	5	10
James, Eugene M. Pratt	Dec 24	1912	1	3
James, Eugenia Malta	Dec 21	1912	1	9
James, daughter of Henry	Feb 22	1918	6	9
James, Nathaniel Henry	Jan 28	1915	1	3
James, Ray	Jun 7	1917	1	3
Janes, William F.	May 27	1926	6	11

NAME	DATE		PG	FL
Jarmon, Hattie Pauline	Nov 26	1920	1	9
Jarmon, Hattie Pauline	Dec 3	1920	2	9
Jeffers, S. L.	Oct 23	1925	1	11
Jeffries, Frank	May 19	1922	6	10
Jenkins, Essie	May 23	1929	1	13
Johannerson, W.	Apr 25	1918	1	3
Johannessen, Lucy	Jan 27	1922	7	10
Johnsey, Cornelia	Mar 25	1915	2	3
Johnson, Asa J. (Estate)	Oct 1	1925	5	11
Johnson, Dr. B. F.	Feb 25	1910	6	7
Johnson, H. T.	Jun 4	1910	3	7
Johnson, Dr. Thomas W.	Jun 24	1915	1	3
Johnston, David E. (Thanks)	Aug 11	1922	3	10
Johnston, James Steptoe (Rev.)	Nov 6	1924	1	10
Jolley, infant	Jun 17	1899	1	1
Jones, A. B.	Apr 21	1909	1	6
Jones, A. B.	Apr 23	1909	1	2
Jones, Arthur G. (Dr.)	May 2	1929	1	13
Jones, Florine	Jan 23	1909	5	5/7
Jones, H. L.	Mar 25	1905	5	4
Jones, infant of Heck	May 22	1909	3	7
Jones, Mrs. J. H. (Ida M.)	Sep 29	1927	2	12
Jones, Mahala	Jan 30	1920	8	9
Jones, Narcissa C. (Estate)	Jul 24	1924	7	10
Jones, Nat B. (Kiowa)	Mar 15	1928	1	12
Jones, Pearl	Apr 5	1928	5	12
Jones, Pettiway	Oct 30	1924	5	10
Jones, son of R. D.	Nov 19	1925	8	11
Jones, child of Rex	Dec 12	1918	1	3
Jones, Robert Littleton	Jan 13	1922	3	10
Jones, W. W.	Mar 17	1906	4	4
Jones, Walter W.	Mar 24	1906	4	4
Jordon, John Robert	Mar 10	1922	3	10
Jordon, William F.	Oct 17	1929	3	13 S2
Josephine, Sister	Nov 15	1923	5	10
Joy, Florence	Jan 18	1908	5	5/7
Joy, Lou	Sep 19	1929	11	13
Joy, R. B.	Feb 24	1906	14	4
Joy, Richard	Feb 3	1927	1	12
Joy, Mrs. Richard	Jul 2	1920	1	9

NAME	DATE		PG	FL
Joy, William A.	Mar 14	1924	3	10
Juarez, Patricio	Apr 1	1926	7	11
Juarez, Pedro	Jun 21	1918	6	9
Juarez, son of Pedro	Jun 21	1918	6	9
Juenke, Katherine Heimann	May 26	1922	2	10
Jump, Mrs. R. E.	Dec 2	1916	1	3
Jung, Adolph	Jul 3	1924	5	10
Jung, Albert	Dec 23	1905	5	4
Jung, Anna	Jan 29	1916	6	9
Jung, Anton	May 30	1918	4	3
Jung, Joe	Oct 24	1929	8	13 S2
Jung, Mrs. Joseph	Nov 1	1917	2	3
Jung, Mrs. Joseph	Nov 2	1917	6	9
Kabell, John	Dec 24	1914	1	3
Kaiser, E. W.	Aug 29	1929	1	13
Kaiser, Mrs. W. C.	Dec 4	1913	1	8
Kaiser, W. C.	Nov 2	1917	1	9
Kaiser, Mrs. W. C. Kaiser (Thanks)	Dec 13	1913	4	9
Kalka, John	Nov 14	1918	1	3
Kammlah Sr., Mrs. Henry	Feb 22	1913	2	9
(Amalia Betz)				
Kane, John	Apr 20	1907	8	4
Karger, Mrs. Coroline	Jul 7	1909	1	2/6
Karger, Caroline	Jul 10	1909	1	5/7
Karger, Walter	Dec 6	1928	1	12
Keese, J.	Mar 9	1916	1	3
Keese, T. H.	Dec 2	1915	1	3
Keese, Thomas	Nov 25	1915	1	3
Keester, Harry G.	Jun 4	1920	7	9
Kehoe, Andrew Patrick	Aug 6	1925	4/5	11
Kehoe, Florence	Dec 15	1927	5	12
Keifer, James Blair	Jun 30	1922	3	10
Keller, Robert	Jan 15	1925	5	11
Kelley, Mrs. Ollie	Jul 5	1923	5	10
Kelly, Mrs. Ben H.	Jan 27	1912	5	9
Kemper, Mrs. Henry	Jun 23	1927	5	12
Kemper, Dr. William (Sr.)	Mar 2	1914	6	9
Kemper, Mrs. William	Feb 5	1925	5	11
Kennedy, A. Milton	Jul 23	1914	1	8
Kennedy, Samuel J.	Nov 14	1929	1	13

NAME	DATE		PG	FL
Kenodie, Robert	Dec 31	1904	4	4
Kensing, Bell	Aug 21	1913	8	3
Kensing, Frank	Aug 24	1913	1	9
Kent, J.	Jan 20	1912	5	9
Kern, Frank H.	Jan 27	1922	3	10
Kerwin, John	Mar 12	1920	9	3
Kidd, Mrs. Bubie	Feb 12	1925	7	11
Kilday, Edward	Jan 31	1929	7	13
Killingworth, David M.	Sep 22	1927	12	12
Killough, B. T.	Aug 18	1927	6	12
Killough, Sarah Elizabeth	Feb 14	1918	1	3
Kincaid, Maggie A.	Jul 25	1929	1	13
King, J. B. (Dr.)	Nov 5	1910	2	7
King, J. E.	Jan 28	1923	1/9	10
King, Lancelot Edmund	Dec 7	1916	1	3
King, Lancelot E.	Jan 4	1917	1	3
King, Launcelot E.	Jan 13	1917	5	9
King, Opal	Mar 22	1917	1	3
King, Mrs. W. A.	Jun 3	1916	1	67*
*Found in the June 2, 1984 Mt. Sun				
King, Mrs. W. A.	Jun 8	1916	1	3
Kingsley, Byron F. (Dr.)	Feb 5	1925	5	11
Kingsley, Ralph Waldo	May 14	1925	7	11
Kirchgrabber, Frank	Jul 19	1923	2	10
Kleck, Sylvester	Aug 27	1914	1	8
Klein, Fred B.	Apr 19	1928	1	12
Klein, Mrs. L.	Jun 25	1914	1	8
Kneese, Eric	Sep 9	1926	11	11
Knight, Mrs. J. M.	Aug 22	1929	1	13
Knopp, Marcus	Sep 10	1925	9	11
Knox, Douglas	Dec 4	1924	9	10
Kolodzey, Ben F.	Oct 15	1925	3	11
Koon, Mrs. J. D. (Thanks)	Apr 17	1924	5	10
Kott, Mrs. Albert	Oct 17	1929	3	13 S2
Kott, Ernst	Sep 13	1928	1	12
Kraus, Jacob	May 26	1922	2	10
Krueger, Anna May Josephine	Jan 20	1912	2	9
Kuehn, Hedwig	Nov 28	1929	5	13
Kuesal, Willian T.	Sep 6	1928	1	12
Kuesal, William T.	Sep 13	1928	7	12

NAME	DATE			PG	FL
Kunz, Mrs. Charles	Jun 20	1929		5	13
Kurtz, daughter of Zada	Mar 24	1922		7	10
Kutzer, Ernestine	Feb 2	1907		8	4
Kyle, Charles S.	Oct 27	1906		3	4
Lacey, Howard G.	Mar 28	1929		1	13
Lackey, Mrs. B. F. (Thanks)	Nov 3	1906		2	4
Lackey, Green	Apr 4	1929		1	13
Lackey, Green	Apr 11	1929		1	13
Lackey, Mrs. Green	Sep 30	1926		1	11
(Lucinda J. Zumwalt)					
Lackey, James	Jul 4	1929		1	13
Lackey, Nona D.	Jun 5	1913		4	3
Lackey, Nona D.	Jun 12	1913		1	3
Lackey, Tom	May 11	1916		1	3
Lacy, James	May 6	1899		1	1
Lamb, George W.	Dec 23	1926		1	11
Lambert, Mary	Jan 20	1927		5	12
Lambert, Mary	Jan 27	1927		7	12
Landry, Ras	Mar 17	1927		12	12
Lane, Mrs. John	Mar 10	1927		11	12
Lang, Floyd	Sep 13	1902		8	4
Langford, Isaac B.	Mar 12	1914		4	8
Langford, Jewel	Dec 2	1926		1	11
Lara, Mrs. Pabla	Jun 16	1927		7	12
Lara, Paula	Nov 4	1926		7	11
Latham, Nina	Mar 15	1928		1	12
Lathrop, K. C.	May 8	1913		1	3
Lathrop, Mrs. K. C.	Jun 19	1913		1	3
Lathrop, Mrs. K. C.	Jun 21	1913		5	9
Laughman, daughter of L. W.	Apr 7	1922		3	1
Laurie, Dudley	Mar 11	1915		1	3
Laurie, Dudley	Mar 13	1915		1	9
Laurie, Dudley	Feb 3	1916		1	3
Lawson, Mrs. A. J.	Jun 2	1909		1	2/6
Lawson, J. C. (Jake)	Sep 26	1929		1	13
Leach, Ben T.	Jul 22	1916		1	65*
*Found in the May 18, 1983 Mt. Sun					
Leasmann, Mrs.	Feb 5	1914		1	8
Leavell, Mrs. J. D. (Louise)	Feb 4	1926		1	11
Leavell, John D.	Apr 30	1925		1	11

NAME	DATE		PG	FL
Leazar, father of W. G.	Sep 22	1922	5	10
Le Bourgeois, Rochelle	May 2	1909	1	7
Le Bourgeois, Rochelle	May 8	1909	1	5/7
Ledbetter, Alby	Sep 14	1926	8	11
Lee, Amaza	Feb 6	1919	4	3
Lee, Annie	Mar 8	1917	1	3
Lee, Annie	Mar 9	1917	8	9
Lee, Fannie	Sep 3	1920	1	9
Lee, Julia	Feb 1	1908	10	5
Lee, Julia A.	Feb 8	1908	8	5/7
Lee, Mrs. J. B.	Jul 30	1920	3	9
Lee, Mrs. Pink	Nov 27	1924	9	10
Lee, daughter of Pink	Jan 8	1925	7	11
Lee, infant son of Paul	Aug 30	1928	11	12
Lee, W. M.	Feb 20	1913	4	3
Leeder, son of August	Dec 3	1925	8	11
Leger, Mrs. Alphin	May 5	1927	7	12
Leigh, George L. (Executor's Note)	Feb 22	1902	8	4
Leigh, Harry	Sep 28	1898	6	10*
*Found in May 5, 1922 Mt. Sun				
Leinweber, Dee	Jun 30	1922	8	10
Leinweber, Mrs. L. A.	Jan 30	1919	1	3
Leinweber, Lonie	Mar 31	1906	4	4
Lemoine, Justine Vareille	Jul 23	1925	5	11
Lemos, Francisco	Dec 12	1918	4	3
Lemos, Francisco	Apr 7	1922	3	10
Lemos, Francisco	Apr 21	1922	3	10
Lemos, Francisco	Apr 28	1922	3	10
Lemos, Francisco	May 26	1922	3	10
Lemos, Pedro	Nov 13	1926	7	11
Leonard, Sarah Jennett	Nov 2	1916	1	3
Leonard, Z.	Aug 6	1920	1	9
Leonard, Z.	Sep 10	1920	1	9
Leotine, Sister	Sep 22	1922	3	10
Le Sturgeon, son of Bert	Nov 25	1915	1	3
Lewis, Danforth R.	Mar 29	1928	1	12
Lewis, George	Jan 27	1922	7	10
Lewis, George B.	Mar 15	1928	1	12
Liberto, John	Aug 8	1929	7	13
Ligon, J. T.	Apr 21	1927	3	12

NAME	DATE		PG	FL
Limberger, male child--age 6	Mar 31	1906	4	4
Lincoln, George T.	Sep 13	1917	4	3
Lindner, Ellen	Jul 5	1928	1	12
Little, Mrs. J. Y.	Jun 28	1928	1	12
Little, John L.	Nov 24	1927	9	12
Locke, Ellen	Mar 14	1903	9	4
Locke, John (Probate Notice)	Nov 19	1904	6	4
Lockett, C. C.	Aug 7	1909	1	5/7
Lockley, A. J.	Oct 30	1898	6	10*
*Found in May 5, 1922 Mt. Sun				
Loesberg, Henry	Oct 17	1918	4	3
Loesburg, Emmet	Oct 24	1913	1	3
Logan, Mrs. A.	Apr 6	1907	3	4
Lopez, Mrs. Camillo	Dec 3	1925	7	11
Lopez, daughter of Guadalupe	Jan 17	1929	5	13
Lopez, Julio	Aug 1	1929	1	13
Lopez, Tomasita	Nov 8	1928	7	12
Lorentz, Emma	May 13	1899	1	1
Lourance, Mrs. Logan	May 12	1927	8	12
Love, Mary Ann	Dec 8	1927	1	12
Lowman, son of Mr.	Sep 4	1913	1	3
Lowrance, Amanda	Mar 12	1914	1	8
Lowrance, George	Dec 12	1918	1	3
Lowrance, John	Jul 23	1920	4	9
Lowrance, John	Apr 21	1927	3	12
Lowrance, John Shelby	Aug 7	1913	1	3
Lowrance, John Shelby	Aug 2	1913	1	9
Lowrance, P. O.	Jun 10	1926	1	11
Lowrance, Thomas	Sep 12	1908	3	7
Lowrance, W. M. (Executor's Note)	Feb 15	1902	4	4
Lowry, Charles Lee	Jun 7	1928	10	12
Lowry, Mrs. J. M. (Hattie)	Jun 4	1914	1	8
Lowry, Jane	Jun 11	1925	2	11
Lowry, Martin D.	Nov 8	1923	7	10
Lozano, Manuela	Apr 21	1927	3	12
Lucas, Theophile Eugene (Jr.)	Mar 11	1926	5	11
Lumpkin, Sarah	Nov 18	1915	1	3
Lund, Horace	Aug 15	1918	4	3
Lund, Walter A.	May 27	1905	5	4
Lundell, Lawrence A.	Jun 10	1926	3	11

NAME	DATE		PG	FL
Lurie, Dudley	Mar 13	1915	1	9
Luse, William	Dec 8	1922	7	10
Luttrel, Claude	Jun 2	1922	7	10
Lynn, Hershel	Dec 31	1925	1	11
Maass, Etta (Estate)	Jan 8	1925	4	11
Maddox, Dorothy Lee	Dec 6	1928	13	12
Madrid, Estelle	Aug 11	1927	7	12
Maegle, Mrs. Otto	Oct 6	1927	5	12
Main, Mrs. R. E.	Sep 30	1926	10	11 S2
Mallory, Fred P.	Dec 4	1913	1	8
Mallory, Fred F. (Thanks)	Dec 13	1913	2	9
Mangum, Ruth	Jan 20	1927	6	12
Manning, Arch	May 23	1908	2	5/7
Manning, "Bud"	Nov 20	1913	1	8
Manny, Matthew	Apr 8	1926	9	11
Mansfield, Georgia Ann	Oct 17	1918	5	3
Mansfield, Georgia Ann	Oct 18	1918	1	9
Mansfield, Herman	Jan 30	1919	1	3
Mansfield, Laura	May 17	1917	1	3
Marschall, Freda	Mar 14	1929	6	13
Marchessaux, Edmund	Mar 13	1913	1	3
Marcias, Prudenciano	Nov 28	1929	5	13
Markham, Mary	Dec 15	1922	23	10
Markloff, Miss Dora	Feb 25	1899	1	1
Marlowe, Nancy	Mar 20	1909	3	5
Marriner, Harry L.	Dec 10	1914	1	3
Marshall, Florence Etta	May 25	1907	5	4
Martin, Elizabeth	Jan 2	1909	7	5
Martin, Garrett	Jun 7	1917	1	3
Martin, P. B.	May 24	1928	1	12
Martin, P. B.	May 31	1928	14	12
Martin, Mrs. P. B.	Feb 17	1927	1	12
Martinez, Concepcion	Jul 19	1928	7	12
Martinez, Florencia	Apr 7	1922	3	10
Mason, Mrs. Charles M.	Feb 10	1922	1	10
Mason, Kearney	May 14	1925	10	11
Massey, --- (Grandma--Thanks)	Aug 14	1924	7	10
Massey, Charles Richard	Sep 2	1926	10	11
Massey, Mrs. Dutch	Apr 9	1925	3	11
Massey, John	Feb 18	1926	1	11

NAME	DATE	PG	FL
Masters, Jake B.	Aug 16 1928	1/11	12
Matthews, Lizzie	Mar 8 1928	1	12
Maudstay, Ellen	Jan 14 1915	1	3
Maxwell, J. H. C. (Rev.)	Jul 16 1925	1	11
Maxwell, Volney	Jul 15 1899	1	1
Mayfield, Mr.	Jan 13 1912	5	9
Mayfield, Mrs. Robert L.	Jan 28 1915	1	3
Mc Alpin, Margaret Johnston	Nov 6 1924	6	10
Mc Ateer, father of Vincent	Oct 26 1926	7	11
Mc Beth, Padgett	Oct 17 1918	1	3
Mc Bryde, Lucy	Dec 4 1913	1	8
Mc Call, Jesse	Jan 4 1908	2	7
Mc Call, Jesse (Thanks)	Jan 4 1908	8	7
Mc Can, James F.	Sep 3 1925	1	11
Mc Carty, Annie	Dec 6 1928	7	12
Mc Cauley, E. B.	Jan 31 1929	1	13
Mc Cleery, Donald C.	Aug 26 1926	2	11
Mc Cleery, Donald C.	Sep 2 1926	10	11
Mc Clenahan, Ben	Feb 5 1910	2	7
Mc Collum, Mrs. Glenn	Jun 20 1929	1	13
Mc Corkle, Mrs. G. P. (Maggie)	Aug 2 1902	5	4
Mc Corquodale, Thelma	May 12 1927	1	12
Mc Crary, Alexander	Feb 20 1913	1	3
Mc Crary, Alexander (Thanks)	Feb 27 1913	1	3
Mc Cullar, B. N. (Thanks)	Jul 27 1912	5	9
Mc Cullough, Kenneth	Jun 26 1924	9	10
Mc Cumsey, "Mack"	Jan 30 1920	1	9
Mc Cumsey, "Mack" (Thanks)	Feb 13 1920	6	9
Mc Curdy, R. J.	Nov 20 1924	1	10
Mc Curdy, Mrs. R. J.	Aug 2 1928	1	12
Mc Daniel, Mrs. Artie	Aug 25 1927	1	12
Mc Donald, Cleo	Feb 21 1929	1	13
Mc Donald, Duncan	Nov 5 1904	8	4
Mc Donald, Mrs. J. T.	Dec 3 1920	7	9
Mc Donald, Margaret Ruth	Nov 4 1926	8	11
Mc Donald, W. A.	May 23 1908	8	7
Mc Donald, W. C.	Aug 18 1927	1	12
Mc Doniel, W. J.	Jul 8 1926	1	11
Mc Elroy, James L.	Nov 7 1929	8	13
Mc Elroy, Mrs. James	Sep 15 1927	6	12

NAME	DATE		PG	FL
Mc Faden, Roy Gaddy	Aug 6	1925	1	11
Mc Farland, Mrs. J. A.	Oct 6	1906	5	4
Mc Farland, John C.	Jul 12	1928	2	12
Mc Gaffey, Mrs. C. N.	Feb 19	1925	1	11
Mc Gaffey, Mrs. J. W.	Feb 19	1925	1	11
Mc Gee, J. N.	Dec 17	1925	8	11
Mc Haney, Mr.	Jun 7	1917	5	3
Mc Kay, Mrs. J. D.	Nov 25	1905	3	4
Mc Kepzie, Donald	Sep 2	1899	4	1
Mc Killip, Mrs. A. W. (Kate)	Jun 25	1925	1	11
Mc Kinney, David	Apr 21	1927	3	12
Mc Kinney, Davis	Apr 14	1927	1	12
Mc Kinney, John	Apr 21	1927	3	12
Mc Kinney, William D.	Sep 12	1929	7	13
Mc Kinnon, Mrs. ----	Jul 17	1924	6	10
Mc Mains, Charles	Apr 21	1927	3	12
Mc Millen, Z. B.	Jul 3	1905	4	4
Mc Neal, Jack	Dec 11	1924	9	10
Mc Neal, Dell (Mrs. Jack--Cordelia)	Jan 8	1925	7	11
Mc Neeley, Henry P.	Jul 24	1913	1	3
Mc Nees, David Franklin (Estate)	Jul 23	1925	7	11
Mc Nees, Jannie	Jan 24	1929	1	13
Mc Rea, Minnie	Mar 5	1914	1	8
Mc Rea, Minnie	Mar 7	1914	1	62*
*Old front page in October 3, 1981 issue Mountain Sun.				
Mc Sween, T. R.	Jan 30	1020	8	9
Mc Vickers, J. R.	Dec 21	1916	1	3
Mc Vickers, Joseph Raymond	Dec 28	1916	1	3
Mc Williams, Tommy	Aug 12	1926	1	11
Meadows, Mary Lucille	Sep 29	1927	1	12
Means, Linda	Apr 29	1926	8	11
Means, Mrs. W. L.	Apr 22	1926	2	11
Means, William L.	Nov 8	1928	1	12
Meaux, Lawrence	Dec 5	1929	2	13
Medkiff, Mattie	May 20	1926	4	11
Meeks, Mary Mc Kinney	Oct 14	1926	8	11
Meisell, Henry E.	Oct 29	1925	1	11
Meiss, John F.	Oct 31	1929	6	13
Meissinger, Hardy	Oct 11	1923	9	10
Melson, Mrs. K. H.	Jun 27	1908	2	5

KERRVILLE MOUNTAIN SUN AND KERRVILLE ADVANCE
1898-1929

NAME	DATE		PG	FL
Menchaca, Rafael	May 31	1928	5	12
Mendez, Librado (Juanita Espana)	Nov 17	1927	5	12
Menendez, Joseph	Nov 29	1928	1	12
Merritt, Floyd Bessner	Dec 30	1921	7	10
Merritt, Harvey	Nov 28	1918	1	3
Merritt, Harvey I.	Jul 23	1920	1	9
Merritt, Mrs. S. R.	Jul 20	1913	1	3
Merritt, Sherwood R.	Aug 22	1918	1	3
Mexican Nun	Jul 15	1916	2	9
Michon, John B.	Feb 2	1907	8	4
Michon, Joseph	Nov 6	1924	5	10
Michon, Lena	Dec 7	1916	1	3
Michon, Mary Balbina	Feb 23	1928	1	12
Michon, Mary Balbina	Mar 1	1928	5	12
Miles, Jess	May 28	1925	2	11
Miller, Eli	Mar 27	1913	1	3
Miller, Eli H.	Mar 29	1913	5	9
Miller, Frank Albert	May 7	1925	5	11
Miller, Mrs. George	Feb 20	1920	8	9
Miller, Lee B.	May 21	1925	8	11
Miller, Robert Nicholas	Aug 4	1922	3	10
Millwee, George W.	Aug 14	1913	1	3
Mirales, Dario	Aug 9	1928	1	12
Mirales, Dario	Aug 16	1928	7	12
Mitchell, Elwood	Nov 24	1927	5	12
Moffet, F. M.	Apr 29	1905	5	4
Mogford, baby	Sep 27	1928	11	12
Mogford, E. A.	Oct 8	1920	1	9
Moncevalles, Theresa	Apr 18	1929	7	13
Monsabellas, Felipe	Jan 6	1920	3	9
Montague, Charles	Apr 27	1916	1	3
Montague, Charles	Apr 29	1916	1	68*
*Found in the Spetember 8, 1984 Mt. Sun				
Montel, Mrs. Chas (Sister of)	Sep 9	1915	8	3
Montello, Nicolette	Apr 21	1927	3	12
Montgomery, Mrs. A. H.	Feb 7	1924	6	10
Moody, George W. (Thanks)	Nov 8	1902	4	4
Moore, Dorothy	Apr 19	1928	8	12
Moore, Ethel	Dec 16	1921	3	10
Moore, F. M.	Mar 13	1909	5	5

37

NAME	DATE	PG	FL
Moore, Francis M.	Mar 20 1909	3	5
Moore, Frank	Mar 20 1909	3	7
Moore, Hughes C.	Jan 21 1915	1	3
Moore, Irving	Feb 23 1907	5	4
Moore, Jim	Mar 10 1927	1/8	12
Moore, Joe	Oct 11 1928	9	12
Moore, Johnnie	May 2 1918	5	3
Moore, John W.	May 7 1920	1	9
Moore, Mary Elizabeth	Dec 27 1928	1	12
Moore, Milton	Apr 18 1918	1	3
Moore, Nellie (Mrs. Buck)	Dec 15 1927	1	12
Moore, Nellie	Dec 22 1927	6	12
Moore, Prudie Ann	Jul 20 1913	1	3
Moore, Mrs. W. P.	Jun 23 1927	1	12
Moose, A. C.	Jan 24 1903	2	4
Moose, son of C.	Nov 23 1898	6	10*
*Found in May 5, 1922 Mt. Sun			
Moose, Mrs. R. A.	Sep 19 1918	1	3
Moreno, Juan Gomez	Jul 31 1924	5	10
Morgan, Mrs. D. (Joe Hiser)	Dec 30 1921	7	10
Morgan, Mrs. Frances J.	Oct 14 1926	8	11
Morgan, Mrs. S. P.	Feb 11 1915	5	3
Morris, Albert	Dec 27 1923	1	10
Morris, Albert	Jan 3 1924	1	10
Morris, C. S.	Aug 20 1914	1	8
Morris, Charles	Mar 3 1927	1	12
Morris, Mrs. Charles	Jan 6 1916	1	3
Morris, Fred (Doc)	Jun 23 1922	6	10
Morris, Mrs. Charles	Jan 13 1916	1	3
Morris, Gilbert	Dec 30 1905	5	4
Morris, George	May 21 1925	1	11
Morris, Hattie Lee	Aug 16 1928	1	12
Morris, H. P.	Jul 5 1928	1	12
Morris, Mrs. J. O.	Jun 22 1989	6	10*
*Found in May 5, 1922 Mt. Sun			
Morris, Lizzie	Sep 4 1909	2	5/7
Morriss, Ed E.	Dec 19 1929	1	13
Morriss, Mary Ann	Mar 1 1917	1	3
Morriss, baby of T. A. (Thanks)	Nov 17 1922	5	10
Mosby, Mrs. L. J.	Mar 9 1907	8	4

NAME	DATE		PG	FL
Mosel, Alex	Nov 13	1909	1	5/7
Mosel, Alex (son of Ben)	Feb 4	1926	5	11
Mosel, Mrs. J. P.	Mar 21	1908	2	5/7
Mosel, John Peter	Oct 17	1918	1	3
Mosel, Peter	Oct 11	1918	6	9
Moser, Ora	Apr 21	1927	3	12
Mosheim, Emil	Jun 21	1928	5	12
Mosley, Ellen	Nov 17	1927	1	12
Mosty, Lee A.	Nov 29	1917	2	3
Motley, Lillie	Jul 10	1924	7	10
Mouton, Caesar	Oct 30	1909	2	5/7
Moyer, Peter	Jun 23	1927	1	12
Moyer, Peter	Jul 28	1927	1	12
Mull, Christina L.	May 25	1916	1	3
Mullen, J. Frank	Sep 27	1902	5	4
Mullen, J, Frank	Oct 11	1902	5	4
Mullen, William Joseph	Jul 14	1922	7	10
Mullins, Grace Lena	Sep 26	1918	1	3
Mullins, Leo	Aug 21	1924	5	10
Murphy, Annie	Dec 13	1913	1	8
Murray, John J.	Mar 12	1925	7	11
Muschec, daughter of J.	Oct 3	1914	6	9
Mussil, Otto	May 31	1928	5	12
Nance, Gypsy May	Jan 14	1926	2	11
Navarro, Miguel	Feb 27	1920	3	9
Neal, Annie	Dec 24	1914	3	3
Neatherlin, C. M. (Thanks)	Oct 17	1929	5	13
Neely, J. I.	Nov 17	1906	5	4
Nelson, A. S.	Nov 11	1915	1	3
Nelson, H. L.	May 19	1922	7	10
Nelson, Paul	Oct 20	1922	6	10
Nelson, S. W.	Feb 4	1899	1	1
Nelson, Tedd Carrico	Nov 14	1918	4	3
Nelson, Mrs. T. J.	Sep 18	1915	1	9
Nelson, Tom	Feb 28	1924	3	10
Nelson, Tom J.	Sep 23	1915	1	3
Nepps, Dollie E.	Dec 20	1928	3	12
Neumann, Joe	Dec 5	1918	4	3
Neunhoffer, Ida	Apr 7	1927	7	12
Nevares, Lucia	Apr 21	1927	3	12

KERRVILLE MOUNTAIN SUN AND KERRVILLE ADVANCE
1898-1929

NAME	DATE	PG	FL
Nevares, Refugio	Apr 21 1927	3	12
New, Mrs. Liberty L.	Mar 14 1924	9	10
New, Sarah (Mrs. W. B.)	Nov 11 1926	11	11
New, Mrs. W. B.	Nov 18 1926	11	11
(Sarah Virginia Rollins)			
New, William B.	Apr 1 1915	4	3
Newman, R. S.	Jul 2 1920	1	9
Newton, Annie May	Feb 4 1899	1	1
Newton, Elmo M.	Nov 19 1914	1	3
Newton, J. E.	Jun 11 1914	5	8
Newton, James Ervin	Jun 18 1914	1	8
Newton, J. E. (Thanks)	Jun 20 1914	1	9
Newton, Lucy	Feb 13 1920	8	9
Newton, mother of Mrs. Mary (Thanks)	Jun 10 1926	10	11
Newton, Mrs. S. M.	Nov 11 1899	7	1
Newton, William Edward	Sep 12 1918	4	3
Nichel, Mrs. E. C.	Dec 10 1925	9	11
Nichols, A. G.	Sep 11 1909	7	5/7
Nichols, Infant of Henry	Nov 14 1908	4	7
Nichols, Mary Abigale Lackey	Feb 18 1899	1	1
Nichols, Milton	Nov 28 1918	1	3
Nichols, William Rowland	Jul 19 1923	5	10
Nichols, William Thomas	Aug 16 1928	1	12
Nieto, Angelita	Mar 22 1913	1	9
Nimitz, Anna	Jun 17 1926	9	11
Nimitz, Charles	Jun 14 1928	1	12
Nimitz, Charles H. (Sr.)	Jun 21 1928	5	12
Nimitz, Ernest A.	Jul 5 1928	8	12
Nimitz, Theresa	Oct 4 1928	1	12
Nimitz, Mrs. William	Feb 19 1925	1/5	11
Noble, G. L.	Oct 15 1920	5	9
Noll, Anna	Jul 30 1920	5	9
Noll, Anna	Aug 6 1920	3	9
Noll, Anna	Sep 10 1920	1	9
Noll, H. (Sr.)	Jun 24 1926	8	11
Noll, Henry (Sr.)	Jul 1 1926	1	11
Noll, Julius (Dr.)	Aug 20 1925	1	11
Noll, Walter	Jul 4 1929	1	13
Nolley, -----	Jul 19 1923	5	10
North, Mrs. T. C. (Edna Stone)	Jan 8 1914	8	8

40

NAME	DATE			PG	FL
North, Thomas Collin	Mar	24	1922	3	10
North, Will	Nov	20	1909	3	5/7
North, Willie James	Nov	27	1909	1	5/7
Northcraft, Claud	Nov	24	1906	10	4
Norwood, Walter D.	Jul	30	1920	3	9
Nottinger, Jacob	Nov	7	1929	7	13
Nowlin, Dr.	Dec	8	1998	6	10*
*Found in May 5, 1922 Mt. Sun					
Nowlin, Benjamin F. (B.F.)	Nov	19	1904	4	4
Nowlin, Benjamin F.	Nov	26	1904	4	4
Nowlin, Benjamin F.	Dec	3	1904	8	4
Nowlin, Daniel C.	Apr	9	1925	1	11
Nowlin, Mrs. F. A.	Oct	1	1925	6	11
Nowlin, Susan Arabelle Gathings	Oct	8	1925	2	11
Nulk, John C.	Jun	6	1908	5	7
Nurenberger, Henry	Feb	11	1915	5	3
Nyc, Babette	Feb	20	1909	2	5/7
Nyc, Billie Ruth	Jun	24	1926	8	11
Oakley, A. T.	Oct	27	1906	4	4
Oatman, Grandma	Mar	2	1916	1	3
Obar, Ann	Jun	3	1926	1	11
Obar, G. T.	Mar	8	1917	7	3
Oberle, Harold	Jun	18	1925	5	11
O'Bryant, Louis (Jr.)	Nov	22	1928	7	12
Ochse, Clara	May	15	1913	5	3
O'Connor, Charles aka	Oct	11	1923	5	10
(Francis Milton Flynn)					
Odell, Elizabeth Jane	Sep	20	1928	1	12
Oeffinger, John	Nov	11	1899	7	1
Oehler, Lockie Lillian	Feb	26	1914	5	8
Oehler, son of Adelbert	Jun	27	1929	5	13
Olejas, Porferio	Feb	27	1920	3	9
O'Neill, Charles James	Feb	10	1927	1	12
O'Neill, Charles James	Feb	17	1927	5	12
Oppermann, Emil	Sep	15	1906	7	4
Oppermann, W.	Mar	26	1902	4	4
Oppert, J. V.	Sep	18	1913	1	3
Ocasco, Ezekiel	Jul	15	1915	2	9
Osborne, Mary Elizabeth	Feb	17	1922	5	10
Osborne, Rachel	Mar	3	1922	5	10

NAME		DATE		PG	FL
Osburn, Mrs. M. C.		Jul 11	1918	1	3
Ottmers, Harry Paul	(Thanks)	Nov 1	1923	5	10
Overton, Mrs. J. D.		Oct 22	1914	1	3
Overton, Rev. J. D.		Dec 10	1914	1	3
Pafford, Rob		Apr 15	1905	4	4
Pafford, William E.		Oct 28	1915	1	3
Page, Children		Feb 22	1908	8	7
Page, Idelia		Feb 15	1917	6	3
Page, Idelia	(Thanks)	Feb 22	1917	4	3
Page, John M.		Sep 9	1926	9	11
Page, John T.		Mar 13	1913	1	3
Page, John T.		Mar 8	1913	4	9
Page, sister of W. H.		Sep 8	1922	7	11
Page, William		Jun 28	1928	10	12
Pais, Lee		Mar 3	1927	7	12
Palmer, S. J.		Jan 14	1915	1	3
Pampell, T. J.		Dec 16	1899	8	1
Pamperton, Mrs. Sesh		Jul 29	1899	1	1
Pankratz, Max		Sep 14	1926	1	11
Pankratz, Mrs. Max		Sep 14	1926	1	11
Pankratz, Theodore		Nov 1	1928	1	12
Park, Cleveland		Sep 22	1906	8	4
Parker, J. H.		Feb 9	1917	1	9
Parker, Lottie		Feb 18	1926	8	11
Parker, Nora		Oct 22	1914	4	3
Parr, J. R.		May 15	1924	8	10
Parrott, Mollie		Jan 21	1899	1	1
Parsons, John H.		Jan 17	1924	1	10
Parsons, Mary A.		Nov 28	1929	1	13
Pate, J. C.		Jun 7	1917	5	3
Paterson, James		Dec 31	1914	1	3
Patterson, Lewis L.		Feb 14	1929	1	13
Patterson, Lowell G.		Oct 24	1918	1	3
Patterson, Mrs. Sam		Jan 17	1929	1	13
Patton, Mrs. Charles		Jan 31	1918	5	3
Patton, Mrs. W. S.		Jul 23	1925	1	11
(Nellie G. Ridgeway)					
Patton, Mrs. W. S.		Sep 24	1925	8	11
Patton, William Warren		Nov 15	1928	1	12
Paullin, J. W.		Mar 13	1909	3	4/7

NAME	DATE		PG	FL
Peabody, Peggy	Sep 20	1923	10	10
Pearson, Mrs. ----	Nov 12	1925	9	11
Pelzer, Gus	Nov 7	1908	5	5
Pemberton, A. B.	Jun 1	1907	5	4
Pennington, Mrs. (Ora)	Apr 14	1927	1	12
Pennignton, Ora	Apr 21	1927	3	12
Pennington, Zola May	Apr 14	1927	1	12
Pennignton, Zola May	Apr 21	1927	3	12
Perez, Andrea	Apr 21	1927	3	12
Perez, David	Apr 18	1918	5	3
Perez, David	Apr 26	1918	6	9
Perez, Dona Carmen	Feb 14	1924	5	10
Perez, Petra	Apr 21	1927	3	12
Perez, Mrs. Rudolph	Jun 16	1927	7	12
(Mathilda Espinosa)				
Peril, Mrs. E. A.	Feb 28	1903	5	4
Peril, Girard	Nov 7	1908	5	5
Peril, Girard A.	Nov 7	1908	4	7
Peril, Girard	Nov 14	1908	5	5
Peril, Girard A.	Nov 14	1908	5	7
Perner, Selma	May 20	1905	5	4
Perry, H. H.	Nov 22	1923	6	10
Perry, Tudie	Jul 29	1915	5	3
Peschel, Emil (Thanks)	Oct 25	1923	3	10
Peschel, Julius	Aug 22	1918	1	3
Peschel, Mrs. Julius	Apr 5	1928	5	12
Petermann, Edmund	Oct 1	1920	3	9
Peters, Mrs. P. E.	Apr 30	1914	1	8
Peterson, Iris Carr (Mrs. Tom)	Jul 16	1925	5	11
Peterson, Lee C.	Feb 24	1927	1	12
Peterson, Ray A. (Thanks)	Jan 6	1927	9	12
Peterson, Tom B.	Jan 11	1917	1	3
Peterson, Tom B.	Jan 13	1917	1	9
Peterson, Susie Phillips	Sep 24	1925	4	11
Peterson, Mrs. W. C.	Jun 18	1925	1	11
Peterson, Mrs. Walter G.	Sep 17	1925	1	11
Peterson, William C.	Sep 18	1924	1	10
Peterson, William S.	Jun 20	1929	1	13
Petmecky, Fleta	Feb 26	1914	1	8
Petmecky, Walter T.	Sep 20	1923	5/9	10

NAME	DATE			PG	FL
Pfeufer, Vide (Victor)	Sep 6	1902		5	4
Pfeuffer, Eugenia	Nov 19	1910		2	7
Pfeuffer, Nicholas George	Jul 17	1913		1	3
Pfeuffer, Richard	Sep 29	1922		6	10
Phansteel, Cornelia	Sep 24	1925		1	11
Phillips, Addie	Apr 18	1903		5	4
Phillips, Earl R.	Jan 21	1899		1	1
Phillips, J. L.	Mar 14	1908		5	5/7
Phillips, Leilla	Mar 9	1907		7	4
Phillips, Walter J.	Aug 30	1902		4	4
Pingleton, Douglas	Sep 27	1923		3	10
Plant, Mrs. W. Y.	Sep 30	1926		12	11 S2
Plummer, Russell L.	Nov 15	1928		1	12
Pogmore, Margaret	Dec 24	1914		1	3
Polk, Mrs.	Feb 24	1922		3	10
Polka, father of Jim	Jul 17	1924		3	10
Pope, Mrs. L. F.	Aug 2	1898		6	10*
*Found in May 5, 1922 Mt. Sun					
Pope, son of Willie	Jul 3	1913		1	3
Porras, Marcelo (Estate)	Mar 22	1928		9	12
Porter, Malta (Mrs. M. R.)	Jul 9	1925		5	11
Posey, W. D. (William D.)	Feb 28	1929		1	13
Powell, Mrs. Henley	Jul 24	1913		1	3
Powell, brother of J. B.	Jun 24	1926		8	11
Powell, J. H.	Mar 3	1922		7	10
Powell, James (Estate)	Jan 8	1925		2	11
Powell, Mrs. Otis	May 24	1928		1	12
Prevost, adopted daughter of Leon	Apr 21	1927		3	12
Price, Mattie Surber	Mar 29	1917		5	3
Price, W. R.	Mar 26	1925		5	11
Prichett, Mrs. L. E.	Sep 14	1898		6	10*
*Found in May 5, 1922 Mt. Sun					
Priday, A. C.	Dec 10	1914		1	3
Primm, Mrs. Frank (Hazel)	May 5	1922		1	10
Prisch, W. G.	Nov 20	1909		1	5/7
Provenzo, Salvador T.	Feb 3	1927		7	12
Provenzano, Salvador	Feb 10	1927		7	12
Provine, Nan	Feb 25	1915		4	3
Pruitt, Edward J.	Feb 22	1908		8	5/7
Purseley, William Wall	Jun 22	1916		1	3

NAME	DATE			PG	FL
Quarles, Sally Bell	Feb 2	1928		9	12
Quigley, John	Jun 21	1928		5	12
Rabalais, Mrs. Harold B.	Feb 10	1927		7	12
Rabalais, Mrs. Milton	Apr 8	1926		5	11
(Victoria Mayeaux)					
Rabb, Early	Aug 5	1899		1	1
Raff, Geroge A.	Apr 28	1918		4	3
Ragland, F. S. (Estate)	Jul 19	1923		4	10
Ragland, Victor E.	Apr 2	1920		5	9
Ragland, William M.	Oct 20	1906		4	4
Raiford, Mrs. Robert	Sep 11	1913		5	3
Rainey, Dr. Frank	Feb 5	1914		5	8
Ralston, Mahala	Dec 12	1918		1	3
Rambie, Mrs. H. E.	Jul 25	1918		1	3
Rambie, Horace	Jul 15	1915		1	3
Ramirez, Aurita	Jan 23	1920		3	9
Ramirez, Georgia	May 12	1927		6	12
Ramos, Ignacio	Jun 11	1920		3	9
Ramos, Jose	Mar 3	1927		7	12
Ramos, Mrs. Sista Perez	Sep 4	1924		5	10
Rankin, Mrs. H. A.	Mar 1	1928		6	12
Rathman, Anton	Jan 17	1929		5	13
Rausch, Jacob	Nov 15	1902		5	4
Rawlings, Charlotte Eliz. Nichols	Jun 28	1918		1	9
Rawlings, Mrs. J. A.	Jun 27	1918		1	3
Rawson, Florence Ann	Jan7	1915		1	3
Rawson, Georgine	Nov 4	1915		1	3
Rawson, Georgine	Apr 18	1929		1	13
Rawson, Mrs. Herbert	May 7	1925		3	11
Ray, Albert S.	Mar 21	1929		5	13
Ray, W. R.	May 10	1917		6	3
Rayfield, N. H.	Apr 21	1906		5	4
Real, Emilie Schreiner	Mar 21	1918		1	3
Real, son of Felix	Dec 23	1921		3	10
Reck, Anna	Jan 31	1929		1	13
Reckham, Mrs. Russell	Dec 8	1922		5	10
(Annie N. Rees)					
Reed, Dan	Apr 11	1908		3	5/7
Reed, W. C.	Apr 14	1922		3	10
Rees, Alonzo	Jan 30	1919		1	3

KERRVILLE MOUNTAIN SUN AND KERRVILLE ADVANCE
1898-1929

NAME	DATE		PG	FL
Rees, Dr. H. Clay	Feb 12	1914	1	8
Rees, Dr. H. Clay	Feb 7	1914	5	9
Rees, James C.	Aug 30	1923	5	10
Rees, Lucy A.	Oct 31	1929	1	13
Rees, Sidney	Dec 11	1909	1	5/7
Reeves, Lorraine	May 31	1928	7	12
Reeves, William	Nov 28	1918	1	3
Regan, Harold A.	Mar 22	1928	6	12
Reichert, Jno. F.	Oct 20	1922	5	10
Reichert, John F.	Oct 27	1922	3	10
Renick, Arthur	Jul 5	1917	5	3
Reno, Henry Irl	Dec 5	1918	4	3
Repka, Frank	Sep 27	1923	5	10
Repsdorph, George	Aug 27	1925	5	11
Reyes, Cristobal	Apr 21	1927	3	12
Reynolds, N. O.	Mar 10	1922	7	10
Reynolds, R. H.	Oct 25	1917	1	3
Reynolds, R?. O.	Apr 8	1899	1	1
Reynolds, W. L.	Sep 6	1917	1	3
Rhea, Della	Dec 3	1914	5	3
Rhodes,----	Feb 22	1908	5	5/7
Richards, C. M. (Thanks)	Aug 27	1920	7	9
Richards, Rolfe	Jan 18	1908	5	5/7
Richardson, C. E.	Aug 25	1922	7	10
Richardson, Mrs. G. L.	Dec 17	1914	5	3
Richardson, Travis Wayne	Sep 4	1913	1	3
Richter, Mrs. Gus	Jun 9	1927	7	12
Riddle, J. B. (Rev.)	Oct 11	1923	6	10
Ridgaway, Julius	Jun 21	1928	1	12
Ridley, Mrs. B. C.(Elizabeth North)	Sep 22	1927	1/8	12
Ridley, Jerome	Mar 30	1907	8	4
Riley, Fred	Apr 5	1929	1	13
Rischworth, Mrs. W. H.	Jul 26	1928	1/6	12
Ritchie, Joseph Harrison	Feb 27	1920	1	9
Roberts, Esther	Mar 1	1917	1	3
Robertson, Oscar	Oct 3	1908	3	5
Robeschung, Hank	May 22	1909	1	5/7
Robinson, Albert C.	Apr 4	1908	2	5/7
Robinson, Emmett Lee	May 2	1908	8	5
Robinson, J. L.	Jun 16	1909	1	2/6

46

NAME	DATE	PG	FL
Robinson, Mrs. Lou	Oct 4 1928	1	12
Robinson, Minnie	Apr 4 1929	1/3	13
Robinson, Walter	Jan 17 1903	4	4
Rodey, William A.	Dec 4 1924	1	10
Rodgers, C. E.	Jul 20 1913	5	3
Rodgers, Silas (Thanks)	Feb 15 1902	1	4
Rodgers, Silas	Feb 22 1902	8	4
Rodriguez, Antonio	Nov 5 1910	1	7
Rodriguez, Canute	Jun 28 1928	7	12
Rodriquez, Rev. Jose Policarpo	Apr 2 1914	1	8
Rodriguez, Narcissa C.	Sep 6 1923	5	10
Roebuck, J. E.	Jan 13 1917	8	9
Roeder, Mrs. Louis nee Friedrich	Apr 9 1920	6	9
Roeder, Mrs. William	Mar 28 1908	8	5/7
Rogers, Gulielma Desdemona Miller	Nov 21 1908	5	5/7
Rogers, Julia D. (Desdemona)	Oct31 1908	8	5/7
Rogers, Julia Miller (Thanks)	Nov 7 1908	4	5/7
Roll, Charles	Mar 16 1907	8	4
Roll, George	Mar 16 1907	8	4
Rollins, Hinchie	Feb 4 1926	9	11
Romero, Louise Jimenez	Nov 11 1926	7	11
Roper, W. E. C.	Feb 11 1915	4	3
Rorer, Ferdinand	Jan 15 1914	8	8
Rose, Frank--infant son	May 13 1910	3	7
Rose, Gabriel M.	Nov 28 1929	1	13
Ross, John K.	Feb 10 1922	7	10
Roteschung, Hank	May 22 1909	1	7
Rotge, Annie	Sep 28 1917	1	9
Rotge, Annie	Oct 11 1917	1	3
Roth, Victor	Jun 27 1929	1	13
Rouff, Leon	Jul 15 1926	3	11
Rouse, J. A.	Dec 20 1917	1	3
Rowinsky, Edward (Jr.)	Jul 15 1926	5	11
Rudasill, J. A.	May 19 1922	7	10
Ruff, Hieronymous	Jan 30 1920	1/3	9
Ruff, Herman Werner	Jun 11 1920	6	9
Ruff, Homer	Jan 30 1920	1	9
Rumsey, Delia	Apr 21 1906	4	4
Rush, T. E.	May 2 1908	8	7
Russell, Don (Estate)	Jul 23 1925	5	11

NAME	DATE		PG	FL
Russell, Mrs. L. A.	Jan 17	1918	3	3
Sager, Jesse (Thanks)	Jul 8	1926	4	11
Sageser, Mrs. D. W.	Jul 3	1925	9	11
Sageser, Lewis E.	Jun 20	1929	1	13
St. John, Lt. Alvin	May 28	1920	7	9
Salmon, Mrs. J. B. (Velma Hodges)	Feb 20	1913	4	3
Salmons, Oscar M.	Aug 16	1928	1	12
Salter, Clarence E.	Jul 18	1929	1	13
Saludis, Annie	Aug 8	1929	1	13
Sanchez, Jesus	Nov 8	1928	7	12
Sanchez, son of Joe	Nov 22	1928	7	12
Sanchez, Simon	Oct 31	1918	4	3
Sandell, Theodore	Jan 12	1928	1	12
Sander, Myrtle Gene	Mar 8	1928	1	12
Sandherr, son of Nat	Nov 21	1908	8	5/7
Sanglier, Justin O.	Mar 18	1899	1	1
Sanglier, Miss Maggie	May 13	1899	1	1
Sansom, John W.	Jun 25	1920	1	9
Saubell, Nicholas	Apr 5	1913	1	9
Sauseda, Richard	Jun 17	1916	6	9
Sawyer, Mrs. E. E.	Nov 17	1906	4	4
Sawyer, George (Thanks)	Feb 18	1899	1	1
Saxon, James A.	Apr 14	1906	4	4
Schaefer, Frank	Oct 25	1928	7	12
Schanafealt, Carrie L.	Jun 9	1927	7	12
Scheel, Louise	Oct 18	1928	1	12
Schellhase, Gottfriend (?)	Oct 17	1929	1	13
Schladoer, Robert	Jan 17	1929	5	13
Schmerbeck, Robert	Mar 18	1899	4	1
Schmidt, Prof. Edward	Jul 15	1915	1	3
Schmidt, Rosie	Aug 4	1922	7	10
Schumacher, Oscar R.	Apr 23	1925	1	11
Schmuacher, Mrs. S. (Sarah A. Braziel)	Nov 13	1924	1/7	10
Scholl, Henry (Sr.)	Sep 11	1909	2	5
Scholl, Henry V.	Jan 13	1912	1	9
Schonette, Harvey	Apr 7	1927	1	12
Schott, Caroline	Feb 14	1929	7	13
Schott, Edward	May 9	1929	7	13
Schneider, John	Oct 11	1918	6	9

NAME	DATE		PG	FL
Schnerr, David	Apr 10	1924	9	10
Schreiber, Albert	Oct 28	1905	8	4
Schreiner, Charles	Feb 10	1927	1	12
Schreiner, Charles	Feb 17	1927	1	12
Schreiner, Charles	Feb 24	1927	1	12
Schumbelt, G.	Sep 28	1917	1	9
Schuster, Mrs. Charles (Thanks)	Oct 10	1908	2	5/7
Schwart, Frank Gerald	Oct 18	1923	5	10
Schwethelm, Henry	Aug 21	1924	1	10
Scoble, Annie E.	Oct 19	1916	1	3
Scott, Alex	May 30	1929	1	13
Scott, S. J.	Jan 16	1919	1	3
Scott, S. J.	Jan 10	1919	1	9
Secrest, Mrs. L. M.	Jul 3	1909	5	5/7
Secrest, Mrs. M. L.	Jun 30	1909	1	2
Seeber, Charles J.	Dec 16	1921	1	10
Seffel, Ed E.	Sep 19	1918	5	3
Seifert, ————	Aug 2	1902	4	4
Selby, Matti	Dec 10	1925	10	11
Shand, Allister	Oct 17	1918	5	3
Shand, John	May 20	1915	1	3
Shand, Mrs.	Jan 31	1918	5	3
Sharp, Ed	Mar 22	1913	1	9
Sharp, W. B.	Mar 21	1908	5	5/7
Shattuck, Gertrude	May 30	1908	2	5
Shattuck, Gertrude	May 30	1908	6	7
Shaver, Mrs. L. R.	Feb 5	1914	1	8
Sheffield, Maurine	Jan 13	1927	3	12
Shekell, Eugene	Jun 10	1926	4	11
Sherer, August	Sep 27	1902	5	4
Sherman, John	Mar 2	1914	6	9
Shiner, Louise West	May 3	1928	1	12
Shirey, J. N.--son of	Feb 20	1913	1	3
Shumard, M. A.	Jul 7	1927	6	12
Siebennchen, John	Feb 20	1913	1	3
Silvas, Clara	Nov 14	1918	4	3
Silvas, Jose	Sep 28	1917	6	9
Silvas, Lamasio	Nov 14	1918	4	3
Silvas, Miguel	Oct 20	1927	5	12
Silvers, John	Jan 18	1908	11	7

NAME	DATE		PG	FL
Silvers, John	Jan 25	1908	5	5
Simmons, nephew of W. A.	Jun 18	1925	8	11
Simmons, W. A.	Jun 9	1927	1	12
Simms, Mrs. B. W. N.	Feb 7	1918	3	3
Simms, Mrs. B. W. N.	Feb 14	1918	5	3
Singleton, John Eldridge	Aug 23	1928	3	12
Skinner, W. L. (Rev.)	Jul 1	1926	6	11
Slaughter, Clifton	Sep 29	1927	5	12
Slaughter, Clifton F.	Sep 22	1927	12	12
Slayden, James L.	Feb 28	1924	10	10
Sleeper, L. G.	Jan 13	1927	10	12
Sloan, Mrs. E. J.	Jan 2	1913	1	3
Slusser, John L.	Jul 18	1929	1	13
Smalley, Isaac	Sep 5	1918	1	3
Smallwood, Edward (Note of Admin.)	Dec 9	1899	8	1
Smallwood, Edward (Note of Admin.)	Dec 16	1899	5	1
Smallwood, Edward (Note of Admin.)	Dec 23	1899	3	1
Smead, Sarah G.	Sep 11	1909	7	5/7
Smith, Mrs. Carey P (Jane)	May 20	1899	4	1
Smith, Cora Dyer	Oct 19	1916	1	3
Smith, D. C.	Jun 11	1914	1	8
Smith, Edgar	Sep 4	1924	10	10
Smith, Freddie	Jan 13	1916	1	3
Smith, Freddie	Jan 15	1916	6	9
Smith, Glenn	Feb 12	1925	1	11
Smith, Mrs. H. B.	Mar 25	1926	1	11
Smith, Jack	Sep 27	1928	1	12
Smith, Leo	Jan 20	1927	10	12
Smith, Mabel	Jun 25	1925	9	11
Smith, Mary Jean	Oct 11	1928	1	12
Smith, Nancy (Mrs. Pat)	Nov 10	1927	1/11	12
Smith, Pat	May 26	1909	1	2/6
Smith, Pat C.	May 29	1909	7	7
Smith, T. D.	Feb 23	1929	1	13
Smith, W. E.	Mar 16	1907	3	4
Smith, William (Saco)	May 26	1927	1	12
Smith-Vaudry, T. (Rev.)	Dec 22	1922	3	10
Sommers, W. H.	Sep 9	1915	1	3
Soto, Marcellino	Nov 19	1925	7/8	11
Sparks, Dan (Thanks)	Jun 12	1915	5	9

NAME	DATE		PG	FL
Sparks, Don	Jul 3	1915	4	3
Speed, Mrs. John	Nov 5	1904	8	4
Speier, Christian	Dec 15	1927	5	12
Spenrath, August	Sep 8	1906	8	4
Spenrath, William (Estate)	Aug 27	1925	9	11
Spicer, Robert Emerson	Nov 28	1913	1	3
Spindler, Sarah Clara	May 11	1912	4	9
Spiers, H. L. (Rev.)	Apr 21	1927	3	12
Spiers, Mrs. H. L.	Apr 21	1927	3	12
Spires, Mrs. H. L.	Apr 14	1927	1	12
Sprinkles, Mr.	Feb 28	1918	1	3
Sproul, Elizabeth	May 3	1917	1	3
Sproul, W. W.	Oct 3	1918	5	3
Sproul, William Walter	Oct 10	1918	1	3
Sproul, William Withroe	Oct 11	1918	1	9
Spruill, J. Fred	Mar 11	1926	10	11
Stallings, N. O. (Nick)	Feb 4	1899	1	1
Starkey, Martha A.	Apr 29	1905	5	4
Staudt, Emil	Jan 17	1929	5	13
Steele, Matilda	Apr 26	1917	1	3
Steele, Mathilda	Apr 27	1917	1	9
Steinlein, Mrs. George	May 16	1908	4	7
Stehling, Lawrence	Sep 15	1922	3	10
Steifel, Louise (Thanks)	Oct 23	1925	7	11
Stell, Infant	Feb 11	1915	1	3
Stevens, Charles Jerome	Jan 2	1920	8	9
Stevens, Charley	May 10	1917	1	3
Stevens, Loyd	Sep 17	1914	1	8
Stewart, Edward J.	Nov 21	1929	1	13
Stewart, Frank	Jun 17	1899	1	1
Stieler, Herman	Nov 15	1928	1	12
Stieler, Herman	Nov 22	1928	7	12
Stinson, W. F. (Thanks)	Apr 30	1920	3	9
Stockard, L. E.	Feb 24	1927	12	12
Stockton, --- (Thanks)	Sep 22	1922	2	10
Stoker, Lydia	Aug 24	1912	5	9
Stokes, Harry	Sep 25	1909	4	5/7
Stokes, Melvin	Feb 7	1913	1	3
Stokes, Walter Y.	Jun 21	1928	1	12
Stone, A. G.	Apr 24	1924	9	10

NAME	DATE			PG	FL
Stone, Elizabeth Ann	Apr	30	1920	3	9
Stone, J. W.	Jul	1	1916	1	9
Stone, Joseph T.	Aug	2	1928	1	12
Stone, Lawrence Woodrow	Feb	19	1914	1	8
Stone, Laurance Woodrow	Feb	22	1914	4	9
Stone, Mary	Jun	13	1929	1	13
Storey, A. B.	Jan	20	1912	2	9
Storey, John	Apr	7	1906	2	4
Storey, Walter	May	26	1909	5	2/6
Storey, Walter	May	29	1909	1	7
Storms, Gilbert C.	Jul	19	1917	1	3
Storms, Jonathon	Dec	24	1904	5	4
Storms, Judge R. H.	May	4	1907	7	4
Storms, Sarah	Jan	30	1909	7	5/7
Storms, Sarah	Sep	22	1922	7	10
Storms, Sylvan T.	Feb	16	1907	7	4
Storms, Mrs. Virgil (Sarah)	Jan	23	1909	4	5/7
Stowe, Rebecca (Ray)	Dec	9	1926	7	11
Strohacker, infant	Oct	18	1902	2	4
Strohacker, Louis	Mar	10	1927	1	12
Stucke, Herbert Carl	May	17	1928	7	12
Stults, Mrs. H. C.	Mar	18	1926	8	11
Sullivan, Dovie	Apr	7	1927	1	12
Sullivan, Sidney S.	Dec	3	1925	7	11
Sultenfuss, Louis E.	Jul	7	1928	7	12
Summers, J. J.	Nov	19	1925	4	11
Sumners, L. B.	Jul	7	1909	8	2/6
Surber, A. B.	Apr	6	1916	1	3
Surber, Elmer Dean	Feb	11	1915	5	3
Surber, Emaline	Jul	29	1915	5	3
Surber, Green C.	Oct	1	1926	1	11
Surber, Mrs. Harrison	Jun	2	1927	6	12
Surber, Joseph	Dec	12	1929	8	13
Surber, Joseph	Dec	19	1929	8	13
Surber, Mrs. L. V.	Mar	14	1918	8	3
Surber, Malinda Louise	Jan	27	1927	4	12
Surber, Mary Anna (Estate)	Jan	8	1925	8	11
Surber, Olga Liebold (Mrs. Orville)	Jan	2	1913	1	3
Surber, Rebecca T. (Mrs. Joseph)	Dec	19	1929	8	13
Surber, W. F.	Sep	22	1922	7	10

NAME	DATE		PG	FL
Surber, W. G.	Mar 21	1929	1	13
Surber, Mrs. W. N.	Mar 7	1918	5	3
Suttner, Raymond	Jun 17	1926	7	11
Sutton, Thomas W. C.	Mar 18	1926	10	11
Swan, Joe B.	Oct 11	1923	5	10
Swan, Joe B.	Oct 18	1923	2	10
Sweatt, Murphy	Oct 17	1929	7	13
Swicegood, Stephen P.	Dec 19	1929	5	13
Tacquard, August	Jul 19	1917	13	3
Tagl, William	Nov 14	1929	1	13
Talley, child of Mr/Mrs John	May 14	1920	3	9
Talley, Jack	May 18	1916	8	3
Talley, John Edward	Oct 8	1020	12	9
Tally, Russell	Nov 28	1908	2	5
Tally, Russell	Nov 28	1908	10	7
Tanner, Ben	Feb 2	1907	5	4
Tatsch, Henry	Jul 5	1928	7	12
Taylor, Mrs. A. G. (Martha Graham)	Feb 10	1927	11	12
Taylor, Mrs. Amos	Feb 3	1927	11	12
Taylor, Mrs. Elijah	Mar 21	1908	8	5/7
Taylor, Florence	Mar 12	1925	5	11
Taylor, Mrs. J. B.	Jun 28	1928	11	12
Taylor, Mrs. J. D.	Sep 3	1920	1	9
Taylor, Jno. F.	Oct 8	1920	12	9
Taylor, Mollie Belle Wharton	Dec 5	1918	1	3
Taylor, Oscar	Nov 13	1924	3	10
Taylor, Sam	Oct 13	1927	11	12
Taylor, William A.	Oct 10	1929	1	13
Teeter, infant of T. E.	Jul 8	1905	5	4
Terrell, W. A.	Apr 25	1908	8	5/7
Terry, Henry	Jan 21	1915	1	3
Terry, Mrs.	Jan 10	1919	3	9
Terry, Sargent	Jan 10	1919	3	9
Thibodeaus, Felician	May 14	1920	3	9
Thomas, ——— (Thanks)	Mar 3	1922	2	10
Thomas, George E.	Jan 10	1935	1	16
Thomas, Lizzie	May 9	1918	5	3
Thomas, Mrs. M. A.	Jun 24	1915	1	3
Thomas, Capt. T. (Thomas)	Dec 9	1915	1	3
Thomas, W. P. (Thank You)	Jun 7	1902	8	4

NAME	DATE		PG	FL
Thompson, John S.	Oct 3	1914	1	9
Thorson, Elsa Christine (Mrs. S. D.)	Oct 21	1926	5	11
Thurman, Emma Joy	Oct 14	1926	11	11
Tice, Mrs. M. C.	Jan 13	1927	3	12
Tichborne, Clarence	Dec 3	1925	8	11
Tipton, Clara Wilbanks	Aug 31	1916	1	3
Tipton, Thomas I.	Jan 7	1926	1	11
Tivy Estate Disposition	Feb 25	1905	2	4
Todd, Mrs. W. I.	Feb 25	1899	1	1
Toepperwein, H. W.	Nov 11	1916	1	62*

* This was on an old front page printed in the September 26,
1981 issue of the Mountain Sun. Some of these old issues
were missing by the time it was decided to film them for
safe keeping.

Toffoli, Victor	Aug 30	1923	5	10
Tolin, M. A.	Mar 19	1914	1	8
Torres, Ambrosio (Pete)	Feb 2	1928	1	12
Torres, Ambrosio (Pete)	Feb 9	1928	5	12
Townsend, Irene (dau. of P. M.)	Sep 2	1926	8	11
Townsend, S. J.	Jan 7	1926	1	11
Tracy, Ed	Sep 25	1914	4	9
Travis, Frank (Thanks)	Jun 11	1910	4	7
Trevino, Mrs. Espirion	Jun 16	1929	7	12
Trimble, Marion	Sep 12	1929	11	13
Tullis, John La Fayette	Mar 1	1928	1	12
Turk, Elizabeth	Apr 11	1935	1	16
Turk, Will	Jan 3	1903	5	4
Turk, Will	Jan 10	1903	2	4
Turner, Belva Ray	Mar 14	1929	1	13
Turner, John B.	Mar 17	1927	1	12
Tuttle, Carrie	Dec 19	1929	1	13
Tuttle, Florence	Feb 21	1929	1	13
Tuttle, Sam (Thanks)	Aug 19	1926	3	11
Tynan, Johanna	Feb 1	1925	5	11
Underwood, Earl W.	Mar 13	1913	1	3
Utterback, Ida Mae	Jul 15	1915	1	3
Valdez, Domingo	Apr 26	1928	1	12
Vallaret, Paul G.	Jun 26	1913	8	3
Vallier, Ruth	Jan 16	1919	1	3
Vanderstucken, Mrs. Alfred	Mar 19	1920	4	9

NAME	DATE		PG	FL
Van Hoozer, Cordelia Dony	Jan 9	1919	1	3
(Mrs. I.W.)				
Van Hoozer, Cordelia Dony	Jan 10	1919	1	9
Vann, Margaret L.	Dec 4	1924	1	10
Vann, Wilson Wade	Sep 22	1906	3	4
Vansickle, F. H.	Jan 10	1919	8	9
Vargas, Mrs. Carlos	Apr 14	1922	7	10
Vargas, Marcello	Apr 16	1920	3	9
Vasbinder, L. J.	Dec 23	1921	7	10
Vaughn, Robert H.	Jan 29	1925	1	11
Venable, Roy Aubrey	Nov 19	1910	5	7
Villanueva, Valeriano	Apr 15	1926	5	11
Vining, Reuben	Dec 13	1909	4	5
Vinning, W. L.	Nov 28	1929	3	13
Voges, Menia	May 19	1922	1	10
Von Rosenberg, Anita	May 1	1909	2	7
Wachter, Mrs. Nancy	Mar 21	1903	2	4
Wages, C. B.	Feb 18	1926	7	11
Wagner, Ann	Mar 27	1913	1	3
Wagner, Ann	Mar 29	1913	2	9
Wahrmund, Otto	Jun 27	1929	12	13
Wahrmund, Mrs. Otto	Oct 24	1929	1	13
Wake, --- (Thanks)	Apr 28	1922	2	10
Wakefield, Nellie	Dec 11	1913	1	8
Wales, H. P.	Apr 19	1920	10	12
Walker, John	Oct 8	1904	5	4
Walker, Mrs. J. W.	Jan 2	1913	4	3
Walker, Mrs. L. E.	Dec 24	1912	1	3
Walker, Mrs. L. E.	Dec 12	1912	1	6
Walker, Porter Grover	Sep 18	1913	1	3
Walker, Thomas R.	Mar 29	1902	5	4
Walker, William B.	Feb 23	1928	1	12
Walker, W. F.	Nov 11	1899	5	1
Wall, M. D.	Oct 15	1920	8	9
Wallace, Mrs. A. C.	Jun 25	1925	10	11
Wallace, father of J. R.	Oct 13	1922	7	10
Walther, Gerald J.	Dec 24	1925	1	11
Walter, Gerald John	Jan 7	1926	7	11
Waltrip, R. A. (Rev.)	Oct 31	1918	1	3
Waltrop, Mrs.	Jun 27	1908	5	5

55

NAME	DATE		PG	FL
Ward, Bulah Mae	Oct 8	1920	12	9
Ward, Mrs. John H.	Jul 26	1928	1	12
Ward, Mrs. W. G.	Sep 1	1927	1	12
Ward, son of W. G.	Jan 14	1926	3	3
Ward, Willis	Aug 27	1920	1	9
Warren, infant daughter of Murray	Apr 12	1928	9	12
Wardlow, Mrs. M. D.	Nov 22	1917	7	3
Washburn, son of John	Sep 2	1899	4	1
Watson, Billy	Apr 19	1928	11	12
Watson, child	Apr 13	1907	5	4
Watson, child (Thanks)	Apr 13	1907	4	4
Watson, Mary Alice	Sep 27	1902	5	4
Watson, Thomas Joseph	May 4	1907	4	4
Webster, Herman H.	Nov 24	1927	1	12
Wehmeyer, Mrs. William	Oct 3	1929	1	13
Weid, Elo	Apr 10	1924	3	10
Weir, Beatrice Harrison	Apr 9	1925	1	11
Weise, Nettie Mae	Dec 3	1920	1	9
Welch, Dorothy L.	Jun 13	1929	1	13
Welge, Conrad C.	Oct 8	1914	1	8
Welge, Henry	Dec 9	1915	1	3
Wellborn, S. H.	Nov 13	1913	1	3
Wells, Brock	Oct 11	1902	4	4
Wells, George	Feb 1	1917	1	3
Wells, Martha E.	May 14	1920	3	9
Wells, W. W.	Jun 2	1922	4	10
Weltner, Mrs. Otto	Mar 17	1927	8	12
Weltner, Mrs. Otto (Minnie Kochmann)	Mar 24	1927	4	12
Wentworth, C. N.	Sep 20	1917	1	3
West, Hattie B.	Feb 24	1906	2	4
West, Hattie B.	Feb 24	1906	4	4
Weston, C. T.	Jan 25	1917	1	3
Weston, Caroline	Feb 28	1924	5	10
Weston, Valma	Dec 3	1904	8	4
Wetherall, Richard	Feb 2	1928	6	12
Whalen, mother of Jim	Mar 21	1929	5	13
Wharton, Mrs. Lee	Oct 26	1926	8	11
Wharton, Lucinda	Mar 25	1926	2	11
Wharton, W. C. (Bud)	Jul 1	1915	1	3

NAME	DATE		PG	FL
Wheat, Mrs. C. E.	Dec 26	1929	1	13
Wheat, Ira L. (Jr.)	Feb 24	1906	10	4
Wheeler, Dollie	May 29	1913	1/4	3
Wheelus, C. A.	Nov 3	1922	1	10
Wheelus, Mrs. Cleveland B.	Oct 11	1923	5	10
Wheelus, mother of Gertrude	Feb 7	1929	5	13
Whetstone, Mrs. T. M.	Apr 16	1925	8	11
Whitaker, Sylvia Phillips	Nov 11	1926	11	11
White, Frank	Jul 24	1913	1	3
White, Mrs. Frank E.	Mar 17	1927	8	12
White, Mrs. L. M.	Mar 24	1922	6	10
White, Mary Irene	Oct 21	1905	4	4
White, O.	May 23	1908	8	5/7
White, Raleigh R. (Rev.)	Jan 23	1919	1	3
White, Rebecca	Sep 24	1910	2	7
Whitley, Jack	Feb 3	1922	3	10
Wicker, Helen	Feb 29	1908	8	7
Wickes, Harry	Sep 20	1928	7	12
Wickes, Harry M.	Sep 13	1928	1	12
Wickson, Mrs. Lee (Bessie Bundick)	Feb 18	1926	2	11
Wickson, Melvin La Fayette	Feb 25	1910	3	7
Wied, May Louise	Nov 14	1918	1	3
Wiedenfeld, Ida Schulze	May 17	1928	5	12
Wiedenfeld, Theodore	Nov 19	1904	4	4
Wiedenfeld, Theodore	Nov 26	1904	8	4
Wiedenfeld, William	Apr 21	1927	3	12
Wilborn, daughter of Robert L.	Sep 13	1902	4/8	4
Wiley, Leonard	May 3	1917	1	3
Will, Mrs. Alva (Blanche)	Sep 15	1927	5/7	12
Williams, Alma Lee	Aug 16	1902	4	4
Williams, Alvan	Mar 9	1916	1	3
Williams, Mrs. D. S.	Oct 23	1905	4	4
Williams, Dellia	Dec 30	1905	6	4
Williams, George	Jul 12	1923	4	10
Williams, Mrs. George	Mar 1	1917	1	3
Williams, infant girl	Jun 17	1899	1	1
Williams, James P. T. (Estate)	Apr 30	1925	9	11
Williams, Mrs. John	Jan 8	1925	1	11
Williams, Joseph W.	Apr 21	1906	8	4
Williams, Mrs. Leroy (Thanks)	Apr 23	1925	6	11

NAME	DATE		PG	FL
Williams, Mrs. M. A.	Aug 16	1929	3	13
Williams, Peggy M.	May 30	1929	1	13
Williams, Richard	Sep 20	1917	1	3
Williams, Richard	Sep 21	1917	1	9
Williams, W. E.	Jul 6	1916	1	3
Williams, Mrs. W. E.	Jan 1	1926	1	11
Williams, W. Eugene	Jul 8	1916	1	9
Williams, Wally	Sep 17	1925	1	11
Williams, William Wright	Apr 22	1915	1	3
Williams, Willie Wright	Apr 24	1915	1	63*
*Old front page found in February 3, 1982 issue of Mt. Sun				
Williamson, Alline	Apr 27	1907	4	4
Williamson, Elizabeth Clark Phillips	Jan 9	1913	5	3
Willkie, Wallace Wills	Oct 24	1918	4	3
Willman, Mrs. J. H. E	May 15	1924	9	10
Willis, Mr.	Apr 14	1927	1	12
Willis, Mrs.	Apr 14	1927	1	12
Willis, Nora	Apr 21	1927	3	12
Wills, Thomas D.	May 23	1929	6	13
Wilson, J. C.	Apr 21	1909	1	6
Wilson, J. C.	Apr 24	1909	8	5
Wilson, J. C.	Apr 24	1909	10	7
Wilson, son of John	Nov 10	1922	5	10
Wilson, Livina	Feb 22	1908	5	5/7
Winebrenner, Ruth	Jan 13	1927	2	12
Wing, Mrs. Henry	Apr 23	1920	3	9
Witt, Brent	Aug 16	1928	1/8	12
Witt, August 23	Aug 23	1928	8	12
Witt, Henry William	Jul 9	1925	5	11
Witt, Mrs. James Monroe	Mar 4	1926	2	11
Witt, Nancy J.	Mar 6	1909	7	5
Witt, Nancy J.	Mar 6	1909	3	7
Witt, William Henry	Jul 3	1925	5	11
Witt, W. L.	Apr 1	1905	5	4
Wittenberg, Frank	Apr 14	1927	1	12
Wittenberg, Mrs. Pete	Apr 14	1927	1	12
Wittenberg, Peter Frank	Apr 21	1927	3	12
Wittenberg, Mrs. Peter Frank	Apr 21	1927	3	12
Wittig, Mrs.	Jul 17	1913	5	3
Wittold, Henry	Jul 24	1913	8	3

KERRVILLE MOUNTAIN SUN AND KERRVILLE ADVANCE
1898-1929

NAME	DATE		PG	FL
Wood, George F.	Jan 2	1913	1	3
Wood, H. E.	May 20	1926	4	11
Woodruff, daughter of Henry	Jun 3	1926	7	11
Woods, ———	Apr 1	1926	11	11
Woolter, R. H. (Bob)	Dec 23	1926	5	11
Works, Professor	Aug 12	1899	4	1
Wren, Ross	Jul 19	1928	1	12
Wright, H. C.	Apr	1928	4	12
Wright, Dr. J. W.	Apr 1	1899	1	1
Wynn, Mrs. W. D.	Aug 6	1925	6	11
Yeary, Mary Alice	Jun 26	1924	2	10
Yoast, Mrs. J. F.	Jan 17	1929	2	13
Young, Clarence	Jan 13	1927	9	12
Young, Edna L. (Mrs. Hy O.)	Nov 25	1926	12	11
Young, James A. (Andy)	Oct 9	1924	6/9	10
Young, John	Mar 3	1922	1	10
Young, Mary Catherine	Apr 8	1915	4	3
Young, Maud Sellers	Jan 9	1909	5	5/7
Young, Walter	Oct 9	1909	9	5/7
Youngblood, J. H. (Thanks)	Dec 9	1926	8	11
Yturri, Mrs. M.	Aug 6	1925	3	11
Zanderson, T. H. (Col.)	Jun 23	1927	9	12
Zoeller, George	Apr 25	1908	8	5/7
Zumwalt, W. C.	Jul 29	1926	6	11

NAME	DATE	PG
Ahr, Frank	Apr 24	7
Alexander, John	Jan 30	8
Alsum, T. F.	Aug 28	8
Austin, Howell	Jan 23	5
Ayala, Mrs Santana (Celsa)	Apr 3	5
Babineau, Edwin	Oct 30	7 & 8
Bacon, Persis M.	Jan 30	5
Bacon, Persis M.	Feb 6	1
Ballard, Philip H.	Apr 3	1
Barton, David	Feb 27	1
Bearb, Mrs. A. B. (Josie)	Dec 4	1
Beitel, Albert (Sr.)	Jan 2	1
Bell, W. C.	Apr 3	1
Benedick, Joseph J.	May 15	1
Bennes, J. M. (Thanks)	Jan 30	7
Bierschwale, Mrs. Fred	Jan 30	1
Blacket, John	Jul 24	1
Blank, Fritz	Nov 20	1
Blanks, Granville	Jul 10	1
Blanks, Isaiah	Dec 4	1
Bradshaw, John W.	Apr 24	1
Branning, Frances D.	Feb 27	1
Bridges, Joe (Estate)	Jul 10	8
Brent, Herbert	Oct 30	1 & 7
Britt, M. O.	Oct 9	1
Brooks, Mrs. Charles S.	May 29	8 & 11
Brown, Robert I. (Thanks)	Aug 7	7
Brysch, Raymond	Jul 24	7
Burge, A. E.	Feb 20	5
Burgess, Olin	Oct 23	1
Burnett, R. L.	Jul 24	7
Coats, C. A.	Jan 9	1
Colbert, Hiram J.(Estate Notice)	Sep 4	7
Coleman, Adaline V.	Jan 16	1
Cook, James R.	Oct 16	8
Cox, Mrs. Frank	Jul 3	1
Cox, Twins of George	Jun 19	11
Crenshaw, Mildred	Apr 24	1
Crow, William Charles	Aug 7	1

NAME	DATE	PG
Cutsinger, Lynnie	Apr 24	11
Daniel, Sarah D.	Mar 13	1
Davis, C. J.	Aug 21	1
De Hymel, Octavia	Sep 18	7
Deibner, Mrs. J. W.	Jan 16	3
Delgadillo, Lucia	Dec 25	7
Denton, Brock	Apr 10	1
Doebler, Richard	Feb 13	1
Du Bose, A. D.	Jul 24	2 & 11
Dusch, Katherine	Apr 24	7
Eames, Mrs. J. A.	Feb 6	11
Edmonds, Henry (Thanks)	Jun 12	7
Faltin, Clara	May 22	1
Faltin, Clara	May 29	4
Fanning, Ira S.	Apr 10	1
Fanning, Ira S.	May 8	2
Ferguson, William B.	Aug 14	1
Ferris, A. H.	Nov 6	8
Fitzsimons, Jay F.	Oct 16	1
Flasseur, Emilie	May 1	7
Foryon, Carl (Dr.)	Sep 11	8
Fourton, Carl (Dr.)	Sep 4	1
Franz, Lola Mae	Jun 5	1
Freeland, Mary	Jan 23	5
Friday, Obie B.	Nov 13	7
Gorman, Lauretta	Jan 2	5
Graham, Mrs. D. H. (?O. H.)	May 1	11
Graham, Mrs. O. H.	May 8	7
Gray, Jessie R.	Jul 17	2
Gregg, Saunders	Oct 2	12
Gregory, Julia	Nov 13	1
Habgood, J. H.	Jan 23	1
Hamburg, Sandy	Jul 3	1
Hamilton, J. M.	Aug 14	1
Harrah, Asahel O.	Oct 30	1
Harris, Fannie	Jul 10	1
Harrison, Thomas S.	Aug 7	1
Harwood, Mrs. Clair L.	Nov 27	1
Henderson, John F.	Sep 11	1
Henke, Richard	Sep 4	1

1930
Film Roll #13

NAME	DATE	PG
Hill, Mrs. P. O.	May 29	12
Hodges, Alfred E.	Sep 11	1
Hogg, Will C.	Sep 18	2
Hollomon, George R.	Nov 6	1
Hood, Twin Boys of Maurice	Mar 20	8
Howard, James L.	Sep 4	1
Hubble, Levi R.	Nov 13	1
Hubble, Mary	May 29	8 & 11
Hudspeth, Ann E.	Mar 6	1
Huffman, Orris	Mar 27	1
Hunnicutt, C. W.	Jan 30	1
Hunter, Mrs. J. B. (Buck)	Oct 9	1
Jackson, James E. (Thanks)	Jun 5	11
Johnston, Charlie H.	Aug 7	1
Jung, Mrs. Charles	Aug 14	12
Karieva, Sophie L.	Jun 26	1
King, Guy M.	Sep 25	3
Konze, Sophie	Feb 6	12
Krebs, Mrs. Ralph	Jan 16	5
Lackey, Theodore	Jul 17	1
La Rue, Clyde A.	Jul 24	12
Lear, Mrs. Robert (Clemmie)	Jun 26	1
Lopez, daughter of Aurelio	Oct 23	7
Lopez, Eusbio	Dec 25	7
Lowrance, Leah Ann	Jan 23	1
Lowry, Robert C.	Oct 2	1
Magee, J. W.	Oct 23	8
Mandry, John	Oct 23	7
Mc Bryde, T. A.	Sep 18	1 & 8
Mc Caleb, M. M. (Jr.)	Aug 21	1
Mc Cauley, Emmet B. (Estate)	Oct 9	11
Mc Corquodale, Ellen D.	Oct 2	12
Mc Killip, A. W.	Nov 6	1
Meredith, Essie T.	Aug 28	1
Moody, Frank	Oct 30	8
Mooney, Mrs. W. M.	Nov 13	8
Moore, Clyde	Aug 28	3
Moose, Andrew M.	Mar 27	1
Moyer, M. P.	May 29	11
Muscato, Tony	Jul 24	7

62

NAME	DATE	PG
Nichols, Eva	Jul 24	1
Nichols, J. L.	Mar 13	1
Oehler, Adolph E.	Jul 10	1
Page, William H.	May 29	11
Paine, George	May 22	1
Pelas, Hyacinth	Sep 4	7
Pendley, Cassie	Jul 31	1
Perkins, Robert E.	Jan 16	1
Polk, Sam	Aug 14	1
Porter, Charles	Oct 23	5
Presley, L. Z.	Oct 30	5
Prestidge, Elizabeth	Sep 4	1
Quigley, Mary	Dec 4	7
Ramirez, Lucia	Dec 4	7
Rauber, Augusta	Mar 20	11
Real, Albert	Jun 19	1
Reindl, Sophie	Dec 25	1
Rice, Frederick A.	Jan 3	3
Ridgaway, Sam	Dec 25	1
Rosenbaum, Dale	Feb 6	1
Rubio, C. C.	Feb 27	1
Sandefer, James	Nov 6	1
Salter, Winfred A.	Mar 6	1
Schilling, Albert	Mar 13	1
Shearin, Anna	Mar 13	3
Shelburne, Callie	Jan 16	1
Smith, J. T. (Thanks)	Sep 25	7
Sowell, Lee	Apr 10	8
Spencer, Frank	Feb 6	11
Sprague, Arthur E.	Jan 23	6
Steves, Johanne	Jun 12	4
Stitt, Joe Bryson	Oct 30	1 & 11
Surber, William N.	Jan 30	1
Suttles, Mamie	Jul 10	1
Tacquard, Lucile S.	Jan 2	1
Thomason, William R.	Jun 12	8
Townsend, Johnnie Marie	Jun 19	7
Tracy, Tommy	Nov 13	1
Trushel, Mrs. John	Mar 13	3
Trvino, Mrs. Leandre	Jan 2	1

1930
Film Roll #13

NAME	DATE	PG
Turner, Mrs. J. B.	May 15	1
Tuttle, Elvira	Jul 3	1
Usener, Ludwig (Thanks)	Jul 10	2
Wade, Annie	Oct 30	1 & 11
Ward, John H.	Mar 27	1
Wallace, James R. (Jr.)	Jul 3	8
Wallace, S. William	Jun 5	1
Webb, J. M.	Feb 27	1
Woody, Maggie	Dec 13	1
Wootton, Claude	Jan 30	1

Officially, there were 190 deaths in Kerr County in 1930.
There are 169 names listed here. Apparently all names did
not get into the paper.

1931
Film Roll # 14

Allen, Mrs. M. E.	Sep 17	8
Allen, Nathan H.	Aug 27	1
Arhelger, Lillian	Jul 2	3
Arthofer, Mrs. Carl	Oct 8	7
Atterberry, James	Mar 19	8
Attwater, H. P.	Oct 1	1 & 11
Austin, J. F.	Oct 8	1
Ayala, Ramon	Jan 1	5
Baker, Benjamin F.	Jun 11	1
Barnes, Mrs. H. C. S.	Nov 12	5
Barton, Willard Mardis	Jan 15	1
Beaver, Mrs. Virgil	Mar 5	11
Beltran, Gilbert	Oct 29	7
Bernhard, Peter	May 28	1
Blanchette, Wallace S.	Aug 20	11
Boyd, Haskell	Feb 12	1
Brasher, Clarence	Sep 10	1
Brightwell, J. H.	Sep 10	1
Briscoe, David R.	Mar 19	1
Brophy, Mary	Sep 10	8

64

NAME	DATE	PG
Brown, Cordelia	Oct 29	1
Brown, Hugh	Apr 2	1
Bruff, John Harper	Sep 24	8
Bruton, David A.	Jan 29	5
Bruton, Mrs. M. E.	Jun 25	12
Carr, Nell Marie	Apr 23	1
Chamberlain, Hugh W.	Mar 19	7
Chambers, Mrs. G. M.	Sep 3	8
Chaney, Joe	Feb 19	11
Charlier, J. J.	May 28	1
Ciomperlik, Isidore	Apr 16	7
Cload, Harry	Mar 19	7
Coffey, Walter L.	Oct 22	12
Coleman, A. W. (Dr.)	May 21	7
Colvin, Molly N.	Jan 8	1 & 11
Comeaux, Essie Pearl	Jan 8	7
Cowsert, E. J.	Apr 16	1
Cox, Joshua	Apr 9	7
Cullom, Charles E.	Feb 26	12
Cummings, Theodore F.	Jun 11	1
Davenport, J. E.	Dec 3	8
Davenport, John F.	Dec 24	1 & 8
Daworzaki, Dimitri	Jul 16	7
Dempsey, B. J.	Oct 22	1
Dempsey, Bartholomew J. (Bat)	Oct 29	7
Derby, W. H.	May 21	5
Dietert, Mrs. Theodore F.	Jan 29	1
Dodd, R. E.	Mar 5	8
Donaldson, David C.	Dec 17	1
Dowdy, Mary A.	Nov 19	1
Driscoll, Thomas J.	Feb 19	7
Duff, Charles A.	Jun 18	1
Duffy, Charles	Jul 2	7
Eckerdt, Mrs. W. R.	Apr 2	1
Elder, Mrs. I. H.	Jun 25	1
Evans, Mrs. A. D.	Jun 25	1
Everett, Mrs. Firth	Apr 23	1
Fanning, Ira S. (Estate)	Apr 23	11
Fatheree, Dora V.	Aug 20	1
Fischer, Mrs. James M.	Apr 23	7

NAME	DATE	PG
Fitz-Simons, Mrs. John T.	Mar 19	7
Ford, Oliver	Sep 3	8
Gannon, Ripple Frazier	Nov 5	1
Garrett, Joe	May 14	1
Garza, Manuel Felix	Mar 5	7
Gonzales, Celstina	Oct 15	9
Gregory, W. B. (Thanks)	Feb 5	10
Gregory, W. V.???	Feb 5	1
Griffin, Alice	Jan 22	1
Habenicht, William	Mar 26	7
Hagelstein, George Henry	Oct 15	1
Hagens, Mason M.	Jan 8	1
Hammond, Mrs. A. K.	Jun 13	1
Harris, E. N.	Jan 29	1
Harris, Miriam	Jan 29	5
Haskin, E. L.	Aug 13	1
Henderson, Mrs. Ed (Callie J.)	Sep 3	1 & 11
Hightower, James I. (Estate)	Feb 12	11
Hodges, Mrs. D. N.	Feb 5	1
Holder, Leland V.	May 14	7
Holekamp, Dan	Jun 4	9
Holland, James S.	Mar 26	1
Holliman, Josephine (Mrs. Tom J.)	Mar 5	12
Hope, Mrs. J. S.	Jun 11	1
Hunter, James B. (Buck)	Aug 27	1
Jackson, Clara B.	May 14	1
Johnson, Ora	Dec 3	1
Jones, Kent L.	Dec 17	1
Jungmann, Mary	Mar 5	7
Kiefer, Grace	May 14	1
Knoppe, Alvin	Jan 8	11
Kruegar, Mrs. Frank	Dec 24	1 & 7
Lachele, Henry L.	Apr 9	1
Landry, Athenor L.	Jul 9	7
Lang, Edward A.	Jun 25	1
Lawhon, Ethel T.	Mar 5	5
Leinweber, Louis A.	Oct 1	1 & 11
Lessing, Rita Elizabeth	Feb 19	7 & 11
Lewis, Mrs. B. M.	Sep 10	1
Liesmann, Ervin	Jul 30	1

1931
Film Roll #14

NAME	DATE	PG
Loeffler, Mrs. Emil	Aug 27	1 & 7
Lormond, Clarence	Nov 19	5
Lund, Freddy	Oct 8	1
Lyle, Carl D.	Feb 26	1
Mandeville, Glenn L.	Jan 8	1
Manuel, Alma S.	Feb 26	2
Martinez, Mrs. Pablo	Mar 26	7
Mc Donald, William F.	Apr 30	1
Melcher, Mrs. Gilbert (Cecelia)	Oct 8	7
Melton, C. B. & Alice (Estate)	Nov 12	5
Merritt, Raymond	Jan 1	1
Mitchell, Cleone	Apr 16	1
Monenti, Gabriel	Oct 8	7
Moore, G. K. (Bud)	Sep 10	1
Morriss, Rawson	Feb 19	1
Morriss, William Rawson	Feb 26	12
Nanny, Mrs. Gela M.	Jan 1	1
Neyland, LAmar	Oct 8	7
Noonan, Thomas E.	Mar 19	1
Norris, Merlin K.	Jul 16	12
Norris, Merlin K.	Jul 23	7
Northrup, John R.	Nov 5	1
Norton, Ellen	Jun 25	1
Owen, Vrnon	Apr 2	7
Patterson, Olive	Jun 18	1
Patton, R. G.	Apr 30	1
Pena, Bertha	Jul 30	1
Peschel, Hemith A.	May 14	8
Phelan, Dick	Jan 29	7
Phelan, Dick	Feb 19	7
Pierce, J. S. (Sr.)	Jun 4	5
Platte, Addie W.	Jan 29	12
Polley, Edward	Jan 8	8
Pue, Earl Lawrence	Apr 2	1
Rawson, W. H.	Apr 9	1
Ray, Ervin	Aug 27	2
Rees, F. A. (Nona)	May 7	8
Reindl, Sophie	Jan 1	5
Reinhardt, Margaret	May 7	8
Rippey, Elva Trent	Jul 16	2

67

NAME	DATE	PG
Robichaux, Junius C. (Thanks)	Oct 29	7
Rowell, Mattie F.	Mar 12	1
Rummel, Ella	Jun 11	1
Sageser, Daniel W.	Oct 15	8
Saner, Mrs. R. C.	Jul 23	2
Saner, Mrs. R. C. (Mary Arminta)	Jul 30	1
Santos, Felix	Nov 19	5
Saur, Fritz	Oct 8	1
Savoie, Hiram	Nov 19	5
Scarborough, Mrs. Jimmie Clara	Dec 10	5
Scheel, Herman W.	Jan 8	1
Schrempp, Richard	Jul 16	7
Schrier, Mrs. T. M.	Jan 29	5
Sherman, Lillian	Sep 10	11
Sieber, Carl	Aug 13	7
Skaggs, Gertie	Sep 10	1
Smith, George H.	Dec 10	1
Smith, L. A.	Jul 16	8
Smotek, John (Thanks)	Feb 12	3 & 7
Sprencel, Anzelem	Aug 20	7
Starling, W. J. B.	Jun 25	1
Stephens, Georgia	Jul 2	1
Stone, Austin A.	Sep 3	1
Stone, Ben Wallace	Feb 26	1 & 11
Stransky, H. R.	May 28	5
Surber, John F.	Nov 19	1
Sutton, Bud	Nov 19	1
Turk, Arthur M.	Jan 29	12
Tuttle, Ben F.	Oct 1	1
Vinson, J. W. (Rev.)	Nov 12	1
Voiss, Henry	Sep 24	7
Waide, Turner O.	Sep 17	1
Wall, Constant A.	Oct 29	1
Wall, R. L.	Dec 17	1
Walther, George W.	Feb 19	1
Warren, Charles	Sep 17	1
Wetherill, Baby/Mrs. R. H. (Thanks)	Feb 5	3
White, Fletcher A. (Rev.)	Jul 2	1 & 8
Wilkinson, Mayfield	Jul 16	8
Williams, Nellie F.	Jul 9	1

1931
Film Roll #14

NAME	DATE	PG
Wills, Harry H.	Mar 12	1
Wright, James H. (Thanks)	Jun 11	7
Yates, John W.	Dec 31	1
Young, John D.	Feb 5	1

1932
Film Roll # 14

Adrian, John C.	Jan 28	1
Baldridge, Mary S.	Jan 7	1
Ballinger, M. L. (Thanks)	Jan 7	7
Baumann, Richard	Apr 28	5
Bednark, F. H.	Nov 24	1
Blair, George W.	Jan 14	3
Blakeslee, Alfred	Apr 7	7
Blatherwick, Mrs. M. L.	Dec 1	1
Brunson, William	Jul 7	1
Bunberry, B. C.	Feb 18	1
Bundick, Roy P.	Jan 7	1
Burch, Dale	Jun 23	1
Burleson, mother of Mrs Z. H.	Mar 24	11
Calderson, Ben	Jul 7	1
Cherry, Lucy	Dec 8	1
Colazo, Nativity (Natividad)	Dec 29	5
Dorsey, Thomas T.	Sep 1	5
Dowd, Arthur S.	Nov 24	1
Dowdy, Frank G.	Feb 4	1 & 9
Downing, Mrs. W. L.	May 5	5
Droddy, Esther	Nov 17	1
Edwards, Maurice	Apr 28	10
Fincher, A. F.	Jan 28	1
Floyd, James W.	Mar 3	1
Folger, John Tristram	Dec 8	1
Folger, Mrs. W. H	Jun 23	1
Fritz, Christian	Jan 14	5
Funk, Emma	Jun 30	1
Fuller, Grady	Dec 1	7
Gallatin, father of Dr. H. H.	Apr 14	10
Glenn, Julius D.	Jun 23	1

1932
Film Roll #14

NAME	DATE	PG
Goldstine, Melville M.	Feb 4	1
Greenleaf, Charles H.	Jul 7	1
Grimes, Joe	Jun 16	1
Guidry, Luke	May 12	5
Haag, P. J.	Dec 29	1
Hamilton, Thomas G.	Jun 16	1
Hankins, Glendora	Nov 17	1
Hawkins, Ellsworth	Nov 10	1
Hawkins, Gertrude	May 19	1
Hicks, Elvious	Mar 24	1
Hollomon, James E.	Apr 7	1
Hollam, W. H.	Feb 4	6
Horner, Thomas J.	Feb 11	1
Hunter, John W.	Nov 24	1
James, Wallace W.	Dec 1	1 & 11
Jarrad, Richard T.	Mar 31	1
Johannessen, Albert	Aug 13	1
Johnson, Mrs. Exa	Aug 13	1
Johnson, Mrs. G. W. (Thanks)	Aug 13	3
Johnson, Mrs. H. J.	Aug 18	1
Jones, Pearle	Jul 21	1
Jungmann, Alvin	Dec 29	5
Kiefer, William	Dec 29	1
Killough, Rowena Lilly	Aug 4	6
Kitchens, Lois	Nov 24	1
Kuhlmann, H. H. (Sr.)	Feb 18	1
Lang, Lloyd	Jun 16	6
Lehmann, Herman	Feb 11	7
Leigh, Edward B.	May 19	1
Littlefield, Lois	Feb 4	9
Littlefield, Mrs. Phillip T.	Feb 4	1
Lopez, ----brano	Jan 14	5
Love, Perry Butler	Mar 17	1
Lowrance, Mrs. Banks (Meble L.)	Feb 4	1
Mabry, Charles	Apr 28	1 & 6
Mc (Mac) Callum, Cleo	Sep 29	1
Mc Cartney, Sylvia	Oct 13	1
Mc Donald, Charles F.	Jan 14	1
Mc Mahon, E. (Dr.)	Feb 25	5
Michon, Frank J.	Apr 7	1

1932
Film Roll # 14

NAME	DATE	PG
Michon, Frank J.	Apr 14	7
Michon, John J.	Dec 22	1
Moore, Rachel	Oct 13	1
Moore, W. B.	Dec 15	1
Morgan, Daniel	Jan 14	6
Morris, Mrs. Fred	Dec 22	1
Morriss, Mrs. Will A.	Oct 27	1
Moseley, Grandma	Jan 14	9
Nance, William F.	Nov 24	1
Neely, Mrs. W. H.	Mar 31	8
New, Ethel	Sep 29	1 & 9
Nichols, Newton Ernest	May 26	1
Nichols, Turner W.	Apr 21	1
Oakley, Anna Kate	Oct 30	1
Odell, Louis M.	Jul 7	1
Ortega, Mrs. Maximina Rabalcaba de	Dec 1	7
Owens, Leo	Sep 22	1
Pampell, Mrs. J. L.	Sep 15	1
Powell, J. B.	Feb 4	6
Priour, Fred T.	Dec 22	1
Ralph, Mrs. Cecil	Dec 1	12
Reed, Mrs.	Dec 22	1
Rees, Ida S.	Feb 4	1
Rees, Louise Blake	Oct 27	6
Robinson, Hope	Nov 17	1
Rogan, Charles	Jan 21	1
Rotge, Mary M.	Sep 29	1
Schilling, Eddie	May 5	1
Schreiner, Mrs. L. A.	Oct 13	3
Schreiner, Mrs. L. A.	Oct 30	1
Schwethelm, Walter	Dec 22	1
Shannon, Nancy E.	Mar 17	5
Skadra, John P.	May 12	5
Smith, Etta Mae	May 19	1 & 11
Smith, Mrs. Sam	Jan 28	1
South, Grover M.	Dec 22	1
Spear, Dick	Mar 17	12
Spencer, Charles A.	Mar 17	1
Spiller, Louis	Feb 25	5
Standefer, Mrs. M. H.	Apr 14	1

NAME	DATE	PG
Staudt, Henry	Nov 24	1
Stieler, Ida	Jul 7	1
Sublett, Ed L.	Nov 24	1
Sutton, James M.	Dec 15	1
Taylor, son of B. A.	May 12	9
Taylor, Harry	Apr 7	1
Templeton, Essie King	Mar 31	1
Thompson, Charles	Jan 21	1
Travis, Mark O.	Jun 23	1
Tullos, Fred	Sep 29	1
Valenta, John	Jul 14	1
Van Berg, Mrs. J. S.	Jun 23	1
Vann, Mrs. E. L.	Apr 28	1 & 9
Vasbinder, Sarah	Mar 24	8
Whitehead, Roy M.	Feb 25	1
Wilkey, William W.	Nov 10	1
Wilson, H. B.	Jan 21	1
Wilson, Horace E.	Jan 28	1
Wilson, Mrs. W. G.	Aug 4	1
Woody, Mrs. A. G.	Jan 14	6

NAME	DATE	PG
Adkins, Arthur T.	Apr 6	1
Adkins, Aubrey	Dec 7	12
Anderson, Guy	Feb 23	1
Ashford, J. T.	Nov 23	1
Auld, John	Apr 6	3
Ayala, Louis	Mar 2	1
Barnett, George W.	Oct 26	8
Beitel, Ally	May 18	1
Bonnell, William H.	Jul 27	1
Bower, Mrs. L. E.	May 11	10
Bradwell, Ellen	Aug 17	1
Burkett, J. C. (Dr.)	Mar 9	1
Burks, William E.	Jul 20	1
Burney, Washington Davis	Mar 9	1
Button, Joseph (Thanks)	Dec 21	3

NAME	DATE	PG
Cates, Craig C.	Feb 23	1
Cathey, Andrew B.	Mar 2	1
Chambers, C. M.	Mar 16	1
Comparette, Louis M.	Mar 23	1
Conden, Adelaide	Jul 13	1
Coombs, E. H.	Jan 12	1
Cowden, Alma	Jun 1	1
Cowden, Washington P.	Mar 2	1
Cowden, William H.	Jul 27	10
Crenshaw, Carey	Jul 27	9
Crenshaw, Earl	Nov 23	1
Cunningham, J. E. (Rev.)	Apr 27	3
David, Reeder	Jan 19	1
Daw, William H.	Apr 6	1 & 9
Dean, W. L.	Jul 20	1
Decker, Lucy	Feb 9	5
Deuster, Herman	Aug 24	1
Dismukes, brother of C. M.	Oct 26	9
Dobbins, Robert	Nov 30	1
Douglas, Richard H.	Mar 30	1
Dryden, George E.	Aug 24	1
Duderstadt, Henry	Dec 14	11
Dykman, Bertha	Feb 9	1 & 9
Eager, Josephine	Aug 24	1
Estes, mother of Ned	Oct 5	9
Fairchild, Erastus S.	Jan 12	1
Field, Littell Rene	Dec 14	1
Forbes, E. D.	May 18	10
Freeman, George L.	Aug 31	1
Garcia, Felipe	Dec 7	1
Garcia, Mrs. Felipe	Dec 7	1
George, James S.	Jul 27	1
Gibson, Mrs. F. M.	Jan 5	1
Goodwin, Sidney G.	May 11	10
Gore, Teresa Vianna	May 18	10
Gourley, Mrs. Leslie L.	Jan 19	1
Gourley, Ruby Mc Elroy	Jan 19	6
Graves, Mrs. E. F.	Aug 24	2
Hammock, J. J.	Mar 2	1
Hanes, Jesse C.	Nov 16	1

NAME	DATE	PG
Harris, Mrs. John A.	Jan 5	1
Herzog, Mrs. N.	Mar 30	1
Hess, Joseph P.	Jan 5	1
Hill, G. B.	May 11	1
Holliman, James	Nov 9	1
Holloman, Mrs. Roger	Jan 12	1
Hull, Charels R.	Jul 13	3
Hyde, Theodore C.	Jan 26	1
Johnson, John	Jul 13	5
Jones, Allen George	Jun 8	1
Jones, Andy	Apr 6	9
Karger, Gilbert A.	Nov 30	1
Kilgore, George C.	Dec 14	1
Leismann, Frieda A.	Sep 23	10
Lessing, Charles A.	Nov 16	1
Linn, Doyle Wayne	Nov 16	1
Lopez, Malinda	Dec 7	1
Lord, John	Nov 2	1
Lovell, Idabell	Mar 16	1
Lyle, Mrs. J. P.	Jul 27	3
Lyons, Rufus M.	Jun 29	1
Martin, Enoch B.	Nov 23	1
Matthews, Kathleen	Feb 9	1
Mayfield, Sam	Sep 7	6
Mc Crosky, Mrs. W. J. (Thanks)	Oct 12	10
Mears, E. L.	Jun 22	9
Mero, Mimi Orfilea	Jul 13	5
Montgomery, Etta Jane Bell	Mar 30	3
Montgomery, Mrs. L. W.	Feb 23	1
Moreno, Maria G.	Jun 8	1
Morris, Carl	Jul 20	1
Morris, Libbie	Nov 23	1
Morris, Robert M.	Jul 13	1 & 9
Mosel, Ed P.	Jun 22	1
Murr, Mrs. Henry	Aug 31	10
Nauwald, Bertha	Nov 2	1
Nelson, Frank H.	Jul 27	1
Nichols, Alice	Mar 23	1
Nowlin, Ruth Marie	Sep 28	1 & 6
Pearson, I. S.	Dec 23	1

NAME	DATE	PG
Pearson, Rayburn	Oct 19	1
Perkins, Lydia L.	Sep 28	1
Peters, Alfred Ganes (Bud)	Oct 26	1
Price, Charles	Oct 12	1
Pumphrey, Joseph R.	Sep 28	1
Rawls, Robert R.	Jul 20	8
Rees, Ruth Walker	Jun 29	6
Reiffert, Annie Megge	Dec 28	1
Reinhardt, John	May 4	1
Riggs, Hannah M.	Jul 13	1
Riley, W. P.	Jan 19	8
Rodgers, Jimmie	Jun 1	1
Rotge, Hippolite (Polite)	Dec 7	1
Ruff, Rudolph	Sep 21	1 & 8
Rutledge, Frank	May 4	1
Saenger, Anna S.	Aug 31	1
Schreiner, Walter R.	Apr 13	1
Schwarz, Harry	Feb 23	1
Schwethelm, Emilie	Jan 12	1
Selfridge, Laurence (Dr.)	Dec 7	12
Sells, Elmer N. Joseph	Jun 1	5
Shumate, Nina	Jan 19	1
Smith, Clifton A.	Sep 21	1
Soloman, Dona	Nov 16	1
Stephenson, Roscoe G.	Dec 14	12
Taylor, Amos (Rev.)	Feb 16	7
Taylor, Amos G. (Rev.)	Feb 23	7
Taylor, Myrtle Lee	Jun 1	1
Thurmond, Joe	Aug 31	10
Tinney, William Thomas	Aug 24	1
Tomerlin, William J.	Aug 17	7
Weesner, Laurence	Nov 23	1
West, Arthur L.	Dec 7	1
Wiedenfeld, Stanley B.	Jan 26	1
Williams, Julia	Jan 12	3
Wood, William H. (Dr.)	Feb 16	1
Woods, William H. (Dr.)	Feb 9	1
Wray, Paul	Jul 27	1

1934
Film Roll #15

NAME	DATE	PG
Deibner, John W.	Apr 19	1
Denton, Elbert (Bert)	Jan 25	1
De Witt, Joseph	Jan 4	1
Diamond, Douglas	May 24	1
Dickey, Jim W.	Oct 4	1 & 9
Doebbler, Ernst	May 3	10
Domingues, Francis J.	Aug 30	1
Donnelley, Garrett J.	Mar 22	1
Dorfman, Charles	Dec 20	12
Duderstadt, Fred	Sep 20	8
Dudley, R. H.	Jan 4	5
Duncan, John	Mar 8	1
Earl, Rebecca H.	Mar 1	1
Farmer, James L.	May 24	1
Erawood, Arvella	Aug 2	3
Fawcett, F. S.	Nov 29	12
Forgason, Sallie B.	Jun 7	1 & 9
Foster, John L.	Nov 22	1
Fox, Ruby Riley	May 3	1
Freeman, James P.	Dec 6	1
Furr, Mrs. Benety	Jan 25	3
Gamel, Herbert	Apr 5	1
Gann, Fred	Aug 30	1
Geron, Harry R.	Jan 25	1
Geron, Harry R.	Feb 1	1
Gibbs, Andrew J.	Jan 25	1
Gibson, John R.	Dec 27	1
Goff, Robert B.	Mar 8	1
Gonzales, Boyer	Feb 22	6
Granberry, Mrs. Charles	Jan 11	1
Guest, Chris M.	Mar 1	1
Habecker, Emil	Jun 21	8
Habecker, Emil (Sr.)	Jun 11	3
Heimann, Jacob A.	Mar 22	1
Hein, Otto A.	Nov 15	1
Herzog, Nathan	Nov 29	1
Holdsworth, Thomas	Jun 21	1
Holekamp, Mrs. George	Jun 11	9
Humphrey, Elizabeth	Apr 5	1
Hutchings, Mrs. Henry	Mar 1	3

76

NAME	DATE	PG
Irving, Mrs. Alvin	Aug 2	1
James, Mary L.	Sep 13	1
Jenon, Frank	Dec 13	1
Jolley, Elida	Apr 19	1
Karger, August	Dec 27	1
Karger, H. Charles	Mar 29	1
Karger, Julius	Mar 29	1
Karger, Lillian	Mar 29	1
Kelly, Ben H.	Aug 9	1
Kelley, Martha	Jun 7	10
Kendrick, Lillian	Oct 11	1
Kerlick, J. G.	Jun 7	10
Klatt, Max	Aug 23	1
Le Blanc, Leo	May 17	5
Leinweber, Emil	May 24	1
Little, Helen Louise	Mar 15	1
Luppy, Victor E.	Mar 8	1
Martin, Mrs. S. J.	Jun 7	1
Mason, Augusta (Mrs, Lee)	Jul 19	1
Mason, mother of C. C.	Aug 30	7
Matthew, Mrs. Tom	Oct 11	10
Mayhugh, Issac (Dr.)	Nov 8	1
Mc Carthy, John (Rev.)	Jul 12	12
Mc Combs, Mrs. George	Oct 4	9
Mc Creary, J. E.	Feb 15	1
Mc Curdy, Joe	Jan 25	1
Merrett, John W. (Dr.)	Dec 27	1
Miers, Mrs. Hal	Feb 8	1
Morriss, Anne Thompson	Apr 19	1
Nelson, Eveline Emma	Nov 1	1
Nelson, William H.	Apr 5	1
Newton, Edward E.	Dec 20	1
Nicholson, Roy	Jan 4	5
Norwood, Sarah F.	Oct 18	1
Oatman, John B.	May 31	1
O'Brien, Dennis Gene	Jun 28	5
O'Bryant, Agnes	Nov 8	3
Orosco, Joe E.	Jun 28	5
Patton, Mrs. R. G.	Mar 15	1
Petersen, Karl	Jul 12	7

NAME	DATE	PG
Petropol, Leon	Jun 11	5
Platte, Alfred G.	Mar 13	1
Pugh, J. H.	Feb 22	5
Raiford, J. C.	Mar 22	11
Raiford, James C.	Mar 15	1
Reimenschneider, Mrs. V. E.	Mar 15	1
Richeson, Mrs. G. L.	Jan 25	1
Rodriguez, E.	Jan 11	5
Russell, Henry Wade	Oct 11	3
Ryan, Ira Frank	Mar 8	5
Sanders, Roswell M.	Oct 25	1
Schmidly, Jesse	Aug 16	1
Self, Mrs. A. E. (Emma Teadford)	May 31	1
Shumaker, George A.	Dec 20	1
Shupak, Doris	Mar 1	1
Smith, Harriet E.	Mar 1	3
Smith, Marjorie Mae	Oct 18	1
Smith, Riley R.	Jun 7	1
Smith, Mrs. Riley R.	Jun 7	1
Spence, Mary J.	Aug 2	10
Spicer, Mrs. James	Jul 26	1
Sutherland, Olson	Mar 13	9
Swanson, Alfred	Jun 28	5
Trushell, John	Jul 5	1
Vallier, Gerald	Oct 11	1
Van Dyke, Mrs. Jacob	Jul 19	10
Vanhoozer, Isaac White	Jun 21	1
Vann, Elisha L.	Jan 11	1 & 9
Vardell, T. W.	Mar 1	6
Walker, Mrs. C. G.	Feb 8	1
Weingarten, Harris	Oct 18	1
Wells, Monroe	Oct 18	1 & 9
Wenzel, W. C.	Feb 8	1
Weston, Charles	May 24	1
Woodruff, Henry	Jul 5	1
Work, Ruby	Dec 20	1
Wright, Lula M.	Aug 16	1
Young, John R. (Jr.)	Aug 9	5

NAME	DATE	PG
Abrams, E. W.	Mar 7	10
Adkins, J. Leslie	Jan 10	1
Anderson, William M.	Nov 14	1
Anglin, J. A.	Jul 4	1
Babb, Mrs. John W.	Jun 20	1
Baker, Mrs. William C. (Rosa M.)	Dec 12	1
Bennett, James A.	Mar 28	3 & 8
Bohnert, Mortiz	Feb 28	1
Bomar, C. V. (Dr.)	Jan 31	5
Breihan, Bertha E.	Jan 10	1
Bridges, Mattie B.	Sep 19	1
Briscoe, Ray	Jan 17	1
Bruff, James M.	Feb 14	1
Bundick, P. A.	May 9	1
Burney, Dee	Oct 10	1
Burns, Prather Jordan	Jul 25	9
Campbell, C. B.	Nov 21	1
Campbell, Charles B.	Nov 14	1
Castleberry, S. C.	Jun 6	1
Childs, Ed I.	Apr 4	1
Cocke, G. W. (Rev.)	Dec 12	1
Cordova, Jose	Sep 5	5
Cozene, Louis N.	Jul 11	5
Crawford, Lem S.	Sep 26	6
Crenshaw, Pleasant A.	Jan 10	1
Daniel, Thomas E.	Oct 10	5
Delavan, Mrs. Y. J.	Nov 14	9
Dilworth, Joe	Jan 24	1
Dodd, Mrs. R. E.	Feb 7	1
Dominguez, Ovey	Nov 21	1 & 5
Dowdy, George	Apr 11	1
Dowdy, infant daughter of C. A.	Jan 10	1
Draper, H. E. (Dr.)	Dec 12	6
Duffefy, Mrs. Jim	Apr 11	1
Durham, Jane	Mar 14	1
Eason, Fred Dixon	Dec 12	5
Easterling, Birdie	Jan 3	10
Erb, Harry Floyd	Jan 17	8
Fariss, Robert L.	May 16	1
Fischer, Augusta	Mar 7	1

NAME	DATE	PG
Flanagan, P. J. (Rev.)	Sep 5	5
Ganter, Lewis F.	Nov 21	1
Garcia, Trinidad	Mar 14	1
Garrett, William G.	Apr 25	1
George, Charles	Aug 8	5
Gibson, John R.	Jan 10	3
Griffin, Cleveland	Nov 28	1
Griffin, Cleveland	Dec 5	11
Grona, Shirley Ann	Apr 18	1
Grona, Mrs. William	Apr 11	1
Habetz, Henry	Apr 25	5
Haeber, Bruno	Sep 5	1
Hampson, Sarah	May 9	1
Harris, John M.	Aug 1	1
Harrison, Robert L.	Sep 19	7
Hazlett, Sarah V.	Oct 31	1
Henderson, Harold	Jun 20	1
Hernandez, Mary	Oct 24	7
Hitzfeld, John	Mar 7	1
Hodge, Mary J.	Mar 28	1
Hoss, Pauline	Mar 7	9
Hull, Edward F.	Jul 11	1
Hunt, Mrs. J. W.	Apr 25	1
Hunter, Margaret	May 16	1 & 8
Huth, Doretta	Nov 14	9
Irving, Elizabeth V.	Jul 11	1
Johnson, son of Boswell	Nov 21	3
Johnston, John W. (Dr.)	Aug 15	1
Jones, William R.	May 9	8
Juarez, Ramon	Aug 15	5
King, Nancy	Apr 4	1
King, W. A. (Dr.)	Nov 7	1
Kingsley, George A.	Jun 20	7
Knapp, Mrs. John L.	Dec 12	3
Kolodzey, John J.	Mar 14	1
Lear, Sam	Mar 7	8
Leech, Mc Donald	Feb 14	1
Lesterjette, Edward	Jun 27	1
Lesterjette, George	Oct 16	1
Lewis, Mrs. Charles T.	May 2	1

NAME	DATE	PG
Love, Margaret	Feb 21	1
Mae, Harriet	Nov 21	5
Mahoney, Charles Patrick	Feb 7	5
Mancha, Estella	Aug 8	5
Mason, Ruby	Mar 28	1
Mc Cormick, Charles H.	May 9	8
Mc Daniel, L. S. (Silas)	Oct 10	4 & 9
Mc Donald, J. D.	Oct 10	1
Mc Gee, Daniel W.	May 9	8
Mc Lain, Victor Lee	Jun 6	8
Mc Mahon, Mrs. E. K.	Nov 28	9
Mc Mahon, Jim	Oct 3	1
Meckel, Charles H.	Sep 19	1
Morales, Guillermo (Estate)	Sep 12	9
Morris, Edith	Mar 14	5
Motte, Mark	Jun 27	1
Munson, Luther	Jun 13	1
Munson, Luther P.	Jun 20	6
Murr, Henry	Jan 10	1
Nelson, Sarah Alice	Aug 1	1 & 6
Oatman, Lillian (Mrs. F. B.)	Apr 25	1
Ochse, Robert	Feb 28	1
Oechsner, Mrs. Lula Blanch	Feb 14	5
Oliff, Betty Jean	Aug 15	9
Parker, D. D. (Doc)	Jun 27	1
Parker, Lela	Jun 27	1
Peril, Fannie	Dec 19	1
Peterson, John	May 30	1
Petsch, Mrs. Joe F.	Apr 13	1
Pfeiffer, Lena	Jan 24	9
Posey, Mrs. Lou	Sep 12	1
Ragland, Samuel G.	Sep 12	1
Rawson, Herbert	Jun 6	1
Rees, Stonewal Jackson	Jan 31	1
Ritcherson, Tommy Gene	May 30	1
Robbins, Edward E. (Thanks)	Feb 14	5
Roberts, W. F. (Jr.)	Oct 24	1
Robison, David F. (Gerald)	Jan 17	1
Robledo, Anestacio	Oct 24	7
Rothschild, William	May 23	8

NAME	DATE	PG
Roundtree, Harvey C.	May 23	8
Rusche, Julius	Jul 25	1
Ryder, Pauline	Oct 10	3
Salinas, Mrs. Librala	Sep 19	1
Sawyer, E. E.	Apr 18	1
Schofield, Sarah	Dec 5	1
Schmidt, Adolph	Sep 5	9
Schreiner, Aime Charles	Nov 21	1
Schwethelm, Ernst	May 2	1
Segesar, Bertram C.	Jan 17	1
Sikes, G. A.	Jul 4	1
Smith, Mrs. Jessie G.	Jul 4	1
Spencer, W. V. (Dr.)	Nov 7	1
Steagall, Josephine	Oct 17	1
Stephens, Christopher S.	Apr 11	8
Stewart, Howard L.	Sep 12	8
Stieler, Emma	Feb 14	1
Stockton, Samuel E.	Aug 1	1
Strange, Olin M.	Spe 19	1
Taylor, Mrs. D. C. C.	Feb 14	1
Taylor, Matthew G.	Dec 12	5
Thomas, George E.	Jan 10	1
Trevino, Leandra	Jul 11	5
Turk, Elizabeth	Apr 11	1
Vecherst, Victor	Feb 28	1
Voigt, Paul	Aug 1	1
Wagner, Cecil	Nov 21	1
Wells, Monroe	Apr 18	1
Wendel, Arthur C.	Nov 14	1
Whitcomb, Orville F.	Nov 28	6
Whitehead, Carl	Aug 29	2
Wilkerson, Steve	Nov 7	1
Wilkins, Oscar L.	Mar 21	1
Williams, Cora	Aug 1	1
Williams, Mrs. Cy	Jun 13	1
Williams, John	May 9	1
Witt, J. Monroe	May 2	1

The last paper of 1935 is missing--December 26, 1935.

1936
Film Roll #16

NAME	DATE	PG
Adams, Sadie Merle	Nov 12	1
Arledge, Elva H.	Feb 13	8
Armstrong, Orville	Oct 8	1
Baethage, Albert	Jan 30	9
Bailey, T. H.	Apr 16	1
Bailey, Wesley	Apr 23	5
Baker, A. W.	Feb 13	4
Baker, Mrs. E. F.	Nov 19	1
Baker, Floyd	Jul 23	8
Baldwin, Mrs. George	Jan 2	1
Ball, Major K.	Jun 4	8
Barnes, Luther (Rev.)	Nov 19	8
Barry, Clarence P.	Feb 6	8
Benson, Willian G.	May 21	1
Berger, Walter	Oct 15	7
Berrien, Bertha	Jan 30	1
Berrien, Jim	Jan 30	1
Bertzyk, Ramon August	Mar 5	5
Bloxom, Bobby A.	Jul 30	10
Boettcher, Christian H.	Jul 30	10
Bonn, Mrs.	??Oct 22	11
Bradwell, Daisy	Mar 26	1
Bundick, Tom M.	Feb 27	1
Burks, Melton	Apr 30	1
Burns, Richard	Nov 19	8
Carew, Julia	Dec 17	5
Carnes, William C.	Mar 26	1
Carpenter, John W.	Dec 24	1
Clabaugh, Mrs. E. C.	Jul 9	3
Coffey, Jesse	Mar 12	9
Colbath, Letabell	Jan 9	1
Coldwell, Mrs. N. (Carrie)	Aug 27	1
Coleman, Mrs. A. D.	Nov 5	3
Coleman, Ernest (Jack)	Jun 25	1
Coleman, Norman	Jul 16	1
Coleman, Norman	Jul 23	3
Collazo, Ramon	Oct 8	5
Collonge, Louise	Oct 29	7
Cravens, George F.	Sep 17	12
Crow, Edith Alberta (Thanks)	Jan 23	9

83

NAME	DATE	PG
Crump, Nettie L.	Apr 2	1
Davis, Mrs. Jack	Nov 12	1
Davis, Tillman B.	May 28	4
De Freest, Harold	Jul 9	1
Dietert, Emil E.	Feb 27	1
Duckworth, Infant of R. B.	Aug 6	1
Dunn, Joseph W.	Aug 13	1
Durant, Henry T.	Mar 19	1
Ed, Saba George	Jul 2	8
Egli, Dick	May 14	5
Elliott, Thelma	Dec 3	1
Evenson, Laura Pope	Apr 23	6
Fairy, Mrs. W. S.	Aug 20	3
Farr, Edwin W.	Jun 18	8
Fellbaum, Ernest	Oct 8	1
Folsom, Edward S.	Jul 16	6
Fox, Margaret	Oct 29	7
Fox, Virgil	Nov 12	1 & 12
Fox, Zalmon F.	Mar 5	1
Frank, George	Jul 9	8
Franke, Ruth H.	Feb 20	1
Franklin, Lurine H.	Sep 24	10
Franz, Lee H.	Aug 6	10
Galbraith, Harry W.	Dec 10	1
Garibay, Cruz	Apr 23	5
Garrett, John Henry	Jun 18	6
Gerrish, David A.	Sep 17	8
Giltner, Paul R.	Mar 5	5 & 8
Gingras, Margaret Lee Ison	Jan 30	1
Goforth, John N.	Jul 16	6
Gore, George C.	Mar 26	8
Green, Edward H. (Dr.)	Jan 2	5
Green, Will	Apr 2	3
Hampson, Dorothy	Apr 2	1
Hancock, Charles W.	Jul 23	1
Hans, Joe Edgar	Oct 29	7
Harbin, Walter G.	Oct 15	8
Harlin, V. S.	Apr 16	10
Hatch, Sarah A.	Feb 6	1
Haufler, Gustave	Dec 17	3

1936
Film Roll #16

NAME	DATE	PG
Hawkins, C. A.	Sep 24	5
Haynes, M. D.	Jan 23	6
Hetton, Arthur E.	Aug 6	10
Hodges, Mary Ellen	Jun 25	1 & 9
Holdsworth, Mrs. Richard	Nov 19	1
Holloman, George	Feb 6	1
Holt, Connie E.	May 28	1
Hopf, Mrs. Max (Mary Cloudt)	Jan 23	3
Hopkins, Clara May	Oct 1	10
Horton, Sallie	Oct 8	1
Houlberg, Mrs. Harry	Mar 12	3
Hurst, Henry C.	Mar 5	8
Inman, James B.	Jul 23	8
Jackson, Barbara	Feb 13	1
Jonas, Lizzie	Jan 23	1
Keith, Sarah J. (Mrs. J. L.)	May 21	1
Kersey, John W.	Apr 30	7
Killinger, John William	Oct 29	7
Kirkland, Paul J.	Feb 6	1
Kroenert, George (Jr.)	Jan 16	1
Kuntz, J. B. (Koontz)	Oct 22	4
Kuntz, Mrs. John J.	May 14	5
Lange, Robert (Sr.)	Dec 10	1
Lee, Martha Ann	Feb 13	1
Lehman, G. H.	Oct 8	3
Leigh, Dalton	Jul 30	1
Leinweber, Charles	Dec 24	1
Lowrance, Tommy Nell	Oct 1	1
Lubbock, Jean Gray	Aug 13	1
Mahavier, Mrs. Kay	Jan 9	5
Martin, Clarence	Sep 3	10
Mata, Dorotea	Oct 15	7
Mattox, Charles Logan	Jan 9	5
Mc Carty, Herbert	Oct 15	1
Mc Cutcheon, L. H. (Rev.)	Dec 17	8
Mc Gaffey, Otis	Apr 23	1
Melcher, Gilbert	Jan 9	5
Miller, Minnie Maude	Jun 18	6
Miller, Reuben	Apr 23	3
Moore, Mrs. Gabe R.	Oct 15	8

NAME	DATE	PG
Moore, J. T.	May 21	1
Moore, Mrs. Jack	Jan 30	1
Moody, John A.	Apr 23	1
Moore, Mrs. Truett	Apr 23	1
Morgan, Harry M.	Dec 3	4
Neal, Ben C.	Oct 29	1
Neff, Joseph	Nov 26	8
Nichols, Sarah Frances	Oct 22	10
Nichols, William A.	Jun 18	1
Nigh, Stella	Oct 29	12
Nutter, Thomas H.	Jul 16	1
Osborne, Bill	Sep 17	1
Palmer, Ernest E. (Dr.)	Oct 15	1
Palmer, Mrs. Ernest E.	Oct 15	1
Payne, Claude	Mar 26	1 & 8
Perdue, Dewey	Jun 25	1
Peters, Mrs. E. M. (Winifred S.)	Jun 25	1
Peterson, Mrs. Hal	May 7	1
Peterson, Mrs. Hal	May 14	1
Peterson, Walter G.	May 28	1
Petsch, Joseph F.	Mar 12	1
Powers, Harold E.	Aug 20	8
Price, Crawford (Thanks)	Mar 5	5
Proffit, Thomas J.	May 28	12
Pruitt, Harvey G.	Jan 23	7
Raute, Otto	Jul 30	1
Ramsey, Adah	Aug 6	3
Rape, Eunice Leon	??Oct 22	11
Real, Theresa	Mar 26	6
Riley, Mark	Apr 16	10
Roberts, Josephine	Jun 11	1
Robertson, Lake	Feb 13	1
Robinson, Thomas E.	Apr 30	7
Rogers, James M.	Nov 26	8
Rogers, Virginia	Apr 16	1
Roots, Mrs. Willie	Jul 2	3
Ruthesell, Robert	Aug 13	8
Sanford, E. B.	Sep 17	1
Saul, James H.	Jun 11	1
Selfridge, Mrs. L. W.	Feb 27	1

NAME	DATE	PG
Sharitz, Claude L.	Oct 8	1
Siebenthal, Ernst	Jan 30	1
Simpson, Noah W.	Mar 5	5
Smith, Charles H.	Nov 12	6
Smith, Robert E.	Jan 9	7
South, Carl W.	Sep 17	1
Sowers, Gerald L.	Jan 30	1
Spence, C. B.	Nov 26	1
Stehling, Joseph	Jul 23	1
Stieler, Mrs. Adolph (Jr.)	Jun 11	3
Stine, August W.	Jul 30	10
Stone, William Lee	Nov 12	3
Swope, A. D.	Oct 8	1
Tiemann, Eugenia S.	May 28	5
Turner, Maurice	Oct 22	1
Vedor, Roberta Lee	Sep 10	3
Wallace, James Harrison	Feb 6	5
Warden, Francis M.	Jul 23	8
Watson, Joe	Aug 27	1
Weldon, George W.	Jan 2	8
Weldon, Oscar	Sep 10	1
Wharton, Lucia Ann	May 7	1
Williams, John B.	Dec 3	1
Williams, Robert	Jan 16	6
Wilson, Earl	Jun 25	6
Woodward, Elizabeth	Jan 9	1
Wright, Thelma	Jun 18	6

1937
Film Roll #17

THE FIRST PAPER AVAILABLE FOR THIS YEAR IS FEBRUARY 11TH.

These obituaries are from the Kerrville Times since January
and early February papers are missing from the Kerrville
Mountain Sun. The first issue of the Kerrvile Times available is January 28, 1937. The Times papers are in very poor
condition.

NAME	DATE	PG
Ahr, Frank	Apr 24	7
Baldwin, Mrs. Cecil	Jan 28	1
Bot, Henry (Jr.)	Jan 28	1 & 10
Brett, Frank T.	Feb 18	1
Bundick, Martha	Feb 18	1
Carroll, Frank	Jan 28	10
Cox, Gertrude	Feb 4	7
Dunkerly, Mrs. Court	Feb 4	1
Kelley, Herman L.	Jan 28	10
Loesburg, (Girl) Thelma Joy	Feb 4	2
Mayhugh, J. R.	Feb 18	1
Meyer, Joe	Feb 4	7
Oehler, Mrs. August	Feb 4	1
Pampell, Mrs. Milton L.	Feb 4	1
Perner, William	Feb 18	1
Prestridge, Dicey Jane	Jan 28	1 & 6
Stonoff, Kris	Jan 28	10
Vaughn, Ronald Lee	Jan 28	4

Film Roll #17

NAME	DATE	PG
Adams, Georgia O.	Feb 25	5
Adams, W. F. (Sr.)	Apr 8	1
Allen, Mrs. W. W.	Oct 28	1
Atwood, Emma Talley	Sep 9	1
Aubey, Horace M.	Sep 23	1 & 7
Baldwin, George	Nov 11	1
Bell, J. L.	Jun 24	1
Bennett, Thomas Roy	Mar 4	5
Benson, Aileen	Sep 9	11
Bevins, Roy	Sep 2	12
Biermann, Louis	Jun 10	7
Billings, Thomas Alex	Sep 23	2
Blair, Raymond	Oct 21	12
Boney, Frank N.	Oct 7	1
Brach, Roger C.	Jul 29	8
Branch, Agnes	Jun 3	9
Brandon, Mrs. W. L. (Emma Jung)	Jun 17	12
Brett, Frank T.	Feb 18	1

NAME	DATE	PG
Browkaw, J. F.	Sep 2	12
Bullard, mother of Dr.	Oct 14	1
Bundick, Martha	Feb 18	1
Burgess, Riley C.	Apr 8	1
Burney, Mrs. De Witt	Jul 29	1
Burney, Mary Louise	Feb 25	1
Byrd, Carl	Aug 5	9
Campbell, Harry L.	Sep 30	1 & 8
Carroone, Richard T.	Jul 15	7
Cherry, T. M.	Nov 11	12
Conn, Isabell O.	Oct 7	1
Cottle, Lee	Mar 11	8
Crowell, Ruth Idella	Sep 16	12
Davis, F. F. (Rev.)	Aug 5	8
Delaney, James Vincent	Jun 17	7
Dietert, Milton E.	Nov 18	1
Dunkerly, Court	Feb 11	1
Eads, Martha Marion	Jul 29	8
Eaos, H. M.	Apr 8	4
Earls, J. M. (Rev.)	Apr 1	9
Ellis, Susan	Dec 9	8
Epperson, D. M.	Feb 25	1
Ernst, Claire Ashford	Apr 1	1
Fain, Mrs. William	Jul 29	11
Fairbanks, Robert	Dec 2	12
Falvey, John Joseph	Jul 29	11
Fielder, Edward	Jul 8	1 & 7
Finley, Emma	Jun 3	4
Forgy, Dee	Aug 5	12
Fritz, Josephine	Dec 16	8
Geisler, Henry	Apr 8	5 & 6
Gifford, Carl	Apr 1	10
Goff, Maggie	Sep 2	12
Goldman, Lillian	Aug 12	7
Gonzales, Mrs. Mauro	Aug 26	7
Goodman, Leo	Jul 15	10
Gore, Mrs. John (Emme Tom Graham)	Mar 25	3
Green, Mrs. William M.	Oct 28	8
Griffith, P. S. (Dr.)	Jun 24	12
Grimland, Roy J.	Dec 23	6

1937
Film Roll #17

NAME	DATE	PG
Gryder, Ruth	Aug 26	8
Guidry, Mrs. Luke	Aug 26	7
Haden, Joey	Aug 5	9
Hamell, Stuart	Apr 15	4
Hammell, Eugene	Jul 1	4
Harwood, John	Mar 4	1
Hatfield, Mrs. William	Apr 15	3
Haufler, Mrs. Gus	Nov 4	1
Hayes, Leah	Oct 14	12
Hazlett, Ira N.	Jun 10	7
Heimann, Elgin A.	Oct 21	1
Henderson, W. Irvin	Aug 26	1
Hill, Cecil E.	Dec 9	12
Hobbs, Pearl	Apr 29	1 & 9
Hollomon, Delilah	Nov 18	1
Holt, Connie	Sep 9	1
Hoover, John S.	Apr 1	1 & 4
Hornbeck, William Walton	Feb 25	6
Houghton, E. S.	Sep 9	8
Howze, Mrs. Jim S. (Annie Garrett)	Apr 22	1
Hull, Harriet	Sep 2	1
Irving, R. L. (Dr.)	Aug 12	8
James, Arnold L.	Dec 23	5
James, Goerge C.	Jun 24	1
James, P. B.	Feb 25	5
James, Pleasant B.	Mar 4	5 & 9
Jennings, William S.	Apr 15	1
Johannessen, Jim D.	Aug 19	1
Jones, Gerry	Nov 11	11
Jorda, Hugo A.	Aug 12	7
Jung, Mrs. H. W.	Mar 18	6
Kendall, Ruby	Oct 14	1
Kensing, William Henry	Dec 30	6
Klarner, Louis	Jul 1	11
Kubelis, Roy	Mar 4	5
Lang, Mrs. E. H.	Nov 18	12
Lange, Mrs. Gottfried	Sep 30	7
Larrimore, William	Sep 23	1
Leonard, Emil	Dec 23	6
Lewis, Lucinda	Dec 16	1

NAME	DATE	PG
Littlefield, P. T.	Nov 25	1
Loesburg, Thelma Joy (Thanks)	Feb 11	5
Love, Frank	Aug 26	3
Lovewell, William miller	Mar 4	1
Ludwig, Mrs. Fred	Jul 8	10
Luigi, James G.	Dec 30	1
Luigi, Lonnie	Dec 30	1
Manade, Maurice	Feb 25	5
Marr, William A.	Nov 11	12
Martin, Walter Gus	Oct 14	5
May, Mrs. M. L. Vivian Barrett	Mar 11	4
Mayhugh, John Rollen	Feb 18	1
Mc Bryde, John Alden	Oct 28	1
Mc Donnell, Robert V.	Sep 16	12
Mc Nealy, Jesse Orville	Mar 4	1
Medina, Apolinar	Jul 8	7
Mosty, Harvey R.	Aug 19	1
Muenker, William	Feb 11	1 & 9
Mullins, Jasper W.	Sep 2	12
Nagel, Theresa	Nov 18	1
Nations, Homer F.	Dec 23	1
Neighbors, Mrs. J. C.	Apr 8	9
Odensal, William C.	Apr 8	4
Orcutt, Mrs. Sam Augustus	Aug 26	1 & 7
Owens, George F.	Feb 18	5
Ozuna, Urban (Rev.)	Feb 18	5
Page, Mrs. John	Jul 15	11
Pehl, Mrs. Ed	Apr 22	8
Permenter, J. N.	Sep 2	8
Permiento, Della	Dec 9	4
Persons, R. W.	Jun 17	12
Pope, Willie	Apr 29	6
Pope, Willie A.	May 6	8
Potter, Mrs.	Jul 29	9
Price, Mrs. W. H.	Mar 18	10
Pruneda, Petra	Jul 8	7
Ramierez, Emmanuel	Dec 30	5
Rawson, Mrs. W. H.	Dec 2	1
Real, Robert	Jun 24	1
Reed, Guy (Dr.)	Nov 11	5

NAME	DATE	PG
Rees, Eleanor Ann	Feb 18	1
Rees, Lenora	Feb 25	6
Remschel, Robert H. (Jr.)	Dec 2	1
Rhodes, Alton L.	Oct 14	1
Riggs, Samuel B. (Dr.)	Jul 1	1
Roberts, Charles A.	Dec 16	8
Roberts, Mrs. Charles A.	Sep 9	12
Robinson, John H.	Nov 11	11
Rogers, Debs	Oct 28	1
Rogers, Ezra	Sep 30	8
Rogers, Jean	Aug 5	1
Ruff, Elmer Elsworth	Jul 8	1 & 8
Ruff, Mary Jane	Dec 30	1
Russell, Louise F.	Apr 15	1
Schupp, Mrs. Lattie	Mar 11	6
Secor, William Lee (Dr.)	Sep 30	1
Shupak, John	Jun 17	7
Smith, Agnes Mary	Jun 3	5 & 9
Smith, Alf H.	Apr 22	1
Smith, Charles Patrick	Apr 8	1
Smith, O. E. (Jr.)	Aug 5	1
Snow, B. L.	Feb 25	10
Speckels, Marie	Apr 15	1
Spicer, James	Dec 2	1 & 6
Stieler, Alfred	Jul 15	12
Stinson, Sam D.	Apr 15	1
Storey, Mrs. John	Aug 26	1
Studley, Robert L.	Apr 1	1
Sturdivant, John Reagan	Nov 4	1
Tatsch, Mrs. Henry	Jul 1	10
Thalman, Fred (Jr.)	Mar 11	6
Thompson, Hoxie H. (Jr.)	Apr 22	1
Thornton, Lucie Tobin	Apr 22	10
Tidwell, Mrs. Stottie	Aug 12	11
Truelove, Betty Rose	Mar 11	10
Vaughn, Mrs. Le Roy	Feb 11	1
Villanueva, Mary	Feb 18	5
Wahrmund, Frank	May 20	10
Watkins, Losson M. (Jr.)	Jun 10	9
Watson, Felix H.	Apr 22	6

```
                          1937
                     Film Roll #17

NAME                          DATE        PG

White, N. H.                  Aug 5       1
Williams, Mrs. T. (Clara W.)  Nov 11      12
Williams, Mrs. Theron         Nov 4       5
Wilson, James W.              Feb 25      1
Wilson, L.                    Jul 29      5
Wilson, Sallie                Sep 23      8
Woody, John D.                Jul 29      8
Wootton, Delcia               Mar 25      5
Yantes, Barnett B.            Dec 30      1 & 7
Youngblood, Edward T.         Jul 1       7


                          1938
                     Film Roll #17

Adams, Mary Eliza             Apr 14      1
Ahrens, Otto George           Nov 10      6
Alexander, Davis M.           Apr 21      5
Allen, Carl Remschel          May 19      1
Anderson, Ralph M.            Jun 23      3 & 8
Anderson, Wiley               Jan 13      8
Anglin, Mrs. J. A.            Mar 17      3
Armistead, J. B. (Ben)        Jul 14      6
Arndt, Otto                   Jul 14      1 & 8
Arombola, Gertrude            Jan 13      5
Baker, Walter                 Jan 27      1
Ball, William F.              Oct 13      5
Bass, Otto                    Jun 16      1
Bass, Otto                    Jun 23      1
Benson, Odis Odell            Jun 30      1
Bigge, Edward H.              Aug 25      6
Blevins, Charles              Feb 3       1 & 8
Blum, Mrs. Max                Feb 3       8
Bradford, George Harris       Apr 7       10
Brasier, Mrs. Frederic M.     Aug 11      1
Brezik, Alfons                Dec 15      7
Bridges, Ed                   Apr 14      8
Bridges, Edward               Apr 21      8
Brown, Mrs. J. S.             May 12      7
Browning, J. E.               Jun 2       7
```

1938
Film Roll #17

NAME	DATE	PG
Brucy, William A.	Dec 29	4
Bundick, Emma Elizabeth	Jan 20	6
Burleson, Ruby Geraldine	Jan 27	6
Burney, Irvy	Jan 13	9
Carroll, Lucian R.	Dec 15	7
Carson, David H. (Dr.)	Nov 3	1
Carson, Stonewall Jackson	Feb 17	6
Chambers, Mary Rose	Jul 28	1
Champenois, Cecil	Aug 25	1
Chapman, Raymond A.	Apr 21	1
Collozo, Edward S.	Jul 21	1
Comparet, J. E.	Mar 3	3
Cosper, J. C.	Apr 14	10
Council, Mrs. W. L. (Lora Mickle)	Oct 13	1
Cowden, Mary Green	Dec 8	1
Cox, Eddie	Jan 20	5
Cunningham, H. T. (Dr.)	Feb 24	5
Davis, Otto E.	Aug 4	2
Delaney, Frank L.	Aug 4	1
Demasters, Milton Odell	Jul 14	1
Denton, J. D.	Apr 21	8
Donald, Viola Penn	Jan 13	6
Dowdy, Richard	Sep 8	1
Draper, Ova M.	Sep 1	12
Duderstadt, Fred	Jun 9	1
Duderstadt, George C.	Oct 20	1
Dufner, infant daughter	Feb 24	4
Duge, Mike	Oct 13	12
Dulnig, Frank G.	Apr 21	7
Durant, Shelby Ben	Dec 22	1
Durrin, Emily J.	Dec 8	1
Eckert, Henry	Dec 22	3
Ellis, John W. (Dr.)	Oct 27	1
Enderle, Mrs. Albert	Apr 28	1
Evans, Leonard (Jr.)	Mar 3	1
Ezdell, Mrs. H. E. (Katie)	Aug 18	10
Fatheree, Mrs. L. B.	Apr 7	10
Faulkner, Inex Nance	Sep 8	9
Fisher, Brown	Mar 17	4
Fisher, Henry	May 26	9

94

NAME	DATE	PG
Fletcher, Howard	Aug 25	1
Fluitt, Mrs. Odel	Dec 15	7
Forgy, Humphry Green	Feb 3	7
Fortner, Commodore P.	Sep 15	4
French, Sharon Gail	Aug 18	5
Friedman, Samuel	Jul 28	1
Goebel, Anna	Feb 10	11
Gold, Jake	Nov 10	1
Graham, Jesse W.	Feb 24	7
Green, William	Feb 10	1
Grosenbacker, Louis	Jan 6	4
Gross, Waller W.	Apr 28	1
Hagens, Robert Mason	Jan 6	1
Haley, Will	Dec 15	7
Hartman, George Henry	Jul 7	5 & 10
Heimann, Mrs. John (Sr.)	Feb 10	1
Henke, Alfred	Dec 15	10
Hensley, M. E.	Jul 28	10
Hensley, Mrs. M. E.	Jul 28	10
Hernandez, Florentino	Nov 10	6
Hodges, Don	Dec 1	12
Hollomon, Thomas Jefferson	Dec 1	1
Holmes, Lloyd	Dec 1	8
Hope, Will	Nov 10	1 & 11
Hopkins, Mrs. M. L.	Feb 24	1
James, Nancy W.	Dec 15	1
Jensen, Lina Huth	Jun 9	1
Johnson, Thomas William	Apr 7	1
Kalkus, Millie	Jan 20	5
Kirkland, Ben	Jan 20	10
Klein,, Roy	May 26	1
Koenig, Henry	Oct 20	5
Kolba, Frank	Jan 27	4
Lackey, Sallie	Sep 8	10
La Fleur, Luke	May 26	1 & 9
Lally, Charles W.	Apr 7	9
Landry, Annie Mae	Dec 15	7
Lantz, Mrs. J. G.	Sep 15	12
Lee, Oscar Arthur	Feb 24	5 & 6
Leonard, Fred A.	Feb 10	7

1938
Film Roll #17

NAME	DATE	PG
Lewis, George W.	May 26	1
Lewis, John C.	Sep 8	6
Linstead, William F.	Sep 29	1
Love, Richard A.	Jun 16	1
Malvin, Golder F.	Sep 29	10
Markham, James S.	Dec 22	8
Marlar, Elizabeth Sherman	Apr 21	12
Masterson, Walter B.	Feb 17	3
Matz, Phillip B. (Dr.)	Jul 14	8
Mayfield, S. S.	Jul 28	6
Maynard, Wesley A. C.	Sep 29	10
Mc Coy, Doris	Apr 28	1
Mc Coy, Mike	Apr 28	1
Mc Coy, Mrs. R. P.	Apr 28	1
Mc Clellan, E. M.	Feb 10	11
Mc Cracken, Charles E.	Jun 23	1
Mc Donald, J. A.	Sep 8	5
Mc Donald, Mrs. J. A.	Sep 8	5
Mc Elroy, S. G. (Steve)	Aug 11	6
Mc Elroy, S. G. (Steve)	Aug 18	1
Mc Gill, Luther G.	Jan 13	10
Mc Nees, J. H.	Feb 17	1
Merritt, Jack Roy	Jun 23	1
Michon, John Peter	Jun 16	1 & 7
Mills, Lloyd	Jun 23	8
Moore, Mrs. H. C. (Alice)	Dec 29	1
Morris, Mattie	Sep 8	1
Morriss, Laurence S.	Jan 27	5
Morriss, Will A.	Feb 3	8
Muller, Mary Sophia	Jan 27	1
Murdock, J. A.	Dec 15	8
Nagel, Mrs. Wilhelm	Jan 27	7
New, Jake A.	Jan 6	10
Nowlin, Claude	Apr 21	1
O'Connor, DAn	Jan 13	5
Oehler, David	Mar 17	1
O'Gorman, Mary	Mar 17	5
O'Neal, L. L. (Rev.)	Jan 13	5
Orcutt, Samuel A.	Jun 30	1 & 7
Ottinger, Mrs. P. A.	Dec 15	1

96

NAME	DATE	PG
Pacheco, Martin	Jun 30	7
Page, Edwin J. L.	Mar 31	5
Parker, William	Feb 24	1 & 6
Pearson, Samuel A.	Oct 13	1
Pennington, Troy	Oct 13	5
Perkins, E. O.	Apr 14	5
Peschel, Rudolph	Jul 7	1
Phillips, Elam R.	Feb 3	7
Pixzini, Esther	Jan 20	5
Powell, Earl	Feb 24	6
Prescott, Eugene H.	Feb 17	1
Prine, Mrs. Homer	Nov 10	1
Raiford, Larry David	Nov 24	6
Rauch, Louise	Jul 21	1
Reagan, Edwin	Oct 13	11
Real, Gertrude (Mrs. Julian)	Jan 6	9
Remschel, Henry	Mar 24	1
Rhodes, Will Henry	Nov 3	8
Rice, Mrs. F. A.	Jan 20	10
Rice, Virginia	Feb 17	3
Rieck, H. W.	Dec 29	8
Robinson, Father of Roy	Jan 20	9
Rodriguez, Polly (Sr.)	Jan 6	1
Rogers, Warren., (Dr.)	Oct 6	1
Romeo, James M.	Oct 20	1 & 8
Rumph, Robert F.	Jun 16	11
Sanchez, Florian	Oct 13	5
Sanger, John Joseph	Dec 15	1 & 7 & 8
Saurer, Henry	Feb 3	11
Schad, Mrs. Frank	Mar 3	1
Schwarz, Mrs. Charles	May 26	1
Seeling, Frederich E.	Feb 3	7
Sheffield, Josephine E.	May 19	1
Shepherd, Margaret	Mar 17	3
Silvas, infant son of Trinidad	Dec 15	7
Sinclair, Carl	Mar 10	1
Sloane, Medwin	Oct 13	8
Smith, John E.	Apr 14	10
Smith, Mrs. Jonas P.	Jul 14	6
Snow, Sarah Ann	Aug 25	6

NAME	DATE	PG
Solomon, Lon	Oct 13	11
Stehling, Mrs. John	Dec 1	7
Stone, Floyd	Oct 13	1
Storms, Robert Jerry	Feb 3	1
Storms, Wayne Powell	Dec 22	8
Swearinagen, Sadie	May 5	12
Swenson, Eric W.	Jun 2	1
Tacquard, Mrs. Faustine	Dec 22	5
Talamantes, Andrew	Feb 3	7
Taylor, Mrs. W. A.	Mar 31	7
Tegener, Frederick B. (Dr.)	Mar 3	5
Terry, Permelia Ray	Jun 9	9
Throckmorton, Richard W.	Jan 27	6
Timmons, J. Grady	Jun 30	12
Tinkham, George Forrest	Sep 8	6
Titus, Mrs. Floyd (Sr.)	Oct 13	7
Tomlinson, Martha Jane	Feb 3	1 & 8
Trapp, Roy C.	Jul 28	5
Tschoepe, Mrs. Alphonse	Jan 20	5
Usener, Ledia	Jan 13	10
Vann, Charlie C.	May 5	1
Walker, John T.	Feb 17	9
Wallace, Joseph	Mar 3	5
Warren, Don	Feb 10	4
Wellborn, Mrs. Clarence E.	Mar 17	9
Wellborn, Robert L.	Sep 8	1
Wharton, David N.	Sep 1	1
Williams, Roy (Thanks)	Jul 28	5
Williamson, James W.	Feb 3	7
Witt, Leonard	Jan 13	1
Wolfmueller, Mrs. Robert (Anita)	Aug 4	1
Woodell, A. F. (Thanks)	Mar 10	7
Yarger, John W.	Mar 10	1
Young, Louis W.	Aug 4	9
Zincke, August	May 26	10

NAME	DATE	PG
Adams, J. D.	Sep 21	1
Ahern, Dan	Jun 29	5
Bailey, Thomas A.	Feb 2	10
Baker, Fidelio C.	Jan 19	6
Banish, John	Apr 20	7
Bartlett, W. F.	Nov 9	3
Beasley, Lulu	Jul 6	10
Bennett, Betty Bob	May 11	1
Bennett, B. F.	Jan 26	1
Bernhard, Allen R.	Sep 7	1
Bernhard, Peter	Mar 16	8
Bittel, Albert	Sep 21	1
Bishop, Mary A.	Mar 23	1
Blanks, Lydia	Jun 22	12
Boyett, William T.	Aug 17	10
Brashear, S. F.	Apr 20	10
Brodie, Stephen L.	Nov 16	12
Brown, Mrs. Archie	Oct 26	10
Buckner, Mrs. T. A.	Aug 17	8
Bundick, Mertie Lee	May 25	8
Burrer, Emilie	Jun 15	6
Cain, J. B.	Jan 19	5
Cannon, J. C. (Dad)	Jan 12	6
Carlisle, Mrs. J. M.	Feb 9	6
Carpenter, James W.	Oct 12	6
Case, Chauncey R.	May 11	8
Clanton, W. M.	Jan 26	1
Clark, Ethlyn	Dec 28	1
Clay, Felix	Apr 20	12
Clay, Mary	Apr 20	12
Cloud, Nell	Sep 1	10
Cobb, F. H.	Dec 21	6
Coke, Bryan L.	Jul 20	1
Coke, Richard (Dr.)	May 18	12
Collozo, Lorenco J.	Jun 22	12
Crider, Mrs. Charles	Mar 19	11
Crotty, Sadie	May 25	1
De Ganahl, Charles F.	May 18	12
Denton, Benjamin F.	Feb 9	1
Dietert, Gus	Sep 28	1

NAME	DATE	PG
Dixon, Hennon E.	Mar 16	12
Dodge, James R.	Jan 12	9
Douglas, Frederick R.	May 4	12
Downard, Richard D.	Feb 9	1
Durant, Shelby	Oct 26	10
Dwyer, Mattie E.	Apr 27	12
Eckert, Mrs. Louis	Mar 30	5
Ellebracht, Mrs. Richard	May 18	5
Elliott, A. R.	Nov 9	9
Enderle, Emma	Jan 5	10
Everett, Joe W.	Feb 9	1
Fitzsimons, J. S.	Jan 12	1
Fly, Montie E.	Apr 27	12
Forsythe, Maude W.	Jul 13	3
Frederich, Albert C.	Aug 10	7
Gallagher, Loren E.	Jan 12	10
Garrett, F. E.	Feb 2	10
Ginocehio, Maggie	Jan 12	3
Gilmer, Mrs. S. H.	Mar 2	5
Glass, Ann Eliza	Oct 12	12
Glenn, Samuel D.	Apr 20	1
Gracey, Quill E.	Mar 19	1
Green, Laura B.	Jun 1	11
Grona, Max	Mar 30	1
Grubert, Mrs. E. H.	Aug 17	6
Guthrie, George W.	Feb 16	1
Harthcock, T. B.	Mar 19	11
Heimann, Frank	Oct 12	1
Hawkins, P. A.	Sep 1	1
Herder, William Kenneth	Jan 5	1
Hilliard, Sallie R.	Mar 23	1
Hines, Julia E.	Apr 13	10
Hutchins, Henry	Aug 3	10
Jackson, John W.	Jun 22	8
Johnson, Margaret A.	May 11	8
Johnston, Charles	Feb 23	11
Johnston, Elizabeth	Dec 28	1
Junkin, Edward D.	Aug 24	1
Kammlah, Louis	Oct 12	6
Keese, Ida (Thanks)	Mar 16	7

NAME	DATE	PG
Kelly, Sue H.	Jun 29	3
Kerr, Joseph N.	Jul 6	5
Kincaid, G. H. (Dr.)	Sep 28	1
King, Catherine	Nov 16	6
Kingsbury, Jerome J.	Mar 2	12
Lackey, Charlie	Nov 16	12
Lesterjette, Mrs. Mintie L.	May 18	11
Lott, John	Aug 3	9
Magner, Patricia	Aug 31	10
Matthews, J. Samuel	Mar 23	10
Mc Bride, Oliver W.	May 4	12
Mc Doniel, Annie (Mrs. W. A.)	Oct 12	6
Mc Kinnon, Ella	Feb 23	8
Mc Lane, Jeffie Lee	Jan 5	1
Miller, Frost W.	Jun 29	1
Mitchell, James H.	Jun 15	1
Mooring, Mrs. Charles E.	Oct 19	1
Morris, Angie	May 11	8
Mosel, Edgar	Dec 14	1
Moses, Margaret	Nov 16	1
Muse, Nora E.	Apr 20	1
Newberry, Mrs. Hubert	Jun 29	3
Newman, John A.	Jul 13	3
Nichols, Bennet	Aug 10	5
Oehler, Mrs. L. F.	Jul 13	12
Oldham, W. S.	Jul 13	4
Page, R. E.	Jun 1	1
Palmer, R. D.	Jun 22	12
Pardue, Howard N.	Sep 21	12
Parish, Benjamin B. (Dr.)	May 4	9
Peterson, Sid C.	Sep 1	1
Pickford, Kingston	Sep 21	8
Poore, Luther F.	Nov 9	10
Priour, Isador	Oct 26	1
Ramsay, William H.	Jan 12	1
Rauch, Ernst	Jan 19	1
Richards, B. C.	Apr 6	1
Riggs, Ella	Apr 13	12
Robinson, H. C.	Mar 3	6
Roeder, William	Mar 16	8

NAME	DATE	PG
Rosenthal, Oscar	Jun 22	1
Savors, Mary A.	Aug 31	6
Schellhase, Anna	Sep 28	11
Schellhase, Henry	Apr 6	1
Schmidt, Helene	Jan 26	1
Schmidt, Paul C.	Apr 6	6
Smith, Leroy E.	Nov 2	1
Speclels, Ed W.	Aug 17	1
Stanley, Margaret	Jan 12	1
Steelman, Harry	Apr 20	12
Steelman, Child (Son)	Apr 20	12
Stevens, Mary E.	Jul 20	10
Stone, Evans	Sep 28	12
Storey, Mrs. A. B.	Apr 13	1
Sylvester, James I.	Apr 6	7
Taylor, Marion L.	Oct 5	1
Traban, Henry	Dec 7	12
Vallier, Elmer E.	Feb 2	10
Vara, Maria	Nov 20	2
Vieno, Mrs. Ollie	Dec 28	6
Warren, James E.	Dec 7	8
Weaver, Mrs. C. H.	Aug 10	6
Webb, Marshall E.	Jun 1	11
Wescott, Orville, D.	Aug 31	1
Weston, Mrs. M. F.	Aug 3	1 & 5
Wheless, Joseph Sidney	Jan 5	1
White, George G.	Jan 12	10
Williams, Mrs. Elizabeth B.	Mar 2	8
Williams, Harry	May 4	1
Williford, H. E.	Jan 5	1
Wilson, Leonard W.	Mar 16	8
Wilson, Richard D.	Oct 26	3
Wilson, Richard D.	Nov 2	1
Woodall, Mrs. Ballard W.	Feb 2	5 & 10
Woodall, Gillette M.	Nov 16	6
Woodley, W. O.	Aug 24	10
Word, Wiley C.	Oct 12	6

NAME	DATE	PG
Adamek, Emil J.	Apr 18	11
Allen, Gertrude	Jul 25	6
Ayala, Trinidad (Jr.)	Sep 12	11
Baermann, Lizzie	Aug 8	3
Baggoatt, Earl S.	May 30	3
Baker, William C.	Sep 19	1
Baldwin, George	Feb 1	12
Baldwin, Lewis	Feb 29	1
Bannecman, R. C.	Feb 29	1
Barfield, Mrs. H. C.	Oct 10	12
Barrett, Mrs. W. J. (Roberta)	Sep 5	1
Barton, baby of Jack	Mar 7	12
Becker, Mrs. L. P.	Jan 4	6
Benton, S. P.	Jun 20	4
Bierschwale, Dan W.	Jul 11	8
Bierschwale, Fritz	Jan 11	10
Blevins, Maxine E.	Dec 26	10
Branch, Calvin	Feb 22	1
Browne, Harold F.	Nov 7	11
Brucks, L. J.	Mar 28	7
Burkett, Mrs. J. H.	Feb 29	10
Burney, Ivy H.	Dec 26	1
Butler, Francis M.	Nov 21	3
Carter, John M.	Apr 25	12
Chaney, Richard H.	Aug 8	1
Chatelle, N. G.	Oct 10	1
Chipman, R. A.	Oct 24	10
Clapp, Lillie B.	Sep 12	1
Colbath, John H.	Nov 21	10
Compton, Otis M.	Aug 22	6
Conners, Lottie	Oct 24	6
Cooper, R. V.	Oct 24	1
Cooper, Reba Ann	May 2	11
Corkerill, Blain	Jun 13	11
Crate, James S.	Dec 19	12
Crawford, Karl W.	Apr 4	1
Crews, Jacob T.	Jun 27	7
Crider, Daniel Dee	Jan 25	10
Danilovez, Steve	Sep 12	11
Davis, John U.	May 30	3

1940
Film Roll #18

NAME	DATE	PG
Day, Pricilla	May 9	5 & 11
Dicken, George D.	Jul 18	8
Dinwiddie, Robert L. (Dr.)	May 30	3
Dozier, James H.	Nov 21	10
Dozier, Mrs. P. H.	Feb 29	5 (11)
Duderstadt, Jane	Dec 19	12
Eldridge, Lewis W.	Feb 29	12
Evertson, Ethel Mae	Apr 11	1
Faris, B. L.	Jan 18	10
Fletcher, Clara	Dec 19	1
Ford, Lonnie L.	Apr 13	11
Forman, Mrs. W. J.	Sep 12	1
Fred, M. K. (Rev.)	Jan 11	10
Gardiner, William	Nov 7	11
Gardnier, William	Nov 7	12
Gelussich, John J.	Jun 27	7
Geray, Frank J.	May 16	5
Glidden, R. T.	Jan 11	3
Gowan, Mary E.	Apr 25	1
Graham, J. H.	Jul 25	8
Gray, Mrs. Luke	Nov 21	10
Green, John N.	Nov 7	11
Grinstead, Miranda P.	Aug 22	10
Guthrie, Clarence Y.	Sep 19	1
Habecker, Mrs. Emil (Gertrude)	Aug 22	1 & 8
Hall, Mrs. D. C.	Feb 29	1
Hamilton, Harry (Rev.)	Dec 19	1
Harris, Lucy B.	Apr 25	8
Harrison, Emmett	May 9	11
Heimann, Louis	Aug 22	1
Heyland, Louis	Jan 18	1
Hight, Joe D.	Jun 13	11
Hill, Eugene	Apr 11	11
Hodges, Dawson N.	Feb 8	1
Holchak II, Stephen J.	Apr 4	5
Hopf, Hugo A.	Apr 11	10
Horne, Nellie	Sep 19	12
Huffstetler, William A.	Jun 27	7
Huntington, Sallie A.	Oct 10	1
Hyde, Mrs. S. E.	Apr 11	12

104

NAME	DATE	PG
Hyde, Sylvia Mae	May 2	1
Jaeggli, Mrs. E. A.	Apr 18	12
Jeffers, Mrs. S. F.	Dec 19	12
Kaiser, C. A.	Sep 5	12
Kallam, H. T.	Apr 4	5
Kellam, Gordon L.	Feb 1	1
Karger, Harry (Jr.)	Jun 13	1
Keller, Robert	Oct 3	1
Kenley, W. J.	Aug 22	10
King, Ollie A.	Oct 17	12
Krueger, Mrs. George	Feb 15	12
Landreth, Andrew C.	Apr 18	11
Landrum, Horace H.	Jun 13	11
Landry, Maurice E.	Aug 8	9
Lang, Garland H.	May 16	1
Langbein, Charles	May 23	12
Leckie, Mrs. John	Apr 11	1
Love, James R.	Jul 25	1
Luna, James H.	Sep 26	12
Martin, C. L.	Feb 22	10
Mathews, James G.	Sep 12	11
Matlock, Lena	Jul 18	8
Mayfield, Marvin K.	Feb 1	8
Mc Cain, George D.	Aug 29	12
Mc Cauley, Phillip H.	Apr 11	11
Mc Croskey, D. D.	Aug 8	1
Mc Donald, James E. (Dr.)	Mar 14	1
Mc Lain, Carlton E.	May 16	5
Merrill, Lillian A.	Jun 27	1
Mobely, Wilford P.	Jun 13	12
Moore, William V.	Oct 31	12
Moreno, Juanita	May 2	11
Morris, Tommie	Dec 26	1
Mosel, Charles B.	Dec 5	1
Mosel, William J.	Feb 22	8
Murrah, Lee Alfred	Jun 6	1
Murphy, Clifton C.	May 30	3
Neal, Mrs. Conley	Jan 4	1
Neal, Irwin	May 2	11
Neunhoffer, Clara	Aug 8	10

NAME	DATE	PG
Nitch, Carl W.	May 2	11
North, T. C.	May 16	12
Norwood, Mrs. Frank C.	May 9	5
Olson, Robert A.	Jun 6	1
Overby, Grace	Jul 25	12
Page, Saragh E.	Oct 24	10
Parks, William K.	Feb 29	12
Paul, Mrs. Dick	Dec 26	10
Pedlar, Russell	Sep 5	1
Perkins, Dorothy	May 2	11
Perry, Mrs. W. P.	Mar 21	1
Peterson, Henry	Jul 25	1
Pincoff, Emma	Jul 11	1
Pinson, Thomas M (Dr.)	Dec 5	1
Pippstine, Edward A.	Aug 8	9
Polak, Emmett	May 9	11
Prickop, Frank	Jun 13	11
Ragland, Mrs. Frank	Mar 14	1
Rauch, Gustav A.	Apr 18	12
Reeves, Urbane R.	May 23	11
Reynolds, Andrew J.	Dec 12	8
Rhame, Robert	Aug 8	9
Rhodes, Willie B.	Nov 7	11
Riggs, Richard	Feb 29	8
Riley, Ethel	Oct 31	8
Roark, Thomas T.	May 23	11
Roberts, Buck	Apr 11	11
Rothrock, Addison M. (Dr.)	Sep 5	1
Rousseau, Robert	Jun 13	11
Russell, Marion A.	Feb 8	12
Sandefer, Annie	Oct 31	9
Schad, Frank X.	Aug 29	12
Scheldrup, Bertha S.	Jun 27	7
Schoolcraft, Shere F.	Aug 29	8
Serber, J. H.	Jan 25	6
Smith, Hal	Jan 18	1
Smith, S. J.	Sep 26	12
Smith, Thomas A.	Jun 27	7
Smith, Thomas J.	Apr 11	11
Sodich, Mrs. Andrew	Feb 29	5 (11)

1940
Film Roll #18

NAME	DATE	PG
Solomon, J. J.	Dec 26	10
Stapp, C. A.	Jan 4	1
Stapp, Mrs. C. A.	Sep 26	1
Staudt, Lawrenc L.	Aug 29	8
Stephenson, Austin	Jun 27	7
Stephenson, Frank W.	Apr 18	11
Sterling, Florence	Mar 28	12
Stevens, Mrs. J. T.	Jul 11	1
Stewart, Richard H.	Jun 13	11
Stewart, S. S.	Apr 18	7
Stokes, Brown H.	Mar 28	1
Strauch, Scott	Oct 10	1
Summers, Thomas O.	Dec 26	1
Tarver, J. M.	Aug 29	6
Thompson, William F.	Jul 25	12
Truadt, Mrs. Nat	Feb 29	12
Tuttle, James E.	Jul 11	6
Walsh, Ferdinand C. (Dr.)	Feb 15	1
Walker, George A.	Mar 14	1
Walker, Walter B.	Aug 8	9
Walther, Mrs. G. W.	Mar 7	1
Weizel, Mrs. Charles	Sep 26	1
Wesch, Charles J.	Oct 31	12
White, John D.	May 16	5
Whitenburg, Clarence C.	Jun 27	7
Wilson, Robert I. (Jr.)	Dec 5	1
Winn, Mrs. John H.	Jan 11	1
Wolcott, Emma	Dec 19	1
Wood, James O.	Jun 27	7

1941
Film Roll #19

Anderson, George R.	Apr 3	1
Arnecke, Gary	Sep 18	6
Arnold, Edwin J.	Mar 27	1
Babinaux, Emily	May 1	10
Babineaux, Wesley E.	Dec 11	11
Bailey, Rebecca A.	May 22	5

107

1941
Film Roll #19

NAME	DATE	PG
Bane, Aurora D.	Dec 25	10
Banta, Helen	May 8	4
Barton, Victoria	Apr 10	10
Bates, Edith Klein	Jan 16	12
Beaver, Daniel A.	May 29	1
Blanks, Gabe	Aug 7	4
Bonnie, Felix	Dec 18	10
Bridges, Elvira	Feb 20	12
Brodie, Louis E.	Mar 13	1
Brothers, Emily Lucretia	Feb 6	5
Brown, Andy Monroe	Nov 6	12
Brown, Charles Lee	Aug 21	1
Brown, J. S.	Apr 24	1
Buie, Neil	Feb 13	3
Burge, Thomas W.	Nov 13	4
Burleson, A. J.	Sep 4	1
Burleson, Luther	Sep 4	1
Carruth, E. B. (Sr.)	Oct 9	1
Carson, W. W.	Apr 17	10
Castillo, Pedro	Jan 23	6
Caulfield, John H.	Dec 18	5
Chamborn, Clarion (Jr.)	Nov 20	1
Chapa, Lupe	Jul 17	1
Chapa, Ramon	Jul 17	1
Clark, Curtis Allen	Aug 28	10
Clark, Howard	Jul 24	5
Clendenin, Mrs. Cecil	Mar 13	1
Coleman, William Pickney	Jan 30	12
Colvin, G. M.	Mar 6	9
Corbell, Charles A.	Oct 30	8
Crawfrod, Charles	Oct 9	12
Crowell, Wade	Dec 4	8
Denton, Ethel A.	Oct 23	1
Denton, Joseph Jasper	Oct 23	1
Derry, Malinda	Jan 2	1
Dietert, Rudolph H.	Oct 23	3
Dismukes, infant dau. of Charles	Mar 20	8
Dixon, Henry Eugene	Apr 10	7
Eddins, Mrs. Charles	Mar 20	1
Elloitt, Mary	May 22	12

NAME	DATE	PG	SEC
Fawcett, E. K.	Sep 25	12	
Fields, Frank	May 22	8	
Flood, Dave	May 15	1	
Forgason, J. W.	Oct 9	12	
Francis, Carlton S. (Dr.)	Mar 13	12	
Frazier, James	Oct 16	3	
Frizzells, Fred	Jun 5	12	
Garven, Edward I.	Dec 25	1	
Gerachi, Nicholas	Jun 5	12	
Goldman, Elza	Jan 16	1	
Goodson, Mollie	May 22	11	
Graham, Sarah	Jul 3	7	
Griffin, Walter	Nov 27	1	
Grobe, Frederich Daniel	Apr 24	10	
Grona, Paul	Oct 9	5	
Grona, William Paul	Oct 16	1	
Guerrero, Josephine	Nov 6	4	
Guerrero, Rosalie	Nov 6	4	
Hart, J. H.	Jul 3	4	2
Henriksen, Herbert M.	Dec 25	10	
Hill, O. M.	Jan 2	1	
Hilliard, Mrs. C. W.	Dec 18	5	
Hood, Mrs. G. W.	Jul 31	2	
Howard, Frank A.	Dec 11	7	
Hoxie, Herbert O.	Jan 30	12	
Ingenhuett, Mrs. Herman	Feb 27	8	
Johnston, Tom C.	Sep 25	1	
Jordan, Betty A.	Feb 13	6	
Kelley, Mrs. Ed	Jan 2	3	
Kingbury, Henry R.	Nov 27	4	
Klaerner, Charles	Jan 9	6	
Lee, J. B.	May 15	1	
Lee, Mattie M.	Mar 20	1	
Lewis, Ruben	Apr 10	12	
Lich, Otto	Feb 6	5	
Linder, Rudolph	Dec 25	10	
Lochte, Marie	Dec 11	3	
Locke, Mrs. Colin C. S.	Sep 25	10	
Long, Willie B.	Jan 16	5	
Lopez, Camilo (Jr.)	Oct 16	3	

1941
Film Roll #19

NAME	DATE	PG	SEC
Lopez, infant daughter of Gilbert	Nov 27	4	
Lowrance, Mrs. Peter Osborne	Jan 23	1	
Lusk, John R. (Smokey)	Jan 16	1	
Mac Dowell, Muriel	Jul 31	1	
Magee, Homer (Rev.)	Jan 16	12	
Marlar, Howard	Oct 9	5	
Marlar, Howard L.	Oct 16	1	
Massey, Myrtle	May 22	12	
Mc Creary, Rose L.	Oct 12	1	
Mc Dougle, James	May 29	5	
Mc Lemore, Grady (Thanks)	Jun 26	8	
Mc Swain, William W.	Oct 9	12	
Merriman, Eli	Jan 30	5	
Mobely, Mollie Reagan	Oct 30	8	
Moore, Charles Woods	Mar 6	9	
Moore, Elizabeth Deal	May 29	8	
Moore, Ouida Mc Leod	Oct 23	12	
Morrow, Benjamin Franklin	Jun 19	4	
Murphy, Willis	Jan 16	8	
Mutchler, Mrs. Frank J.	Nov 27	4	
Parker, Gifford Cleveland	Dec 11	3	
Parks, Mrs. Jessy C.	Aug 28	10	
Polley, James B.	May 15	8	
Powell, Angie	Aug 21	1	
Priour, Ambrose B.	Jun 19	1	
Randolph, Charles P.	May 8	12	
Randolph, William R.	Mar 6	1	
Reagan, Roy	Jul 10	2	
Reed, Mrs. J. R.	Jun 5	8	
Reiffert, Walter	Dec 25	10	
Reiter, Mrs. Charles	Mar 20	1	
Reiter, Mrs. Charles	Mar 27	10	
Reynolds, Jesse C.	Oct 23	12	
Richardson, Jack P.	Oct 2	10	
Rishworth, William I.	Jul 10	6	
Rose, Charles (Jr.)	Oct 16	1	
Roth, Gene	Jan 2	10	
Saner, Robert C.	Oct 9	1	
Shallowhorne, W. E. (Dr.)	Oct 23	8	
Shand, William S.	Sep 18	1	

110

NAME	DATE	PG	SEC
Sharp, Donald	Jul 10	10	
Skeen, Douglas S.	Aug 28	10	
Smith, Ella	Apr 24	1	
Soto, Rachel	Jun 12	1	
Speakmon, L. S.	Dec 18	12	
Stacy, Mrs. W. H.	Mar 20	12	
Stahmann, Robert	Oct 23	9	
Stevens, John B.	Jul 24	8	
Steves, Mrs. Henry	Aug 28	1	
Stieler, Walter	Jul 17	1	
Stone, J. D.	Sep 4	1	
Sullivan, John L.	Oct 16	11	
Surber, Otto Brooks	Aug 7	10	
Surber, Visa Ann	Apr 24	1	
Sutherland, J. D.	Jul 31	2	
Sweeten, Frank R.	Aug 7	4	
Tarr, Ernest George	Dec 4	12	
Tarver, William T.	Jul 3	11	(7)
Tatom, Granville C.	Nov 20	1	
Taylor, Beal (Presley Beal)	Oct 16	11	
Taylor, U. T.	May 29	11	
Templeton, Roy Ealter	Jan 23	1	
Thompson, Adrian A.	Dec 4	10	
Thraves, Martha C.	Jan 30	12	
Tippit, Jeanette	May 15	1	
Trant, James Alfred (Jr.)	Dec 18	10	
Tucker, George D.	Apr 10	10	
Turknett, Mrs. Charles N.	Dec 4	12	
Valicek, August	Nov 27	4	
Vining, Mrs. J. L.	Dec 18	5	
Walker, Otis	Apr 24	10	
Walker, W. P.	Feb 6	12	
Wickson, Thomas D.	Jan 30	12	
Wilbanks, H. A.	Apr 24	10	
Williams, Alphon Edens	May 15	12	
Williams, Samuel R.	Sep 18	6	
Williamson, Jim	Jan 16	8	
Wilson, Sarah Mattie	Oct 30	12	
Witt, Ethel	Mar 27	8	
Witt, Mrs. W. T.	Jan 23	6	

NAME	DATE	PG	SEC
Winkey, Francis L.	Feb 13	1	

1942
Film Roll #18

Allen, William Marcus	May 17	12
Baker, Elizabeth Wright	Jan 8	1
Ballinger, Murray	Jul 6	10
Bernhardt, Arthur	Aug 13	1
Bierschwale, Dewitt Clinton	Jan 15	1
Bond, L. A.	Mar 12	10
Brachbill, Charles S.	Sep 10	10
Breautigan, Nellie	Aug 20	1
Brent, Mrs. Henry	Mar 26	12
Brice, William C.	Nov 26	1
Burney, Delma Carrol	Feb 19	1
Burney, Guy	May 28	1
Burris, Newton	Apr 23	4
Bush, Norval E.	Mar 12	6
Butt, Mrs. Kearney	Aug 27	1
Campbell, Thelma	Aug 27	12
Carl, John Arthur	Sep 17	9
Carter, J. J.	Mar 5	1
Chapman, Finis	May 28	5
Charlier, Rosalie Priour	Jun 4	1
Chisholm, Henrietta E.	May 21	12
Clayton, J. W.	Sep 10	10
Collier, Waldo E.	Mar 19	7
Cook, Joseph	Jan 15	6
Counts, Numerous E.	Sep 10	3
Craig, Bertha Mae Rees	Jul 30	6
Cranfield, Susan Sackville	Aug 20	5
Cutsinger, Walter C.	Dec 3	1
Davey, B. A.	Apr 23	1
Dawson, Mrs. John (Mary)	Aug 6	1
Dowdy, Gayle E.	Dec 10	1
Du Bose, Mrs. W. C. (Martha C.)	Jan 29	12
Dunahoo, John Edward	Nov 5	1
Duncan, Rebecca E.	Sep 10	1

NAME	DATE	PG
Eckstein, Mrs. Henry	Apr 16	1
Edens, N. S.	Feb 26	6
Edmondson, W. F.	Oct 1	12
Erwin, Charles Henry	Jan 8	1
Evans, Arthur (Thanks)	May 28	3
Ewing, Joseph Newton	Jun 11	1
Ezzell, Alice Rees	Jan 15	3
Farrish, William S.	Oct 29	7
Floyd, Mrs. M. E.	Aug 20	1
Forman, Hubert Anderson	Aug 20	12
Foster, W. H.	Apr 30	10
Francis, John David	Oct 8	3
Gonzales, Jose	May 21	1
Grinstead, Jesse	Dec 10	1
Grobe, Harry Gus	Oct 8	1
Francisco, A. J.	Jan 22	1
Haby, Mrs. George	Feb 26	3
Hartmann, Mrs. Moritz (Anna H.)	Feb 12	12
Heard, John Jesse (Jr.)	Aug 13	1
Heffernan, J. L.	Feb 26	10
Hendrix, Walter Powell (Jr.)	Jul 16	1
Henke, Mrs. Henry	Oct 1	1
Herrera, Mrs. Jose Maria	Jun 25	4
Herzog, Oswald, A.	Sep 17	1
Hibdon, Annie	Nov 12	10
Hildebrandt, Mrs. L. F.	May 28	8
Hope, John James	Oct 8	3
Horlacker, James Levi	Dec 31	1
Houck, Ida	Apr 9	6
Hough, W. W.	Jan 15	4
Howell, Mrs. Claude (Thanks)	Aug 20	4
Howell, Mrs. Jim	Dec 3	1
Howell, Landy Walker	Dec 10	10
Howell, Samuel Edward	Aug 27	3
Ingram, Sarah	Dec 17	1
Jackson, Enoch H.	Jun 25	4 & 8
Jeter, Samuel Le Roy	May 14	12
Jowell, Spencer	Jun 4	6
Juenke, Adolph	Nov 19	8
Justice, William J.	Mar 26	6

1942
Film Roll #20

NAME	DATE	PG
Kammlah, Henry	Jun 21	1
Karger, Arthur	Dec 17	1
Keller, William H.	Nov 5	10
Kelley, Maude	Aug 27	3
Kilgore, Mary E.	Oct 8	10
Klum, Mrs. Jacob	Sep 3	1
Lackey, Wanda Lee	Dec 31	6
Ladson, Beatrice Blanks	Jan 1	8
Lemos, Mrs. Pedro	Jun 25	4
Leydecker, Mrs. Arthur (Emma)	Aug 6	10
Lochte, Werner	Apr 2	5
Lochte, Werner	Apr 9	9
Lowry, Mrs. E. B.	Mar 26	12
Maris, Roscoe L.	Oct 29	1
Markwordt, Mrs. Berthold	Nov 26	1
Mason, Lee	May 28	1
Mc Bryde, Charles E.	Mar 26	1
Mc Cain, Helen	Jan 1	3
Mc Caleb, Mrs. T. W.	Oct 8	10
Mc Cleery, Mrs. J. S.	Aug 13	10
Mc Coy, L. W.	Mar 12	1
Mc Coy, Lucretia	Jul 9	7
Mc Cormick, Harvey C.	Jan 8	1
Mc Daniel, Ben	Jan 15	10
Mears, Jonathon G.	Apr 2	12
Michon, Louis R.	Dec 17	6
Miller, Mrs. H. E.	Apr 9	6
Miller, Tarleton E.	Jan 8	1
Mirro, Anthony J.	Oct 29	1
Modreno, Dominic T.	Sep 10	10
Moos, William G.	Jun 25	11
Morris, Mrs. Clayton	Feb 12	1
Myers, Mrs. Anna M.	Oct 8	10
Naul, William Henry	Jul 2	5
Naylon, Thomas A.	Sep 10	10
Newcomb, Jennie Carr	Feb 26	9
Newton, Dona Mary	Jan 1	1
Oldham, Alma	Apr 23	6
Ottinger, Philip Alexander	Oct 1	12
Patterson, Chester A.	May 7	10

1942
Film Roll #20

NAME	DATE	PG
Petsch, Walter	Dec 3	1
Pillow, Harold Lee	May 7	1
Rankin, Hugh D.	Jan 1	4
Real, Casper	Jan 1	1
Real, Oscar	Jun 4	7
Reddy, Kenneth E.	Sep 10	10
Reese, Samuel E.	Apr 2	1
Richardson, Franklin Wade	Sep 17	1
Richeson, Mrs. W. E.	Feb 12	12
Ridenhour, Jesse W.	Sep 3	1
Roberts, Thomas T.	Sep 10	10
Rogers, Ray	Aug 6	9
Rosss, Oran James	Jun 25	11
Saunders, Ella Pafford	Jun 4	6
Short, Mrs. Clyde	Mar 12	3
Smith, Benjamin Newton	Aug 20	1
Smith, Mrs. Gus	Nov 12	12 (10)
Snow, Amanda	Nov 5	1
Spurgeon, Marjorie Lee	Aug 27	1
Stacy, W. Gillespie	Dec 10	1
Stevens, Ella Jane	Jun 13	1
Stevenson, Mrs. Coke	Jan 8	10
Stitt, John	Jul 2	11
Taylor, Mrs. N. E.	Jan 22	6
Taylor, William Henry	Oct 15	1
Tomlinson, Lillie Patton	Sep 17	10
Tracy, Laura Anna	Jul 23	12
Trejo, Timoteo	Dec 31	8
Varger, John Webster	Jul 9	1
Varner, Mrs. Newton D.	Jun 18	1
Wedekind, John	Mar 26	12
Wellborn, Tom	May 21	12
Wells, Bonnie Lee	Jun 25	1
Wells, Mrs. Ervin C.	Feb 5	1
Wilkie, Ernest Eddie	Dec 17	1
Williams, Mrs. S. R.	Dec 17	1
Woodward, Mrs. J. C.	Nov 12	1
Worthington, William H.	May 14	12
Wuerpul, Ted	Jun 4	1
Youngblood, Thomas Waine	Dec 10	1

```
                        1942
                   Film Roll #20

NAME                    DATE        PG

Zigler, twin daughters of Paul    Jan 29    5



                        1943
                   Film Roll #21

Ahrens, Henry                    Oct 28        10
Angerstein, Mabel Rohre          Feb 18        7
Anthony, A. B.                   Sep 30        2
Anthony, Mrs. A. B.              Sep 18        2
Armstrong, Charles M. (Jr.)      Aug 12        6
Avant, J. L.                     Aug 26        7
Avera, John Powell               May 13        10
Baker, E. T.                     Jan 14        1
Baker, Edna (Thanks)             Jul 29        3
Baker, Nolan B.                  Jul 15        1
Beddingfield, James Clark        Aug 12        1
Below, Lee Williams              Feb 23        7
Bieler, Annie Mae                Apr 29        1
Bierschwale, Frank               Mar 25        10
Bierschwale, William (Rev.)      Mar 18  (17)  1
Billings, Roy Stuart             Apr 8         10
Bishop, Mrs. J. A. (Ima)         Jan 7         1
Bradley, Fenton Maurice          Oct 14        1
Bradley, Kenneth                 Aug 12        1
Brooks, John R.                  Sep 16        4
Buffington, Harvey               Feb 18        6
Burlingame, George Lewis         May 27        5
Burney, Mrs. Guy                 Aug 19        1
Burney, Tommie                   Oct 28        9
Bushong, Luther Davis            Jan 7         1
Butt, Mary Elizabeth             Dec 2         1
Carlisle, Willis                 Aug 5         1
Carr, Edward G. (Ted)            Aug 19        8
Carr, Edward G. (Ted)            Aug 26        1
Carson, Angie Lena               Nov 4         5
Carter, J. B.                    Nov 13        8
Cerda, Jesus                     Apr 22        1
Cocke, M. T.                     Feb 4         6
Coleman, Walter A.               Feb 11        10

                        116
```

NAME	DATE	PG
Coleman, William Perry	Jul 15	1
Crandall, Clarence L.	Apr 8	1
Curry, Lucy Damron	Oct 21	12
Daniels, Mary	Dec 9	7
De Montel, Charles	Nov 11	10
Dibrell, Charles Ethridge	Feb 23	1
Dickey, Clarence Weldon	Nov 13	1
Donson, Charlie	Nov 4	3
Doran, Mrs. William	Mar 11	6
Draper, Jack	Feb 4	1
Dufner, Frances Lois	Jan 7	1
Eckstein, Lena	Aug 26	1
Fairchild, Presley Oliver	Dec 16	1
Farris, John L.	Jul 15	1
Fisher, O. E.	Dec 30	5
Fisher, Sterling (Rev.)	Apr 29	10
Flach, Felix	Mar 11	7
Freeman, George Pierce	Aug 5	1
Gelleman, Ida Charlotte	Dec 30	1
Gillespie, John Darrington	May 27	10
Glenn, Mrs. Samuel Donnelly	May 13	10
Goode, Clarence P.	Feb 4	10
Haines, Lee C.	Mar 25	1
Hansen, Mrs. Pete	Oct 7	12
Haralson, La Rue	Apr 29	10
Hart, George W.	Oct 28	1
Heard, John	Jun 3	1
Heinen, Mrs. Otto	May 27	10
Hodges, James N.	Jan 7	2
Hollimon, Raymond Carroll	Sep 9	1
Hollomon, J. L.	Jun 24	4
Holloway, Mrs. S. G.	May 13	10
Holman, S. L.	Oct 28	9
Howell, Elsie Ann (Memorian)	Dec 9	7
Hughes, Frank Ollie	Mar 4	8
Hurst, Sandy	Mar 25	6
Iley, Lillie Dale	Feb 11	3
Irwin, A. G.	Jan 21	5
Jackson, Murray	Mar 18 (17)	8
Jenschke, Patrick Walter	Jan 7	7

NAME	DATE	PG
Johnson, W. T.	Sep 30	12
Jones, Tom	Sep 16	4
Jordan, Mrs. John	Dec 16	1
Key, Harold Gene	Sep 2	1
King, Mrs. J. E.	Dec 16	1
King, Jackson J.	Mar 4	8
King, Mrs. William Hardy	Nov 25	1
Lancaster, J. J.	Aug 5	1
Lane, Margaret C.	Aug 12	6
Lee, J. H.	Nov 4	8
Leigh, William B.	Sep 30	1
Leigh, William Brewster	Oct 7	3
Leinweber, Mrs. Robert	Oct 14	11
Lewis, Wesley Earl	Feb 23	6
Love, Mrs. Ollie M.	Feb 23	5
Masterson, Lydia Elizabeth	May 6	1
Mathis, Ally N.	Apr 8	1
Mc Bride, Mrs. A. D.	Mar 18 (17)	1
Mc Coun, Tillman	Sep 16	4
Mc Daniel, Mrs. Fred	Jan 14	1
Mc Donald, Julia Henrietta	Oct 21	1
Mc Leod, Dwight Ennis	Mar 18 (17)	1
Mc Nabb, Mrs. C. L.	Nov 25	10
Merritt, Vernon	Mar 11	8
Metcafe, C. Minor,	Jan 14	1
Metcalf, Mrs. Minor (Edna L.)	Jul 22	1
Minsch, Walter A. (Dr.)	May 27	1
Monks, Jennings (Thanks)	Apr 22	3
Moore, Ella Steves	Mar 11	3
Mulvey, George	Dec 2	10
Nichols, Charles Henry	Dec 23	8
Nimitz, William	Feb 11	1
Noonan, Helena Estella	Dec 23	1
North, Billy Leon	Jun 24	7
Oehler, Paul	May 6	1
Pate, Florida	Jan 7	4
Paxton, Ernest B (Jr.)	Apr 8	1
Perkins, Walter Robert	Jul 88	4
Peschel, Lee Emil	Apr 4	1
Peters, Mrs. Alfred Ganes	Dec 30	8

1943
Film Roll #21

NAME	DATE	PG
Pflueger, Mrs. E. W.	Mar 18 (17)	3
Phillips, Walter	Sep 16	1
Piper, Madison C.	Apr 8	10
Powell, H. O.	Sep 9	1
Proctor, Edna Dean	Jun 24	10
Rambie, H. E.	Dec 2	2
Rape, Eunice Leon	Dec 30	1
Rawson, John	Sep 2	1
Rees, Daniel Richard	Jul 1	1
Reinhardt, Ray Brooks	Sep 22	7
Ritz, Emil	Dec 2	1
Robertson, Frank C.	Feb 4	1
Robey, Mrs. Horace D.	Jun 10	1
Rose, Edward Oliver	Apr 22	5
St. Clair, S. P.	Jul 22	1
Saul, Vic	Nov 11	12
Sandabal, Cruz	Feb 18	5 & 7
Schellhase, Walter	Feb 11	1
Schreiner, Mrs. Gus	Jul 22	1
Schwethelm, Bruno	Apr 15	1
Scott, Ray	Apr 15	1
Scott, Mrs. Willie	Feb 23	5
Sholars, Louis T.	Aug 26	1
Sibson, Eunavae	Sep 9	1
Smith, Augustus	May 13	1
Smith, Mrs. L. B.	Feb 18	3
Spiller, R. H.	Aug 19	8
Stone, Mrs. Harvey	Nov 11	1
Stroup, Carl	Nov 13	1
Sturdivant, Alice Lane	Feb 11	8
Surber, Benjamin F.	Dec 30	1
Swearingen, Hamp F.	Sep 30	1
Taylor, James P.	May 27	1
Tyler, Frank A.	Jul 29	3
Vann, John W.	Jun 24	1
Varner, Gus	Jan 21	8
Waite, Catherine	Oct 7	12
Walker, Mrs. R. S.	Feb 4	6
Warren, H. C.	Dec 23	1
Watson, John W.	Mar 4	8

119

1943
Film Roll #21

NAME	DATE		PG
Weber, Lena	Oct 7		12
Welch, Mrs. C. J.	Jul 1		12
Wellborn, Nettie Viola	Nov 11		12
Wells, Elbert Goodrich	Jan 7		1
White, Holly C.	Apr 4		7
Whitworth, William Henry	Jun 24		1
Wills,, Mrs. Richard	Oct 14		1
Wilson, Mrs. Henry Bailey	Feb 23		3
Witt, Joseph Denton	Mar 4		1
Worcester, Roy Greene	Mar 18	(17)	1
Yoast, Samuel H.	Apr 15		12
Young, Mrs. Willis (Thanks)	Sep 23		7
Zavala, Viviano	Jan 14		1
Zumwalt, Ben F.	May 27		1
Zumwalt, Ben F.	Jun 3		8

1944
Film Roll #22

Adams, Mrs. Ben	Jun 15	4
Ahr, Joseph Louis	Jan 27	1
Allen, Mrs. T. M.	Dec 7	1
Armistead, Joseph D. (Rev.)	Jan 13	1
Armistead, Joseph D. (Rev.)	Jan 20	9
Atkins, Nancy E.	Mar 30	1
Bartholomew, Essie Maye	Aug 24	1
Bates, William W.	Jul 20	1
Beaver, Henry H.	May 25	10
Beaver, Virgil F.	Apr 27	1
Beakly, F. C.	Jan 6	2
Bland, Kathleen	Jun 29	8
Blevins, Nancy S.	Feb 24	1
Boehmer, Mrs. Harry F.	Apr 20	10
Boekmann, William	Apr 20	1
Bonn, Mrs. Henry (Thanks)	Jan 6	7
Bonnell, Mrs. Allie Hootoon	Mar 16	1
Brady, Herman F.	Sep 14	1
Bunch, Mary Lee	Mar 9	1
Cass, Loren R.	Jun 15	9

NAME	DATE	PG
Castillo, Pete	Aug 31	1
Chamberlain, William Thomas	Jan 13	1
Coar, Henry Livingston	Jul 27	4
Comeaux, Dallas Louis	Jun 8	5
Cooke, Annie A.	Jan 13	8
Crabb, Pearl Pelina	Oct 5	1
Cruckshank, Gordon	Jul 20	12
Cruckshank, Mrs. Walter Scott	Jan 20	1
Cunningham, Mrs. H. T.	Aug 17	5
Daniel, Floyd	Jun 22	1
Davidson, W. R.	Aug 10	8
Denton, J. W.	Jan 6	10
Dietert, Henry	Jun 8	1
Dondlinger, Ida	Nov 2	1
Durrett, Mrs. George	Feb 3	3
Eakin, Mrs. Ike C.	May 4	1
Eaton, Mrs. Frank	Dec 7	12
Edwards, Mrs. Charles	May 11	1
Emshoff, Johanna	Sep 28	1
Fairchild, Mrs. W. A.	Apr 20	10
Faulkner, Anna Elizabeth	Apr 6	1
Ferris, Elizabeth	Feb 24	6
Foesling, William E.	Jul 27	5
Francis, J. P. (Penny)	Jun 22	9
Garrett, Jimmie	Nov 23	1
Gill, Joe	Jun 22	1
Gillan, Mrs. R. M.	Jul 6	10
Gillis, William	Oct 26	1
Griffin, David Spencer	Dec 7	1
Grona, Charles A.	Nov 16	1
Guilhem, Charles S.	Jan 6	10
Hamilton, Clyde	Dec 28	8
Hardin, L. L.	Feb 10	10
Hardin, Lafayette Lee	Feb 17	1
Harris, John H.	Jun 22	1
Hendricks, J. O.	Jul 27	4
Herrera, Ruben B.	Sep 21	10
Hodges, J. R.	Jun 1	1 & 10
James, William Walter	Nov 23	1
Jones, Enid H.	May 11	4

1944
Film Roll #21

NAME	DATE	PG
Joy, Ada	Dec 21	12
Karger, Fritz Albert	Dec 28	1
Keeney, Randall	Feb 24	6
Kincaid, Mrs. John I.	Mar 2	1
King, mother of R. B.	Aug 31	12
Kirkmeyer, Charles Rudolph	Apr 20	1
Kittrell, John	Jan 13	8
Kornegay, Clifford	Jul 13	8
La Rue, Newton	Mar 16	1
Lochte, Ernest	Dec 28	8
Locke, Joel H.	Feb 3	1 & 6
Lockley, E. G.	Jul 6	1
Markwordt, Berthold William	Dec 7	12
Marlowe, Robert Wilson	Jul 13	5
Martin, M. S.	Mar 16	5
Masters, John D.	Nov 9	1
Mauldin, Ibfant of Buddie	Mar 23	7
Mayfield, Albert Walter	Nov 23	8
Mc Adams, W. J.	Oct 19	1
Mc Nabb, Crawford	May 18	1
Mc Mealy, Earl	Aug 10	1
Mc Nealy, Mrs. J. O.	Aug 24	1
Mc Nees, Sarah	Jul 27	1
Meadow, Wayne	Jan 13	8
Means, Mrs. Elliott A.	Nov 23	4
Meredith, Mrs. J. H.	Jan 20	1
Merrill, R. W. (Rev.)	Dec 21	6
Merritt, Mrs. B. F.	Oct 26	1
Methvin, Gordon T.	May 11	10
Miller, Mrs. ----	Jun 8	10
Miller, Cyrus W.	Oct 12	1
Milliard, Mrs. F. L.	Jun 8	5
Mills, Robert George	Mar 30	1
Moose, Alvin	Jul 20	12
Nankervis, Mrs. B. J.	Jul 20	2
Neunhoffer, Mrs. Oscar	Jul 13	1
Newson, Claude	Nov 9	1
Nichols, Everett Earle	Mar 23	1
Noble, Delmar A. C.	Mar 16	5
Oberlin, Mrs. Leroy E.	Nov 30	1

1944
Film Roll #21

NAME	DATE	PG
Orr, John Wesley (Rev.)	Mar 2	1
Peril, Mary Olive	Dec 14	1
Peschel, Mrs. Albert	Jul 20	1
Phares, Lonnie	Sep 28	10
Phillips, John E.	Mar 30	1
Pincoff, Charles	Mar 30	1
Pittman, Leslie L.	Jul 6	10
Porter, Fred	Aug 3	6
Real, Julius	Jun 1	1
Real, Mrs. Julius	Nov 2	1
Rees, Ivy (Jr.)	Mar 23	1 & 10
Rembold, Peter James	Dec 28	8
Rhoden, Emmett	Jul 20	1
Rhoden, Emmett	Sep 28	1
Robinson, Grace	Nov 30	8
Ridgaway, Eugene Salter	Jul 27	1
Rogers, John H.	Apr 20	1
Rogers, Lieuen (Dr.)	Sep 14	6
Rutherford, William B.	Sep 14	10
Sachry, Emma F.	Mar 23	5
Schmidt, William	Nov 23	10
Self, Roger	Dec 28	1
Sellers, Fannie	Nov 23	1
Chanks, E. A.	Jan 27	1
Shreve, Mrs. Omar	Sep 14	1
Simpson, Samuel	Dec 21	7
Smart, Lon R. (Sr.)	Mar 30	4
Sparks, Fannie	Apr 6	1
Steed, J. F.	Apr 13	1
Steves, Henry	May 18	1
Stockton, Mrs. Samuel E.	Mar 23	4
Storms, William R.	Apr 6	1
Strauch, Mrs. A. O.	Mar 9	1
Strauch, Anton	Jul 13	1
Taylor, Leslie Thomas	Aug 24	8
Thompson, Effie	Apr 20	1
Todd, Richard E.	Mar 2	1
True, Susie Agnes	Nov 23	10
Turner, Edgar H.	Jan 27	1
Turner, Oris Ray (Shorty)	Oct 19	10

123

1944
Film Roll #21

NAME	DATE	PG
Tuttle, Eleanor Gregg	Dec 21	12
Usener, Mrs. Ludwig	Aug 24	8
Vellenga, Charles	Aug 31	1
Vellenga, Charles	Sep 7	6
Vetter, Alvin	Jul 27	1
Villareal, Alfredo M.	Aug 10	1
Webb, Mary L.	Jan 6	1
Wellborn, Clarence	May 4	3
West, Mrs. A. E.	Oct 12	10
Wharton, Mrs. Edward R.	Jul 27	1
Wiedenfeld, Hugo	Sep 21	1
Yelvington, Henry B.	Mar 2	10
Zorzillio, R. Louis	Jun 29	7

1945
Film Roll #23

Aguerre, Ysidro	Feb 1	1
Allen, Terry (Thanks)	May 31	5
Allen, Mrs. W. M.	Nov 29	10
Allstott, Arthur Lee	Apr 12	5
Armstrong, Quinton	Oct 18	1
Bacon, Mrs. Del	Oct 4	1
Bass, Mrs. R. L. (Leona Murff)	Oct 4	1
Bean, R. C.	Apr 12	4
Bittel, Mrs. Albert	Aug 16	1
Blieden, Joe	Aug 16	9
Bodkin, Clyde	Jul 19	7
Borgfield, H. O.	Apr 19	5
Boulware, Mrs. Carl E.	Aug 23	1
Bowman, Edgar Earl	Aug 16	10
Breihan, Sophie	Nov 29	1
Carr, Cathlyn Louise	May 24	1
Carter, Clifton	Mar 22	4
Champion, Frank	Feb 1	8
Combs, Joseph E.	Jun 29	7
Crider, Harlan Dale	May 24	1
Crider, Elmer Patrick	May 31	10
David, Joe Buck	May 17	1

1945
Film Roll #23

NAME	DATE	PG
Davis, Lewis T. (Jr.)	Feb 22	1
Deering, Clyde	Aug 16	1
De La Cruz, Bonefacio	Mar 15	1
De La Cruz, Bonefacio	Mar 22	1
Dowd, Mary	Sep 20	1
Dubose, Mrs. A. D. (May)	May 24	1
Egan, William Earl	Jul 26	7
Elder, Ira Hill	May 17	7
Elkins, Francis L.	May 24	1
Ethridge, Trave	Oct 4	1
Evans, Moss	Mar 29	6
Fairchild, Levi	Nov 1	10
Francis, George Edward	Nov 22	1
Friedman, Mrs. Samuel	May 10	1
Fuller, Sam (Jr.)	Mar 8	1
Garrett, Mack	Nov 22	1
Gillespie, William E.	Sep 13	10
Godwin, Claude L. (Jr.)	May 3	1
Graham, William M.	May 10	7
Graves, Alonzo	Jan 14	8
Hackley, Mrs. Oscar	Dec 6	1
Hamilton, Mrs. Jack	Oct 4	1
Hardin, Don	Jul 26	1
Harless, Mrs. Isaac Newton	May 10	7
Harrison, Mrs. Sam	Apr 26	4
Hartong, Robert C. (Dr.)	Jun 7	1
Hatcher, Maurice	Mar 29	1
Hatcher, Maurice E.	Apr 5	1
Hebdon, George M.	Nov 8	12
Heimann, John (Sr.)	Mar 1	1
Henke, Henry	Mar 1	1
Henson, Mrs. Walter	Feb 15	1
Herman, John (Sr.)	Mar 1	1
Hitzfeld, Mrs. Gabe	Mar 1	8
Holchack, Mrs. S. J.	Jul 26	11
Holekamp, Cecil Martin	Jun 29	8
Hudspeth, Minnie	Feb 15	1
Huntoon, Mae	Jan 25	8
Ingenhuett, Matilde	May 3	1
Inscore, Richard D.	May 24	6

125

NAME	DATE	PG
Jackson, J. A. (Rev.)	May 24	6
James, Estelle Myers	Nov 8	1
Jorda, Albert Laron	Feb 1	1
Journeay, Mrs. David	Jun 7	1
Juarze, Gilbert O.	Feb 1	1
Juenke, Louis C.	Mar 29	1
Keese, Emily	Dec 27	1
Kennedy, Mrs. S. J.	Jul 19	1
Kenney, Stanley E.	Sep 13	10
Kieth, John L.	Jan 14	4
Killough, Sam D.	Jan 18	4
Kincaid, John Ervin	Feb 8	8
Kreyger, Frank R.	May 10	12
Kulka, Anthony L.	May 17	12
Lamb, Arthur Milton	Jan 5	1
Leatherman, William O.	Jan 25	8
Leazer, William G.	Jan 14	8
Lee, Otis	May 31	1
Lee, Otis	Jun 7	1
Liles, Thomas (Jr.)	Mar 8	1
Lindberg, Carolina	Mar 8	8
Lock, Albert (Jr.)	Mar 1	1
Lock, Albert (Jr.)	Mar 8	1
Loeffler, Hubert	Jan 5	4
Loring, E. H.	Jun 29	8
Lowrance, Kenneth	Jul 19	1
Maginn, Hugh	Mar 29	10
Maguire, William H.	Sep 20	1
Masters, Mary L.	Jun 7	10
Maverick, W. H.	Aug 2	1
Mayes, Ted Cunningham	Jun 29	12
Mc Bryde, Andrew Douglas	Sep 6	1
Mc Bryde, Martha	Aug 16	5
Mc Caleb, Mrs. Hugh W.	Aug 16	1
Mc Cormick, H. C.	Aug 23	1
Mc Coy, J. B.	Jul 12	10
Mc Donald, Hollis O.	Apr 5	1
Menchaca, Isaac	Feb 8	1
Merritt, Elizabeth	Nov 1	1
Meyer, Louisa E.	Sep 6	1

NAME	DATE	PG
Michon, August D.	Nov 29	1
Miller, Mrs. A. B.	Jul 5	1
Mogford, Mrs. E. A.	Nov 8	12
Moore, A. J.	Apr 5	1
Moore, Maggie	Jul 19	6
Moose, Laura	Aug 2	1
Morris, Mrs. Eugene C.	Sep 20	1
Morriss, Airs Gilmer	Jun 29	1
Mosel, Mrs. Charles	Feb 8	5
Mosel, Mrs. Ed	Feb 22	1
Mosty, Mrs. L. A.	Nov 22	1
Nelson, Bert Etheridge	Jul 19	1
Neunhoffer, Mrs. Albert	Apr 12	5
Noell, George A.	Sep 27	1
Oatman, Mrs. Julius F.	Jan 18	1
O'Bryant, Ben Jack	Mar 1	1
Park, Sarah Cynthia	Mar 22	1
Poland, N. L.	Sep 27	1
Pope, Jesse Frank	Dec 27	1
Posey, Dan	Nov 22	1
Priour, Mrs. Isadore	May 31	1
Priour, Mrs. Isadore	Jun 7	1
Probst, Otto W.	Jul 5	10
Rankhorn, Christy Howard	Mar 8	1
Rankin, Maude (Mrs. W. B.)	Feb 15	8
Rankin, W. B.	Jan 25	1
Ratliff, Mts. Gertrude Major	Aug 16	5
Real, Walter	Nov 15	1
Ridgaway, James A.	May 17	4
Ritzenthaler, Henry W.	Jun 29	1
Robertson, Mrs. Ralph Waldo	Dec 20	5
Robertson, Thomas Andrew	Oct 25	4
Robinson, Allen D.	Jun 7	10
Rotge, Joseph	Jan 14	1
Rotge, Louise M.	Feb 15	8
Roundtree, Mrs. Payne	Jul 5	6
Roundtrees, Samuel D.	Jan 18	1
Russell, Anna	May 10	6
Saludis, Jim	May 10	5
Schafer, W. H.	Oct 25	6

NAME	DATE	PG
Schmerbeck, Emma C.	Apr 19	10
Schmerbeck, Robert Louis	Jan 18	1
Schnerr, Henry	Jul 19	5
Schumacher, John Randolph	Aug 30	1
Scott, John Wesley	Nov 8	12
Seeders, Mrs. F. W.	Feb 1	8
Shearn III, Charles	Aug 2	1
Sheffield, Frank D.	Jan 25	1
Sheffield, Frank D.	Feb 1	8
Shepard, Harry (Dr.)	Oct 25	1
Shuford, Sidney	May 17	7
Smith, Charles W.	Aug 9	1
Smith, Otto	Mar 29	1
Smith, William A. (Dr.)	Sep 20	1
Snelgrave, George	Mar 29	1
Stehling, James E.	Jun 29	1
Stephenson, Marion Gill	Apr 5	8
Stewart, Mrs. T. E.	Jan 5	8
Stone, Raymond	Mar 15	1
Stone, Raymond	Mar 22	1
Templeton, Mrs. A. W.	Jan 5	4
Thurman, John E.	Dec 6	1
Tupin, Bessie	Nov 22	6
Turknett, Thomas P.	Aug 30	1
Turner, Charles (Dr.)	Jan 14	1
Turner, Mrs. E. L.	Feb 1	8
Turner, Mrs. E. L.	Feb 8	1
Turner, Mrs. Hugh E.	Apr 19	1
Ward, Mrs. B. F.	Mar 29	5
Watkins, Mrs. Elizabeth H.	May 24	7
Weldon, Mildred J. Parker	Jan 18	1
Whetstone, Mrs. D. H.	Apr 5	8
Whisenhunt, Mrs. Fred (Louise)	Dec 20	5
White, Wood E.	Mar 29	5
Wiggins, Warren	Apr 19	1
Williams, Mrs. Thomas P.	Sep 27	1
Wilson, Claude William	Dec 6	12
Winkler, Ernest F. (Rev.)	Jun 21	1
Witt, James T.	May 3	10
Yarbrough, J. L.	Apr 5	5

NAME	DATE	PG
Yarger, Mrs. John H.	Jan 25	1
Young, Joseph Clarence	Jan 5	8
Zachry, Lyle	Mar 22	1

1946
Film Roll #24

Abbey, Mrs. Fred (Carrie B.)	May 2	1
Albrecht, William A.	Dec 12	3
Alexander, Christopher Columbus	Dec 19	1
Alexander, J. M.	Mar 7	1
Anderson, Hester	Jan 3	1
Arnold, J. T.	Feb 7	9
Ayala, Afonso	Jul 11	1
Bailey, Mrs. Ray	Jul 18	7
Baldwin, Tom S.	Nov 7	1
Baker, Virginia C.	May 23	12
Baker, Weaver	Sep 26	1
Bell, Bertha H.	Feb 7	1
Below, Max	Oct 31	4
Benson, Wesley	Jul 4	1
Bode, Ethel Iva Mc Donald	Jul 4	1
Bode, Leo Ellis	Jul 4	1
Bode, Oscar Robert	Jul 4	1
Boechmann, Henrietta Lawson	Dec 12	8
Boehmer, Nina Louise (Estate)	Nov 28	10
Bonn, Henry	Nov 21	1
Booth, Zelma Louise	Jul 25	8
Bradford, W. M. (Ned)	Aug 8	3
Brady, Ralph	Jun 6	12
Bratton, John C.	Oct 24	1
Bratton, John C.	Oct 31	5
Brauer, Henry E.	Jul 18	1
Brown, Edgar George	Dec 12	8
Burnett, Thomas W.	Jul 4	10
Burney, Jesse G.	May 16	12
Burton, Allie B.	Sep 19	1
Cade, Cecil Ernest	Jun 27	1
Carlin, J. W.	Feb 14	6

NAME	DATE	PG	SEC
Carnes, Katherine Louise	Nov 14	10	1
Caulfield, Mrs. Thomas	May 23	5	1
Clark, Emma Leona	Feb 28	12	1
Clement, Jerome B.	Jun 20	12	1
Clements, Gayle Joy	Jun 27	10	1
Cloudt, W. O.	Jun 13	12	1
Clyce, J. S. (Dr.)	Mar 7	12	1
Cocke, Fannie	Jan 17	10	1
Conn, Isaac James	Jan 24	1	1
Cook, W. W.	Apr 25	12	1
Cornmiller, Elizabeth Ann	Jan 10	10	1
Couch, Frederick Leon	Feb 28	5	1
Cox, Mrs. R. P. (Mary Ann)	Feb 21	1	1
Crider, Charles Joseph	May 16	12	1
Crumley, Thomas A.	May 23	9	1
Cunningham, Mrs. C. E.	May 2	8	1
Davis, Mrs. John C.	Apr 11	1	1
Denton, Susan May	Aug 8	1	1
Devall, Elmer E.	Oct 17	10	1
De Vore, Laverne Kay	Dec 26	6	1
Dobkins, O. J. (Teet)	Jun 27	5	1
Domingues, Mrs. P. J.	Nov 28	1	1
Dozier, Charles	Jan 3	1	1
Dreiss, E. A.	May 9	10	1
Eaton, Thomas Ellington	Feb 21	1	1
Eickenroht, Hugo C.	Jun 27	2	1
Ellis, Jordon B.	Jan 17	3	1
Ellis, Wilbur	Feb 28	1	1
Emerson, Murrell	Sep 5	1	1
Emerson, Murrell (Jr.)	Jul 4	10	1
Enderle, Albert	Mar 7	1	1
Ethridge, Beulah May	Apr 4	1	1
Ethridge, H. L.	Mar 14	9	1
Fagan, D. W.	Jan 3	6	1
Faust, Mrs. Louis F.	Jan 24	6	1
Finlayson, Archie M.	Nov 14	6	1
Fisher, Joe	Feb 21	3	1
Foster, Charles	Feb 7	1	1
Foster, Mrs. W. H.	Nov 28	12	1
Fox, Lottie Dean	Mar 21	1	1

1946
Film Roll #24

NAME	DATE	PG	SEC
French, Thomas	Sep 12	10	1
Garland, Orris	Apr 25	1	1
Gillasgy, Grace Moore	Aug 15	1	1
Glenn, George Arrington	May 30	1	1
Glenn, Samuel James	May 2	12	1
Goff, James Rowland	Feb 14	1	1
Gold, Mrs. Lawrence H.	Mar 28	10	1
Goodman, Juanita Ruth	May 16	12	1
Goss, Clinton Hughes	May 30	12	1
Goss, Mrs. John Lee	Sep 5	1	1
Gray, Thomas	Dec 19	3	2
Gregory, John Burel	Feb 28	1	1
Grinstead, Mrs. J. E.	Oct 24	1	1
Hale, Mrs. Johnson	Apr 25	7	1
Hardin, Harris I.	Jan 10	1	1
Harless, Isaac Newton	Mar 7	12	1
Hirth, Doris May	May 16	1	1
Holliday, Everett P.	Jun 20	12	1
Hughes, J. M.	Feb 28	5	1
Hyde, Hiram Preston	Mar 14	1	1
Inscore, Freddie	Jan 31	3	1
Jackson, John Dee (Dr.)	Jan 3	1	1
Johnson, J. Ross	Dec 19	10	1
Johnson, Marvin A.	Dec 26	10	1
Jung, Jim	Oct 3	1	1
Kimball, C. M.	Jul 25	3	2
Knox, Charlie	Jan 31	1	1
Kohler, John F. M.	Aug 22	1	1
Koon, John D.	Jan 3	1	1
Lackey, Oscar	Feb 7	1	1
Laird, Bessie Pope	Jun 6	8	1
Lane, Frank	Nov 21	8	1
Lange, Mollie E.	Nov 21	12	1
Lawson, Roger Craig	Sep 19	1	1
Lawson, Mrs. Roger	Sep 19	12	1
Lee, Mrs. Samuel M.	Apr 4	12	1
Lee, William James	Aug 1	1	1
Leigh, Virginia	Jan 24	1	1
Lendermann, Ike Carson	Jan 17	1	1
Lich, Alwine	Aug 15	1	1

131

NAME	DATE	PG	SEC
Light, Rufus Hardy	Aug 22	7	1
Lookingbill, Zach H.	Aug 22	7	1
Love, Jeff L.	Feb 28	1	1
Lowrance, Joeph Kenneth	Jul 11	1	1
Luther, Olive Dexter	Mar 14	7	1
Mac Donald, Malcolmn	Jan 24	1	1
Masters, Thomas Dudley	Apr 25	12	1
Mc Caleb, Thomas W. (Kid)	Nov 14	1	1
Mc Call, Mrs. Shelby	Sep 12	8	1
Mc Clellan, Emma	Oct 13	10	1
Mc Nealy, Orville	Feb 7	10	1
Miers, C. Hal	Apr 25	1	1
Miller, Rhea	Jan 17	1	1
Monahan, Martin L.	Oct 24	1	1
Moore, Gabe R.	Nov 21	1	1
Moose, Charles Edwin	Mar 7	12	1
Morgan, John F.	Jan 17	1	1
Null, Charles C.	Dec 12	6	1
Oliver, Mrs. Eran Miller	Apr 4	7	1
Paradowski, Mrs. Ed	Aug 8	10	1
Parker, Sarah Evalina	Feb 21	5	1
Parker, Tom P.	Dec 12	8	1
Parks, Royal E.	Aug 22	12	1
Paul, H. L.	Jun 13	1	1
Pearson, Lester Albert	Dec 5	1	1
Pearson, W. M.	Nov 7	1	1
Peril, William Randolph	Apr 4	1	1
Peter, William (Sr.)	Sep 12	1	1
Peterson, Mrs. Lee	Oct 10	1	1
Pope, John Edgar	Mar 14	5	1
Pope, Mattie (Martha Minerva)	Aug 15	12	1
Prince, Mrs. A. E.	Oct 24	9	1
Rankin, Mrs. Henry A.	Jan 31	1	1
Redley, Ertha Vaughn	Oct 24	8	1
Reed, Harrison Patton (Dr.)	Jul 4	1	1
Reeder, Edward	Aug 29	1	1
Rees, Nic Howard	Mar 14	1	1
Richardson, Champ Conrad	Aug 1	1	1
Robinson, J. E.	Apr 4	1	1
Rose, Benjamin Franklin	Dec 26	10	1

1946
Film Roll #24

NAME	DATE	PG	SEC
Rosenthal, Annie	Aug 8	1	1
Ross, Mrs. R. R. (Orlena Nelson)	Dec 26	10	1
Saenger, Mrs. Robert (Jr.)	Dec 19	1	1
St. John, Mrs. Walter	Nov 7	12	1
Sammonsa, Vernon Howard	Feb 21	1	1
Schellhase, Chester	Jul 11	1	1
Schuh, Mrs. Charles	Oct 24	7	1
Schulze, Herman	Mar 7	1	1
Scroggs, Wick	Jul 25	8	1
Shelburne, Russell	May 9	1	1
Shelton, Mrs. J. S.	Apr 11	8	1
Sherfesee, M. F.	May 23	5	1
Sherman, Emma Secrest	Oct 17	1	1
Simmons, Myra Louise	Sep 5	12	1
Smith, Don	Mar 14	10	1
Sorsby, Charles Earl	Mar 28	1	1
Starkey, Alonzo Lycurgus	May 16	1	1
Stowers, Mrs. G. A.	Aug 1	12	1
Strackbein, Mrs. W. C. (Amma)	Aug 15	3	1
Strube, Henry V.	Nov 7	12	1
Surber, Levi	Mar 7	12	1
Surber, Levi Johnson	Mar 14	6	1
Swearingen, Harris E.	Jul 4	10	1
Talbert, Walter Monroe	Apr 18	1	1
Tomlinson, Mrs. Pete	Oct 10	4	1
Turner, Elmer Wilbur	Dec 12	8	1
Turner, Martha E.	Jul 25	1	1
Walden, Albert Wendell	Jan 31	1	1
Walker, F. M. (Jr.)	Nov 21	12	1
Wharey, J. B. (Dr.)	Aug 1	9	1
Whitewood, James Spencer	May 2	7	1
Whitewood, James Spencer	May 23	12	1
Wilson, Mrs. Adam	Oct 31	1	1
Wilson, Ida	Oct 17	1	1
Woodell, John	Apr 11	1	1
Wright, Drury Mitchell	Sep 12	12	1

1947
Film Roll #25

NAME	DATE	PG	SEC
Buell, Allen (Jr.)	Apr 24	7	1
Burkhardt, Edward Rudolph	Oct 23	10	1
Bushong, Mrs. E. E.	Aug 28	1	1
Cannon, Otis A.	Nov 20	10	1
Cappock, Charles Stanley	Apr 3	1	1
Clark, John Thomas	Sep 4	1	1
Clower, William P.	Sep 4	1	1
Cobb, Leslie Randolph	Oct 30	1	1
Cobb, Robert Leslie	Oct 30	1	1
Cole, Mrs. Ira M.	Nov 6	10	1
Collins, Samuel	Aug 14	10	1
Colungo, Victor	Feb 6	1	1
Cone, Mrs. G. W.	Feb 27	12	1
Cooke, Mrs. J. R.	Jul 10	12	1
Copple, Virgil Oscar	Nov 20	10	1
Corder, John L.	Aug 7	5	1
Cotton, Lou Emma	Feb 6	12	1
Cox, William Frederick	Jun 5	7	1
Cox, William Frederick	Jun 12	6	1
Crider, Mrs. M. M. (Martha H.)	May 1	12	1
Crutcher, A. V. D.	Jan 2	10	1
Davis, Robert M.	Jul 24	12	1
Denton, Aaron	Jun 5	12	1
Denton, Cora	Feb 20	10	1
Dickey, Chester Dunlap	Nov 20	6	1
Doerffler, R. A.	Feb 20	10	1
Dowdy, Martha Ellen (Mrs. T. L.)	Jun 26	10	1
Downard, Mrs. R. W.	Jan 2	3	1
Dual, Mrs. O. L. (Willie Annie)	Aug 7	1	1
Du Bose, Benjamin L.	Dec 18	1	1
Duncan, William R.	Nov 20	10	1
Dye, Ernest	May 8	1	1
Eckles, Amanda C.	Oct 16	1	1
Edenborough, Charles A.	Jul 31	1	1
Emsley, Henry C.	Jan 2	10	1
Emsley, Mrs. W. R.	Nov 13	10	1
Ezzell, Samuel Augustin	Jul 10	7	1
Faifer, John Joseph	Apr 17	12	1
Faltin, August S.	Mar 13	1	1
Farrell, Bernard F.	Jan 16	12	1

134

1947
Film Roll #25

NAME	DATE	PG	SEC
Flettcher, Haden Cooper	Dec 4	8	1
Floyd, Frank	Jun 26	7	2
Forehand, Norman Elmo	Nov 20	1	1
Fritz, Adolph O.	Feb 13	10	1
Gardner, Joe M. (Jr.)	Nov 13	10	1
George, Marcus Ralph	Nov 27	1	1
Gilmer, John	Jul 24	12	1
Goldman, Sylvester	Oct 16	8	1
Goodman, Ellen J.	Nov 20	10	1
Goodman, Otto	Apr 10	12	1
Granville, J. B. (Dr.)	Jul 10	9	1
Granville, M. F.	Aug 21	7	1
Gregory, E.	Apr 3	10	1
Greunwald, Louis Clifford (Jr.)	Jan 2	1	1
Griesbach, George	Oct 30	1	1
Groves, Jeptha	Feb 27	12	1
Hall, John	Sep 4	3	1
Hamilton, Hugo Alexander	Jul 3	10	1
Hankins, Clay	Mar 6	8	1
Harris, Mrs. ----	Sep 25	5	1
Haufler, Joseph	May 29	10	1
Heimann, Maria Gottliebe	Feb 20	10	1
Heinen, Arthur	Jul 3	7	1
Holekamp, Mrs. ----	Aug 28	4	1
Holt, Eddie Homer	Jun 19	1	1
Hope, Ellen	Jul 10	12	1
Humphreys, Ruth Elizabeth	Jan 2	6	1
Hutson, Samuel Wesley	Oct 9	12	1
Johnson, Mary	Dec 11	5	1
Johnson, W. T. (Jr.)	Jul 31	10	1
Jones, Alonzo T.	Oct 2	9	1
Jones, Ronald Dale	May 29	6	1
Journey, Jimmie Irving	Sep 18	5	1
Keith, J. L. (Probate)	Jan 30	5	1
Kirkpatrick, Mrs. M. C.	Sep 25	12	1
Koenig, Roy	May 29	10	1
Lange, Alvin	Dec 4	1	1
Leinweber, Tidy Marie	Apr 17	1	1
Lennox, Emma	Apr 17	2	1
Levingston, Mrs. G. M..	Nov 27	1	1

135

NAME	DATE	PG	SEC
Lock, Albert Francis	Mar 13	1	1
Mahon, L. S. (Dr.)	Dec 25	7	1
Manning, Mrs. J. R.	Jun 12	9	1
Marschall, Mrs. Pat	Apr 17	10	1
Mason, Clarenc A.	Oct 9	4	1
Mayhugh, Mrs. J. R.	Jul 3	1	1
Mayhugh, Mrs. J. R.	Jul 10	10	1
Mc Bride, Arthur E.	Jan 23	12	1
Mc Bryde, Thomas A.	May 15	12	1
Mc Dade, Edward J.	Aug 21	12	1
Mc Donald, A. L.	Jan 23	5	1
Mc Kinght, W. J.	Jul 3	10	1
Mc Neal, Alfred	Apr 10	1	1
Merz, Mrs. Adolph (Thanks)	Sep 18	14	1
Mills, Roger Q.	Oct 16	8	1
Monroe, E. M. (Dr.)	Nov 27	10	1
Moore, Mrs. Thomas J.	Aug 7	1	1
Moose, John William	Apr 24	12	1
Morgan, George Frank	May 8	10	1
Murray, Frederick M.	Jul 10	1	1
Nabors, Cranfil L.	Jan 9	1	1
Nash, Emma	Oct 2	6	1
New, William Isaac	Jan 9	6	1
Nichols, Ernest Benton	Feb 13	1	1
Noel, Mrs. William A.	Oct 9	10	1
Nugent, Tolbert Alexander	Nov 6	10	1
Pankratz, Louise Haufler	Jul 17	1	1
Partee, Mrs. Hiram	May 29	9	1
Pelton, James Isaac	Jul 24	12	1
Penn, Hugh Samuel	Aug 14	1	1
Pettus, Mrs. W. P.	Jul 17	8	1
Pfeuffer, Rosa	Feb 20	10	1
Porter, E. H.	Aug 21	1	1
Powers, Edwin	Sep 14	6	1
Pray, Harry V. B.	Jan 2	10	1
Prentice, Maude E.	Sep 11	7	1
Rawson, Charles W.	Oct 16	1	1
Ray, James C.	Apr 10	12	1
Reagan, John Green	Apr 24	7	1
Real, Arthur	May 15	1	1

1947
Film Roll #25

NAME	DATE	PG	SEC
Redwine, Mrs. D. P.	Feb 13	10	1
Reed, Mary Hamburg	Oct 2	1	1
Reynolds, Mrs. N. O.	May 1	12	1
Richerson, Mrs. C. H.	Feb 6	1	1
Richey, Sarah Jane	Jan 9	1	1
Rishworth, William H.	May 15	1	1
Robertson, Sharon Gail	Jul 10	11	1
Rogers, Charles C.	Aug 21	12	1
Ross, Orlena Nelson (Thanks)	Jan 9	6	1
Roussell, C. A. (Thanks)	Dec 11	3	4
Ruse, Katherine	Jan 30	12	1
Russom, John P.	Aug 7	5	1
Seffel, Ed	Apr 3	11	1
Sewell, Arminta Madeline	Apr 24	7	1
Shaw, Mrs. Vernon	Oct 16	1	1
Sinclair, Mrs. William Carl	Jun 19	10	1
Skidmore, Mrs. T. V.	Jun 19	1	1
Smith, C. R.	Dec 4	5	1
Speice, William C.	Jan 16	1	1
Spiker, Mary Louise	Jan 23	12	1
Stapleton, Carolina A.	Jul 17	8	1
Staudt, Rudolph	Jul 24	1	1
Stevens, Lewis A.	Feb 27	12	1
Stewart, Thomas Eli	Sep 11	7	1
Strube, Anna M.	Jan 16	12	1
Sublett, Jesse J.	May 8	1	1
Suggs, T. K.	Feb 6	12	1
Suttle, Homer	Apr 24	12	1
Sutton, James M.	Jan 30	1	1
Switzer, Charles H. (Jr.)	Jun 12	1	1
Tate, Tom	Nov 13	9	1
Templeton, Walter W.	Jan 2	10	1
Thomas, Caleb	Feb 27	1	1
Thomas, James F.	Apr 10	12	1
Thrav----, William V.	Jan 2	3	1
Turner, Hudson (Dr.)	Oct 9	11	1
Vallier, Eliza Bernice	Aug 7	12	1
Vanham, Joseph Henry	Apr 24	7	1
Vetter, Alvin	Dec 18	7	1
Walden, Darrell Gene	May 29	6	1

137

NAME	DATE	PG	SEC
Wesch, Mrs. C. J.	Jul 3	8	1
White, Marion Carter	Sep 18	10	1
Whitehouse, John Cleaver	Sep 4	1	1
Whittemore, W. J.	Jul 10	1	1
Whittle, Edward Forrester	Oct 9	9	1
Winters, Clyde	Jul 10	1	1
Woods, Dwight Everett	Sep 18	10	1
Zachry, Frances	Mar 27	12	1
Zachry, Frances Payne	Apr 3	12	1
Zamora, Teofilo (Thanks)	Feb 27	3	1

Alexander, Hattie Lee	Mar 18	9	1
Allen, Tom	Oct 28	8	1
Atkinson, Mrs. G. F.	Apr 22	5	1
Barnett, Mrs. J. D.	Sep 30	10	1
Beaver, Louis Leander	Aug 12	10	1
Bigger, Samuel Kennedy	Jun 24	3	1
Blevins, Maxey Buster	Jul 29	14	1
Bode, Fritz	Jul 1	7	1
Bode, Paul O.	Jun 3	7	1
Brauer, Josephine	Mar 11	6	1
Brown, Hugh Warren	Jul 1	6	1
Brown, John Thomas	Apr 1	8	1
Brown, Roy N.	Nov 11	16	1
Buckalew, Robert Hall	Jan 15	8	1
Buie, N. D. (Dr.)	Feb 12	5	1
Burkhardt, Annie	Jan 22	6	1
Burns, Julia C.	May 20	6	1
Burrer, Edwin	Apr 15	1	1
Byrd, Mrs. Andrew Jackson (Mary E.)	Apr 15	10	1
Carlisle, Willis	Jul 29	12	1
Carr, Jim Tom	Jan 15	3	1
Carroll, Mrs. Charles L.	Jul 22	5	2
Cason, Allen C.	Jan 22	10	1
Cleveland, Myrtie May	Jul 22	2	1
Cobb, David H.	Apr 15	11	1

1948
Film Roll #26

NAME	DATE	PG	Sec
Cobb, David H. (Jr.)	May 6	11	1
Cole, Mrs. W. S.	Dec 30	1	1
Connolly, F. R.	Jun 17	16	1
Cowden, Mary S.	Feb 5	7	1
Cowen, Charles Franklin	Jul 1	8	1
Cox, Mrs. James G.	May 13	8	1
Graey, Mrs. R. (Mary Ann)	Aug 26	7	1
Crick, Mittie J.	Jan 22	10	1
Crider, Austin	Apr 1	7	1
Culver, Charles F. (Dr.)	Jul 8	1	1
Culwell, Mrs. J. J.	Mar 4	1	1
Dainwood, Donald Lynn	Mar 18	10	1
Davenport, Mrs. John H. (Maggie)	Apr 1	8	1
Davis, John Chelton	Jul 22	1	1
Deering, Lawrence	Jan 8	12	1
Dekle, Mrs. J. A.	Feb 5	14	1
De La Cruz, Bonifacio	Dec 16	1	1
Diepenbrock, Mrs. O. P.	Nov 18	16	1
Dixon, J. E.	Mar 4	5	1
Doss, Grady Ray	Nov 18	8	1
Doss, Mrs. Grady Ray	Nov 18	8	1
Doss, Mrs. Ray	Nov 11	8	1
Dowd, Patricia	Jul 1	1	1
Doyle, Mary	Feb 12	8	1
Edwards, F. M.	Dec 23	8	1
Evans, Luther Eliss	Nov 4	7	1
Evertson, Mary Florence	Apr 15	1	1
Falvey, T. S. (Dr.)	Mar 18	10	1
Feller, Olfen A.	Feb 5	8	1
Flach, Melvin	Feb 12	1	1
Flach, Melvin	Feb 5	1	1
Floyd, Eulie	Aug 5	1	1
Fowler, Alex	Jul 22	3	1
Frederick, Mrs. Albert (Mattie)	Mar 25	7	1
Furr, E. P.	Oct 21	8	1
Gallat, Ernest Otto	Sep 9	16	1
Garrett, Mrs. Willie	Dec 9	8	1
Gavenda, Mrs. Otto (Jr.)	Jan 29	9	1
Gerganess, J. I.	Nov 18	16	1
Gibbs, Charles E.	Aug 26	6	1

1948
Film Roll #26

NAME	DATE	PG	Sec
Glenny, James	May 20	3	1
Grantham, Jewel Inez	Jan 8	7	1
Graves, William Jeptha	Jun 10	8	1
Gray, Luke G.	Dec 23	8	1
Griffin, Danny Ray	Aug 19	10	1
Grinstead, Jesse Edward	Mar 4	1	1
Grona, Mrs. Max	Mar 18	1	1
Hagen, Eda Haynes	Sep 9	5	1
Hahn, Fred	Apr 15	10	1
Harlan, Thomas Pickney	Dec 2	8	1
Harper, Frank J.	Dec 9	7	1
Harper, Mary Elsie	Feb 19	8	1
Hart, Bertina	Jun 17	16	1
Hart, Mrs. J. R.	Apr 8	1	1
Heimann, Harry A.	Sep 9	10	1
Heimann, Mrs. Jacob E.	Mar 4	5	1
Henke, Hugo (Jackie)	Jan 8	12	1
Hertel, Charles Frederick	Apr 22	12	1
Herzog, Walter	Jun 17	16	1
Hickerman, Lee Hill	Apr 1	8	1
Hicks, Benjamin Franklin	Sep 2	8	1
Hill, Mrs. T. W. (Armintea M.)	Jan 29	9	1
Holdsworth, Mrs. Tom	Sep 9	1	1
Holloway, Berniece	May 27	2	2
Howell, Richard Levi	Jul 15	8	1
Hubble, Mrs. B. M.	Feb 12	5	1
Huitt, brother of J. L.	Feb 5	3	1
Hutt, J. W.	May 20	11	1
Jackson, James A.	Sep 30	6	1
Jackson, Robert Franklin	Feb 26	12	1
Johnson, Mary Hasley	Apr 8	11	1
Jones, Charles D.	Jul 29	6	1
Jones, Mrs. George A.	May 13	1	1
Jones, Gwendolyn	Jun 10	15	1
Jones, Jo	Mar 18	1	1
Jones, Jo	Mar 25	1	1
Joy, Awilda	Apr 15	10	1
Juarez, Gilbert	Oct 7	1	1
Juarez, Gilbert C.	Aug 19	10	1
Karger, Mary	Sep 2	1	1

140

NAME	DATE	PG	Sec
Kelton, O. T.	May 13	1	1
Kelton, Mrs. S. M.	Apr 22	12	1
Kent, Alice	Jul 29	14	1
Kettel, Otto	Nov 25	7	1
Knapp, John	Feb 26	2	1
Knox, George	May 27	8	1
Kott, Mrs. Ernst	Jun 24	12	1
Leach, Mrs. E. R.	Jan 1	10	1
Lehmann, Mrs. C. Ferd	Feb 5	7	1
Littlefield, Roy	Feb 19	8	1
Lock, Albert F. (Jr.)	Jul 8	1	1
Lowrance, Kenneth	Oct 14	8	1
Lowry, son of Rev. Dick	Sep 30	6	1
Lucas, Sammie	Dec 9	18	1
Mathews, Somers	Aug 26	1	1
Maxwell, Jesse J.	May 20	1	1
Mayhugh, Chestney	Feb 19	1	1
Mc Donald, H. A.	May 27	8	1
Mc Donald, Hollis O.	Jul 15	1	1
Mc Donald, Jesse Thomas	Nov 25	8	1
Mc Elroy, Sweet Nellie	Feb 26	1	1
Mc Gauhey, Mrs. H. B.	Apr 1	1	1
Mc Innes, Zetha	Oct 28	9	1
Mc Leod, Nannie Taylor	Oct 21	7	1
Mc Williams, David A.	Jun 17	12	1
Meikle, Mrs. Edward	Apr 8	8	1
Meyers, Walter	Jan 22	1	1
Miller, Mrs. T. L.	Oct 14	16	1
Moore, John James	Jan 22	5	1
Moore, Shelby	Apr 29	6	1
Moran, Daniel J.	Apr 8	9	1
Morriss, Mrs. Ed E.	Jul 29	1	1
Morrow, Robert Jefferson	Jul 8	1	1
Moss, mother of Walter	Oct 7	1	1
Motte, Mrs. J. N.	Apr 29	6	1
Mosher, W. S.	Jan 15	5	1
Myers, Mrs. Eddie Lee	Feb 5	6	1
Nabors, George Robert	Aug 19	10	1
Neal, Henry Earl (Jr.)	Sep 2	1	1
Nowlin, Henry Moore	Feb 12	1	1

NAME	DATE	PG	Sec
Nyc, Frederick Francis	Dec 2	1	1
Owens, John G. (Jr.)	Jun 3	2	1
Paradoski, Edward	Dce 2	16	1
Parks, Mrs. M. B.	Jul 8	12	1
Parks, Sarah Elizabeth	Mar 18	10	1
Pearl, George Clark (Jr.)	Mar 18	1	1
Pearson, Daniel	Jan 8	12	1
Pearson, Leonard Forrest	Dec 30	12	1
Polansky, Henry Lee	Jul 29	14	1
Purl, George (Jr)	Mar 25	1	1
Quinn, Janie Althea	May 27	3	1
Raaz, Paul L.	Mar 11	1	1
Reeve, W. H.	Aug 5	10	1
Reeves, William	Jan 8	1	1
Reeves, William	Jan 22	1	1
Reeves, William	Jan 29	12	1
Rhoden, Emmett	Dec 2	6	1
Richards, George	Dec 16	8	1
Richards, Harold	Nov 4	6	1
Robert, L. B.	Mar 4	5	1
Robertson, Adge	Aug 5	1	1
Robison, Charles Otis	Oct 7	1	1
Roland, mother of C. A.	Feb 19	6	1
Rose, J. D.	Aug 12	8	1
Rosson, Beatrice Milton	Mar 4	10	1
Rouse, Thomas B.	Feb 12	14	1
Saenger, Richard	Aug 5	10	1
Sales, Sam	Aug 5	3	1
Salyers, Danny Yount	Aug 5	10	1
Scarbrough, J. M.	Nov 25	8	1
Schofield, Hinsan Herbert	May 6	8	1
Scott, Ray	Aug 5	3	1
Shearn, Charles B.	Feb 19	14	1
Sheffield, Frank	Apr 1	1	1
Sheffield, Frank	Apr 29	1	1
Shelton, Mrs. S. C.	Jul 15	8	1
Shirley, Mary Elizabeth	May 13	8	1
Simmons, Mrs. N. B.	Dec 9	16	1
Smith, Edward F. or H.	Dec 9	1	1
Smith, Joe A.	Jan 8	12	1

NAME	DATE	PG	Sec
Smith, Joseph Alfred	Jan 15	8	1
Smith, Katherine	Aug 12	10	1
Starr, Sarah Elizabeth	Jan 29	1	1
Stevens, Mrs. H. N. (Dorothy)	Feb 5	1	1
Stone, John Isaac	Apr 15	9	1
Switzer, Myrna Fae	Nov 11	8	1
Thalmann, Fred	Jul 22	4	2
Thomas, J. E.	Apr 29	1	1
Thompson, Billy Jeff	Dec 30	1	1
Thompson, mother of H. G.	Jul 22	9	2
Trimble, Martha B.	Jan 8	7	1
Vaughn, Douglas E.	Jul 8	10	1
Vaughn, Douglas E.	Aug 12	10	1
Vilterol, Alfredo	Nov 25	1	1
Wachter, Isaac Johnson	Jul 29	1	1
Wagner, David Dale	Apr 22	1	1
Waldrip, Mrs. John W.	Jun 24	8	1
Walker II, Glenn David	Sep 30	10	1
Ward, Willis Gaenes	Aug 26	1	1
Warren, Evelyn Wood	Feb 19	8	1
Warren, Mrs. Murray	Sep 9	15	1
Watson, Frank	Apr 22	11	1
Webner, Gertrude	May 20	8	1
Wehmeyer, William Adam	Feb 12	1	1
Wehmeyer, William Adam	Feb 19	6	1
Wells, Mrs. Ed. G.	Dec 9	8	1
White, J. R.	Feb 5	8	1
White, May Hannah	Jan 22	6	1
Wiggins, Warren	Jul 22	7	1
Williamson, Albert Bonaparte	Jan 29	1	1
Wills, Eva Melinda	Sep 9	16	1
Windsor, Joe W.	Jan 29	8	1
Woodward, John C.	Jan 1	10	1
Worthington, William P.	Jul 8	10	1
Wright, Jessie	Jan 8	7	1
Yoast, Joe D.	Mar 4	10	1
Young, E. V.	Mar 18	1	1
Zander, Mary W.	Sep 23	6	1

NAME	DATE	PG	SEC
Anderson, Louise Edna	Mar 17	8	1
Anz, "Shorty"	Jul 14	7	1
Arnold, Allen Morris	Jul 17	1	1
Attaway, Elisha Ford	Sep 8	1	1
Auld, Archie	Sep 1	8	1
Babb, William Garnet	Sep 8	6	1
Baker, Charles T.	Jan 20	8	1
Ball, F. H.	Feb 3	12	1
Beaver, Mrs. Hubert H.	Feb 3	6	1
Bernard, Max Jones	Jul 14	1	1
Biedenharn, O. L.	Feb 10	8	1
Boggs, Luther Hamilton	Feb 17	10	1
Bollman, George	Dec 1	5	1
Brown, Betty Jo	Jul 28	5	1
Brown, Horace M.	Feb 3	3	1
Buckner, Suzanne	Dec 8	8	1
Burleson, Zack Henry	Jan 20	8	1
Burrer, Charles	Nov 17	1/16	1
Busby, John H.	Nov 3	8	1
Butler, Ogburn D.	Nov 24	8	1
Byas, William	Jun 10	10	1
Cabbiness, William J.	Jun 23	8	1
Campbell, Mrs. J. W.	Apr 28	1	1
Campbell, Mrs. J. W.	May 5	3	1
Carels, Harold	Dec 29	1	1
Chanout, James	Jan 13	6	1
Chandler, Cassandra Eunice	Mar 3	8	1
Clabaugh, E. E.	Oct 20	6/8	1
Clay, Mrs. J. L.	Oct 13	5	1
Cobb, William Bryan	Dec 15	16	1
Coke, Mrs. Richard	Jan 27	12	1
Colbath, Virginia	May 12	5	1
Collins, Thomas J.	Oct 13	8	1
Conard, Carrol (Dr.)	Jul 28	5	1
Cooke, Joe Richardson	Sep 29	6	1
Corbett, Mary Rose	May 5	6	1
Cox, Walter W.	Feb 17	5	1
Coyle, Margaret Louise	Jun 23	8	1
Crider, Harlan Dale	Feb 10	1	1
Cross, Charles W.	Oct 13	16	1

NAME	DATE	PG	SEC
Culwell, J. J.	Jun 16	7	1
Deal, B. P.	Jul 21	8	1
Dove, Lois	Aug 11	3	1
Doyle, Lyle Jacob	Dec 29	1	1
Ellisor, Mrs. G. C.	Apr 28	3	1
Fleming, Slaytor	Feb 3	8	1
Franks, Robert Allen (Thanks)	Jun 10	10	1
Freeman, Clarence Warren	Nov 3	14	1
Friedrich, Mrs. Hubert (Ada)	Jan 6	1	1
Gentry, Johanna E.	Mar 3	7	1
George, James Albert	Jul 21	16	1
George, Thomas Elmo	Jan 6	3	1
Gillman, Mrs. H.	Jun 30	5	2
Girdwood, Mrs. David	Jul 14	13	1
Glenn, Rhoda	Feb 3	14	1
Grisham, George Rudolph	Oct 6	1	1
Haggerton, Samuel	Jun 10	6	1
Hankamer, Harold Monroe	Jun 2	16	1
Hardin, Don C.	Apr 21	1	1
Harris, Mrs. J. J.	Jul 28	6	1
Harrison, Mrs. Henry M.	Nov 24	1	1
Haygood, Perry Allen	Jan 13	16	1
Heinen, Lena	Jul 7	5	1
Helmke, A. W. (Bob)	Mar 24	1	1
Helmke, Mrs. A. W.	Mar 24	1	1
Henderson, Mrs. Charles (Cynthia)	Apr 28	16	1
Henry, Emerson	Dec 1	1	1
Hodges, Blanche	Sep 1	15	1
Hogg, Thomas E.	Mar 10	1	1
Howell, Jim	Jun 16	8	1
Hughes, William F.	Oct 20	8	1
Huntington, Spencer Hinsdale	Feb 17	10	1
Johns, Jack	Oct 20	1	1
Johnson, Earl A.	Jan 13	10	1
Jones, John Henry	Jun 10	1	1
Jones, Mary	Jul 21	16	1
Jones, Mary Jane	Aug 4	7	1
Jones, Nellie Rees	Jun 10	6	1
Kaiser, Gus	Feb 10	8	1
Kennedy, Harwood S.	Nov 17	1	1

1949
Film Roll #27

NAME	DATE	PG	SEC
Kennedy, Ira	Jul 7	1	1
Key, Mrs. J. F.	Sep 22	1	1
Kieth, William	Jun 10	16	1
Kingsley, Henry	Oct 27	5	1
Knopp, Paul	Mar 10	10	1
Kott, Alfred	Feb 3	1	1
Kott, Alfred	Feb 10	8	1
Kramer, Elmer	Jan 20	8	1
Kuhlmann, Mrs. Henry H.	Jun 16	1	1
Le Blanc, Mrs. Elodie	Jun 30	7	1
Lee, Otis Gentry	Jan 20	8	1
Lee, Otis Gentry	Feb 10	1	1
Leggitt, William Wesley	Jul 28	10	1
Lehmann, Frank Allen	May 12	6	1
Lewis, Clement	Jun 10	8	1
Maher, Jennie M.	Oct 20	8	1
Marberry, Mrs. Francis Peter	May 26	8	1
Martin, Mrs. C. H.	Oct 20	6	1
Martin, Inez	Mar 24	3	1
Martinez, MRs. Frank	Dec 1	8	1
May, L. R.	Oct 13	8	1
Meredith, Raymond Carter	Jan 27	1	1
Merritt, Robert R.	Aug 18	1	1
Miller, Cyrus W.	Feb 10	2	2
Mittanck, Mrs. J. F.	Feb 17	10	1
Moeller, Mrs. A. H.	Mar 3	7	1
Moore, Wilton Wattress	Mar 3	1	1
Moreno, Rafael E.	Apr 28	1	1
Nichols, Alexander Newton	Dec 22	1	1
Odem, William T.	Nov 24	14/16	1
Parvin, Mrs. Joe	May 19	8	1
Patton, Ellen Frances	Mar 31	5	1
Patton, Robert Greer	Dec 1	7	1
Pennington, W. G. (Dr.)	Feb 3	8	1
Pickett, John Jefferson	Nov 3	11	1
Randle, George	Mar 3	8	1
Real, Mrs. Albert (Ida Fricke)	Mar 24	1	1
Reick, Flo Spillar	Jun 30	6	2
Priour, William Monroe	Jan 6	8	1
Rhoden, Emmett Durwood	Jan 13	1	1

146

NAME	DATE	PG	SEC
Robinson, John Weldon	Dec 29	3	1
Rockey, Winnifred Victoria	Oct 20	5	1
Rosenberg, Arthur F.	Apr 21	11	1
Rosenthal, Mrs. Oscar	Sep 22	16	1
Rossburg, Arthur Carl	Feb 10	1	1
Rotge. Mrs. Ernest (Esther Surber)	Aug 25	7	1
Sabban, Mrs. John	Jul 14	15	1
Saner, Orlando Bryant	Jul 14	1	1
Saner, Orlando Byrant	Jul 21	16	1
Saur, George	Mar 17	12	1
Schoenwolf, Adolph Felix	Jan 27	1	1
Schott, Bruno	Sep 1	1	1
Scott, Roy Dolan	Jun 30	6	1
Settle, Ralph	Oct 13	5	1
Shahan, Alta Wellborn	Mar 17	7	1
Sherman, Mrs. Claud	Mar 17	8	1
Sherrill, Mrs. C. S.	Jan 20	1	1
Simmons, Carl Wayne	Feb 17	10	1
Simpsin, Mrs. Goerge (Thanks)	Jul 14	16	1
Simpson, D. E.	Jun 10	1	1
Simpson, Mrs. George	Jul 7	1	1
Sims, Cecil	Jan 20	8	1
Singletarry, Ophelia	Jun 2	8	1
Smith, William Clayton	Aug 4	1	1
Spalding, Mrs. Art	Sep 8	8	1
Spann, Albert Leonard (Jr.)	Mar 17	1	1
Springall, Herbert S.	Mar 17	1	1
Stanley, Mrs. Tom	Nov 24	1	1
Stanley, William M.	Nov 24	8	1
Stehling, James	Feb 24	1	1
Stehling, Jimmie	Mar 24	1	1
Stieler, Anna	Jan 20	3	1
Stone, Mrs. W. L.	Oct 6	8	1
Sublett, Mrs. E. L.	Jun 30	1	1
Surber, Mrs. Green C. (Sarah E.)	Mar 31	1	1
Taylor, Daniel C. C.	Jun 16	1	1
Thomas, Charles (Dr.)	Jul 7	14	1
Tobey, W. A.	Dec 15	15	1
Tolar, William C.	Jul 14	7	1
Tomlinson, Peter M.	Jun 16	16	1

1949
Film Roll #27

NAME	DATE	PG	SEC
Tomlinson, Mrs. S. P.	Apr 21	3	1
Trejo, Christine	Apr 7	7	1
Unnasch, Herman	Nov 17	6	1
Walker, Jimmie A.	Feb 3	14	1
Whipple, Alfred H.	Sep 15	1	1
Williams, Laura Youree	Apr 21	5	1
Williamson, J. B. (Jr.)	Feb 10	12	1
Vinyard, Mrs. John Henry	May 12	5	1
Von Roeder, Mrs. R. O.	Jun 10	1	1
Wall, Herbert	Nov 30	16	1
Walsh, Ralph Hain	Jul 14	8	1
Waterman, Vernice E.	Jun 2	5	1
Wharton, Mrs. David W.	Nov 10	1	1
Witt, Martha Ellen	Oct 6	1	1
Wootton, Cora May	Dec 8	16	1
Worthen, William Roy	Aug 4	5	1
Zumwalt, Mrs. W. T.	Nov 17	7	1

1950
Film Roll #28

NAME	DATE	PG	SEC
Aguero, Domingo	Dec 28	1	1
Albe, Frank	Nov 9	7	1
Ammons, Cyrus	Jan 26	3	1
Ault, John P.	May 25	8	1
Babineaux, Damouville J.	Mar 16	14	1
Barnes, William W.	Jul 27	12	1
Baron, Alfredo	Jun 22	8	1
Benson, Bennie C.	Mar 9	1	1
Bennett, Mrs. Benjamin F.	Mar 23	8	1
Bevill, George P.	Jun 1	1	1
Black, William	Sep 28	3	1
Blessinger, John	Aug 3	15	1
Blevins, Samuel W.	Dec 14	16	1
Blount, Claude	Oct 5	6	1
Breen, Frank M.	Mar 11	1	1
Brown, Mrs. H. B.	Jan 26	1	2
Caddell, John T.	May 4	1	1
Cantwell, James A.	Aug 17	15	1

148

1950
Film Roll #28

NAME	DATE	PG
Carson, A. J. (Rev.)	Sep 7	14
Carson, Thomas E.	Jun 15	14
Chipman, Mrs. Emmett	Jul 6	16
Cobb, Farr H.	Jun 8	1
Cole, Samuel A.	Apr 20	8
Cooke, Mrs. George O.	Feb 2	16
Conn, Francis M.	Dec 7	13
Council, William L.	Feb 9	1
Covert, Mrs. C. C.	Apr 13	1
Cowden, Jerry W.	Aug 17	1
Crooks, Mrs. W. A.	Sep 28	8
Crumrine, Leslie B. (Dr.)	Mar 30	5
Decker, John E.	Apr 20	11
Dickey, Sanford E.	Sep 21	10
Doyle, George M.	Nov 16	1
Ellis, Joseph W.	Mar 30	8
Ellebracht, Richard	Jun 22	3
Ernst, Carrie	Oct 5	10
Evans, Tyler R.	Feb 9	7
Evins, John T.	Jan 19	8
Fatheree, Edgar H.	Mar 23	10
Finley, Harry L.	Oct 26	1
Ford, R. W. (Sr.)	Apr 13	3
Foslein, Clifford A.	Feb 23	12
Franks, Charles G.	Jan 12	8
Gammon, James S.	Jun 22	12
Gammon, James Thomas S.	Jun 8	1
Gary, Odis	Apr 6	6
Gilliland, J. E.	Mar 30	8
Gleason, Mrs. Edith J.	Dec 21	1
Glenn, Mrs. Robert C.	Oct 19	16
Guthrie, Mrs. L. M.	Oct 19	8
Hall, Hiram L.	Feb 9	1
Hammond, Mrs. Emma	Aug 3	16
Hanzen, Harry C.	Aug 31	1
Haver, Stanley (Rev.)	Apr 13	11
Henke, Mrs. August W.	Nov 30	1
Hickman, Charles N.	Feb 9	6
Hicks, J. D.	Jun 15	8
Hill, John W.	Jun 8	1

NAME	DATE	PG
Hobby, Mattie Lee	Jul 27	12
Holdsworth, Richard	Jan 12	1
Hornbeck, Ann T.	Aug 10	6
Horner, Mary C.	Dec 7	7
House, Mrs. W. H.	Mar 16	11
Hutchings, Richard B.	Mar 2	16
Irving, Forrest W.	Aug 3	6
Ivison, Tom	Nov 2	5
Jackson, John	Apr 20	8
Jackson, Mrs. R. F.	Nov 16	6
James, Tom	Feb 2	7
Jerrett, Joseph D.	May 18	8
Kelley, O. A.	Nov 16	8
Kelly, Mrs. Rex	Nov 23	1
Kieth, Edward H.	Dec 28	1
Kilpatrick, Monroe C.	Apr 20	8
Kirkmeyer, Isabella	Mar 30	5
Klein, Mrs. Harry	Jun 15	8
Klein, Jacob	Nov 16	6
Knox, Mrs. J. C.	Jun 8	8
Lackey, Mrs. G. O.	Jun 22	8
Landrum, Lemuel R.	Oct 12	8
Lange, William G.	Dec 7	1
Langham, Mrs. E. E.	Oct 12	11
Lear, Sophie	Feb 23	1
Leatherwood, Ollie G.	Nov 2	6
Le Blanc, Bernard	Apr 20	8
Leinweber, Mrs. Goerge	Aug 3	6
Lett, Sallie G.	Oct 26	15
Lewallen, Bill	May 4	1
Leyendecker, Arthur	Nov 9	8
Lowrance, Edward D.	Nov 23	8
Lucas, Mrs. C. C.	May 25	1
Lucas, D.C.	Nov 2	8
Lunn, Edward	Sep 28	7
Luse, S. D. (Dr.)	Jul 27	5
Manney, Mrs. W. F.	Mar 16	1
Manning, Eliza L. (Dr.)	Jan 5	1
Maples, Pascal L.	Apr 27	8
Mattingly, Benjamin J.	Nov 23	8

1950
Film Roll #28

NAME	DATE	PG
Mc Cullough, infant of Dr. D.	Apr 20	1
Mc Nealy, Walter W.	Apr 6	14
Messick, Bryan W.	Jan 5	4
Miller, Mrs. Hattie	May 25	5
Minear, Mrs. E. W.	Feb 2	1
Moore, Andrew F.	Mar 30	1
Moore, Mrs. Martha H.	Feb 9	15
Mooring, Charles E.	Aug 17	7
Newman, Peggy L.	Mar 30	10
Nichols, John F.	Nov 16	1
Niermon, J. L. (Dr.)	Oct 12	8
Norwood, George	Nov 30	8
Norwood, Mrs. George	Nov 30	8
Null, Donald H.	Feb 2	1
Orchard, Mrs. Fannie	Jan 19	7
Owens, John E,	Dec 21	1
Palmer, Mrs. J. E.	Mar 2	1
Pani, George H.	Apr 6	3
Parsons, Bert C.	Nov 23	13
Pattee, Callie	May 18	3
Paul, Henry T.	Mar 30	1
Perry, Haynie A.	Jun 8	16
Priour, Henry I.	Aug	1
Rankin, Edmond H.	Jun 3	5
Rawls, Mrs. Martha L.	May 25	16
Reed, Emma	Oct 26	16
Reed, Rufus	Apr 6	16
Rees, Albert	Oct 19	1
Reeves, Robert E.	Nov 2	1
Reinhardt, Mrs. Joe	Apr 6	11
Remschel, Mrs. Henry	Oct 26	1
Robertson, Mrs. R. L.	Feb 2	8
Robbins, Laura E.	Nov 23	13
Rowland, George	Aug 17	6
Sabins, James S.	Aug 3	14
Saenger, Walter E.	Aug 3	1
Sandel, Mrs. Daniel W.	Mar 11	7
Schulze, Mrs. Herman	Mar 23	3
Schumacher, William C.	Jul 6	1
Schwethelm, Arno	Oct 5	15

151

NAME	DATE	PG
Scoggins, Eugene	Jul 27	12
Scruggs, Marion A.	Jul 20	10
Sessions, Mrs. John	Aug 24	3
Shackleford, Mrs. C. E.	Feb 2	7
Shelton, Collen M.	Nov 16	1
Shelton, Harvey W. C.	Mar 11	6
Shilling, Mrs. Albert	Jan 26	3
Smith, Mrs. Alf H.	Nov 16	16
Smith, J. B.	Jan 19	8
Smith, Lewis A.	Sep 21	16
Snowden, Jeff C.	Feb 23	1
Stancil, Edgar A.	Feb 23	1
Starkweather, Walter	Dec 14	16
Staudt, Mrs. Emil	Jun 15	8
Stewart, Ida	Sep 14	1
Stirling, Joseph H.	Jun 22	5
Sutton, Mrs. James M.	Apr 20	1
Swayze, Harry L. (Dr.)	Aug 31	1
Taylor, James E.	Dec 21	8
Terry, Autry A.	Sep 14	8
Townsend, Donald F.	Sep 14	1
Townsend, Donald F.	Sep 21	10
Vann, Blache	Oct 12	1
Vann, Stewart	Aug 10	1
Walker, Mrs. Howe	Sep 7	14
Wallace, John C.	Aug 17	8
Wahburn, Patrick	Oct 5	10
Washburn, Mrs. Pat	Aug 17	12
Watson, David R.	Feb 9	1
Wedekind, Dorothy Mariette	Jun 15	8
Weeks, Mrs. N. W.	Sep 21	6
Whetstone, A. T.	Jun 15	8
Whitehead, Leona Ethel	Apr 27	16
Willson, T. Morris	Aug 3	1
Woody, Hugh	May 25	8
Wright, William H.	Jun 15	8
Young, Pete	Apr 27	8

1951
Film Roll #28A

NAME	DATE	PG	SEC
Allen, E. V.	Oct 25	1	1
Amend, Mrs. Algie	May 24	5	1
Anderson, Temple B. (Rev.)	May 24	6	1
Armintor, Mrs. F.	Apr 26	4	1
Banta, Gerald	Mar 15	14	2
Beard, Dalton D.	Jul 12	1	1
Bell, Sam	Feb 8	3	1
Barker, Mrs. Andy	Mar 8	1	1
Bigger, James C.	Mar 8	11	2
Blackburn, Edward M.	Jun 21	8	1
Blair, Mrs. L. F. (Thanks)	Apr 19	2	2
Blake, James H.	Aug 2	1	1
Blythe, Ison	Oct 11	6	2
Bolton, Mrs. Cleve M.	Dec 27	6	2
Branch, Milton	Mar 29	8	1
Brandon, W. L.	Mar 29	1	1
Bresee, Florence	Feb 22	8	1
Bundick, Mrs. Leonard	Jul 19	8	2
Burleson, Mrs. Bill	Jul 26	8	1
Burnett, James R.	Aug 30	1	1
Burnett, Jefferson D.	Apr 12	8	1
Burnett, Mrs. W. W.	Apr 5	6	1
Buswell, Calvin E. (Dr.)	Jun 21	8	1
Carson, Joseph F.	Nov 1	8	1
Chaney, Mrs. R. H.	Aug 30	1	1
Chenault, James E.	Sep 6	1	1
Chenault, James E.	Nov 22	1	1
Chester, Mary C.	Jan 18	8	1
Clark, Mrs. J. T.	Jul 23	5	2
Clark, Roy	Jan 11	3	1
Cole, Helen C.	Apr 26	1	2
Cook, Wiley L.	Aug 2	6	2
Coppedge, James P.	Aug 30	1	1
Corn, Mrs. Sherwood	Sep 20	8	1
Darden, Ed	Jan 4	12	1
Davis, Minnie	Aug 2	6	2
Deats, George W. M.	Sep 6	6	2
Deckert, August	Jan 25	6	1
Deering, Mrs. J. T	Jan 25	1	1
Deike, Walter	Mar 8	8	1

153

NAME	DATE		PG	SEC
De Vore, James A.	Jul 26		6	1
Dick, Phillip	May 31		1	1
Dickey, Robert C.	Dec 6		1	1
Dickey, Walter L.	Nov 2?	(8)	6	2
Dietert, Ernest	Sep 13		8	1
Dillingham, Emma A.	Oct 4		8	1
Dowding, Mrs. Bill	May 10		7	1
Dwyer, John	Nov 22		1	1
Dyson, Pearl E.	Aug 9		8	1
Eathrone, Albert L.	Aug 30		8	1
Espinosa, infant son (Thanks)	Dec 6		7	1
Evans, James M.	Aug 23		1	1
Fawcett, Willis A.	Mar 8		1	1
Fenlon, Mrs. Thomas	Dec 20		8	1
Fessenden, Le Roy	Mar 15		1	1
Fluitt, Linda M.	Jul 12		1	1
Fordtran, Mrs. F. L.	Jun 21		1	1
French, J. T.	Aug 23		8	1
Fryer, Thomas V. (Dr.)	Aug 2		8	1
Furr, Arthur	Mar 1		7	1
Gary, Marvin C.	Feb 8		11	1
Gilmer, Street H.	Feb 15		16	2
Goodwyn, Francis E.	Jun 21		8	1
Goss, George	Aug 23		8	1
Graces, John C.	Aug 23		6	2
Griffin, Mrs. J. E.	Jan 18		8	1
Grinstead, Eugene D.	Aug 16		8	1
Hackworth, Victor W.	Feb 15		3	1
Hardy, William T.	Jan 4		3	1
Harrigal, Mrs. J. A.	Sep 6		2	2
Harrison, John A.	Oct 18		8	1
Harrison, Mrs. T. J.	Apr 26		6	2
Harwood, John A.	Nov 29		6	2
Heimann, Eddie L.	Jul 26		8	1
Henderson, Mrs. M. L.	Jun 28		8	1
Hitzfeld, Gebhardt	Nov 22		8	1
Holkes, Emory B.	Feb 1		16	1
Hollier, Mrs. A. D.	Nov 22		5	1
Hooten, William F.	Feb 8		8	1
Hurt, Bea	Jan 4		10	1

NAME	DATE		PG	SEC
Irving, Richard J.	Jun 28		7	1
Ivey, Prentice	Nov 22		8	1
James, Morris C.	Mar 22		1	1
Jarmon, Walter W.	Aug 16		1	1
Jeffrey, Mrs. Gus	Mar 29		1	1
Kasey, Mrs. E. H.	Dec 20		5	1
Keller, Dora E.	Jan 4		12	1
Kelsey, J. W.	Feb 22		8	1
Kerr, Mrs. H. H.	Apr 5		8	1
Koon, John E.	Nov 2?	(8)	1	1
Lackey, Benjamin F.	May 15		7	1
La Rue, Mrs. Newton	Dec 27		6	1
Layton, Mrs. Fletcher P.	May 31		6	2
Lee, W. Albert	Nov 29		8	1
Lewis, Mrs. Dave	Jun 14		6	1
Lich, Mrs. Julia	Mar 8		15	2
Loesberg, George	Jul 5		2	2
Louy, Frank A.	Dec 27		6	1
Lowery, Mrs. John T.	Jul 26		8	1
Marberry, J. T.	Oct 11		4	2
Marshall, Laura	Feb 8		11	1
Masters, J. W.	Jul 5		1	1
Mauldin, Nettie W.	Jun 7		8	1
Mayer, Charles (Jr.)	Dec 6		1	1
Mc Caleb, John W.	Aug 9		8	1
Mc Call, John V. (Dr.)	Aug 2		8	1
Mc Cartney, Mrs. T. V.	Aug 16		8	1
Mc Faddin, Maude	Apr 26		7	1
Mc Manus, Alma	Jan 25		1	1
Mc Nealy, Ralph	Nov 15		7	1
Meadow, Martha E.	Feb 1		16	1
Merritt, Mrs. Robert	Mar 15		10	1
Merritt, Solen B.	Aug 9		5	2
Michamore, Calvin g. (Jr.)	Sep 27		8	1
Michon, Bernard F.	Nov 2?	(8)	1	1
Michon, Bernard F.	Nov 2?	(8)	8	1
Miers, William T.	Jan 11		3	1
Miers, William T.	Nov 2?	(8)	6	1
Miller, Charles	Jan 4		1	1
Miller, E. L. (Dr.)	Aug 9		6	1

NAME	DATE	PG	SEC
Miller, William W.	Aug 23	1	1
Mittanck, Julius F.	Jun 21	1	1
Moore, Thomas	Mar 1	8	1
Morris, Eugene G.	Feb 8	8	1
Morris, William B.	Sep 27	8	1
Mosel, Herman	Mar 1	1	1
Murphy, Clarence	Oct 4	8	1
Murphy, Martha Jo	May 10	6	2
Murphy, Mrs. Tom	Oct 18	6	2
Nelson, Harry E.	Dec 6	7	1
Nichols, Martin E.	Oct 4	8	1
Noll, George	Sep 20	8	1
Oldham, Clarence M.	Aug 2	6	2
Oliver, E. D.	Jan 11	7	1
Ortega, Louis	Sep 13	8	1
Parker, Mrs. J. E.	Jun 21	8	1
Parker, John	Apr 19	8	1
Parks, M. E.	Jun 7	8	1
Pauley, Richard A.	Mar 29	8	1
Peril, James A.	Aug 2	1	1
Petersine, David F.	Sep 6	6	2
Peterson, Mrs. Sid C.	Sep 27	1	1
Phillips, Warren	Dec 13	8	1
Raiford, Nancy T.	Jun 21	1	1
Raimond, Martin V.	Jul 26	8	1
Reisterer, Bobbie Nell	Jan 11	10	1
Richards, Mrs. B. C.	Dec 20	1	1
Ridgeway, Lena S.	Oct 18	8	1
Rishworth, Harry	Dec 13	8	1
Rutherford, William W.	Nov 22	6	2
Sanger, Robert (Sr.)	Nov 15	1	1
Schleuter, Allen F.	Oct 11	8	1
Schneider, Mrs. Albert	Jun 21	8	1
Schuh, Richard L.	May 17	1	1
Schulze, Walter	Jan 4	1	1
Schwethelm, Mrs. Bruno	Nov 1	1	1
Scott, Annie B.	Feb 15	16	2
Secrest, Mrs. F. H.	Apr 26	6	2
Shinn, Mrs. J. W.	May 10	6	2
Simmonds, James M.	Nov 15	8	1

NAME	DATE	PG S
Singleton, Robert M.	Feb 1	2
Skeen, Leon	Apr 19	6
Skiles, Orvil J.	Jul 19	8
Smith, Rodolph P.	Dec 20	1
Snodgrass, Volney B.	Aug 2	1
Spicer, Mrs. J. S. A. (Jr.)	Aug 9	1
Starkey, Alice	Aug 9	1
Starkwater, David	Dec 13	1
Starkwater, Lois	Dec 13	1
Stephenson, Mrs. William T.	Apr 5	6
Strackbein, Mrs. Louis	Oct 25	6
Strube, Fritz	Jan 18	1
Sublett, Elwynn L.	Apr 12	6
Tatsch, Mrs. Fred	Jun 28	8
Taylor, Nancy Jane	May 17	8
Thomas, Mrs. John J.	May 24	8
Thallmann, Louise	Jul 5	6
Tinney, Thomas T.	Feb 15	16
Treiber, Mathias C.	May 17	7
Trejo, Mrs. D. L.	Jul 26	8
Vann, Mrs. Walter W.	Feb 8	1
Verble, Lillie B.	May 17	6
Wagner, J. Joseph	May 3	1
Walker, Olive	Aug 20	4
Ward, Arthur	Apr 26	6
Ward, August	May 15	15
Weber, L. R.	May 31	6
White, Mrs. F. A.	Nov 29	6
Wiley, Mary M.	Sep 27	6
Williams, Charles R.	Apr 19	8
Williford, Louis O.	Jul 12	8
Wilson, J. W.	Jan 11	3
Wolf, Rudolph	Jan 25	16
Wisner, Mary	Jun 28	3
Yariger, Mrs. E. H.	Jul 26	8
Yates, Mrs, W. H.	May 3	8
Young, John Phillip	May 31	1
Young, Mary Ellen	Oct 4	8

NAME	DATE	PG	SEC
Craddock, Mary E.	Aug 14	6	2
Crate, Herbert L.	Nov 6	8	1
Crooks, William A.	May 29	4	1
Daniels, George M.	Mar 20	6	2
Darby, John W. (D.D.)	Mar 13	1	1
Davis, W. A.	Apr 17	1	1
Davis, Wilbur L.	Dec 11	8	2
Dawson, Cyrus A.	Oct 16	1	1
Dechert, Harry G.	Nov 6	6	2
Deece, Mrs. Francis	Apr 17	5	1
Dennis, Joe	May 29	8	1
Denton, Howard A.	Aug 28	8	1
Desbrow, Donald L.	Oct 30	1	1
Dishinger, Edwin R.	Jun 5	1	1
Dodgen, Dudley	Mar 6	8	1
Dowling, Mrs. Edward J.	Jul 10	1	1
Dubose, Harold	Dec 18	1	1
Duderstadt, Ernest H.	Aug 14	1	1
Durham, Phipps F.	Sep 25	8	1
Durst, Charles	Apr 3	8	1
Eckstein, Henry W.	Aug 14	6	2
Eckstein, Mrs. Henry	Jan 31	1	1
Eggeling, Walter	Dec 4	8	1
Eldridge, Louis W.	Feb 7	1	1
Engel, Albert F.	Oct 9	6	1
Englemann, Mrs. Hugh B.	Jul 3	4	2
Ernst, Edwin F.	Dec 11	8	1
Everett, Leonard (Red)	Mar 6	1	1
Everett, Leonard D.	Mar 20	1	1
Fine, Charles D. (Jr.)	Feb 7	1	1
Freeman, Clifford W.	Aug 21	6	2
Fuller, Delia K.	Apr 10	6	1
Fullwood, Edward H.	Mar 13	6	2
Fussell, Mrs. J. W. (Willie A.)	Jan 31	1	1
Gaddy, Elijah J.	Jun 5	1	1
Garrett, Mrs. William G.	Aug 7	1	1
Gatz, Bertha	Aug 21	1	1
Gaywood, Mrs. J. G. (Dora)	Mar 20	6	1
Goode, J.	Mar 6	6	2
Gottschalk, Gus	Mar 27	6	2

NAME	DATE	PG	SEC
Grantham, Jesse	Apr 3	8	1
Gray, George S.	Sep 18	8	1
Gray, Ralph A.	Aug 21	6	1
Green, Kate L.	Jun 19	4	1
Grona, William	Nov 13	6	2
Hahn, Harry C. (Jr.)	May 29	1	1
Hancock, Albert F.	Mar 27	8	1
Hardin, Mrs. Harris I. (Rosa)	Nov 6	6	2
Harris, Mrs. Artie M.	Nov 6	6	2
Harrison, John M.	Jun 12	3	1
Hauk, Frank J.	Nov 20	1	1
Hawley, James L (Dr.)	Oct 22	6	1
Holden, Mary F.	Sep 25	6	2
Hollier, Aduet D.	Sep 4	6	1
Hollomon, R. E.	Oct 9	6	2
Honse, Mrs. Frank	Jul 3	8	1
Hopkins, Mrs. M. L.	Nov 13	8	1
Hough, Annie	Jan 3	6	1
Howell, Mrs. Jim	Apr 10	3	3
Hurlburt, Mrs. B. E.	Sep 4	6	1
Hutchinson, Frederick M.	Apr 17	1	1
Hyde, Joe	Jul 24	6	2
Ingram, Adelbert (Star)	Jun 26	7	1
Johnson, Eleanor L.	Mar 20	8	1
Johnson, Harold	Oct 16	1	1
Jung, Thomas	Oct 30	5	2
Keidel, Felix (Dr.)	Nov 13	6	2
Keidel, Victor (Dr.)	Nov 13	6	2
Kelly, John J.	Jun 12	1	1
Keys, Jess	Oct 30	7	2
King, Mrs. Austin	Apr 3	5	1
King, Mrs. Rufus	Apr 3	1	1
Knopp, Richard W.	Aug 14	8	1
Kurtz, Albert W.	Sep 11	6	1
Lackey, Franklin (Bo)	Mar 6	1	2
Lamoreauz, Leslie W.	Dec 11	8	1
Larnard, Ray R.	Nov 27	1	1
Lawson, Mary J.	Feb 21	4	1
Le Clere, L. P.	Nov 6	8	1
Lemaux, I. W.	May 15	1	1

NAME	DATE	PG	SEC
Lochte, Charles M.	Jan 3	6	1
Marcho, James H.	Aug 14	4	1
May, Mrs. Elmo P.	Jan 10	8	1
Mc Donnold, Irenos G.	Mar 20	5	2
Mc Grew, Ode	Dec 11	8	1
Mc Kean, Mariertta	Oct 16	8	1
Miller, Charlie R.	Jan 24	1	1
Miller, E. H.	Jul 10	6	2
Miller, Robert S.	Jan 17	8	1
Molesworth, Mrs. M. M.	Jul 10	6	2
Morriss, Robert H.	Jun 5	1	1
Morrow, Leonard A. (Jr.)	Nov 13	8	1
Mullinax, P. H.	Oct 30	7	1
Murdock, A. E.	Jul 24	1	1
Nance, John A.	Dec 25	1	1
Neimann, Mrs. C. H.	Oct 2	6	1
Nelson, Frank C.	Jul 17	4	1
Oakes, Harriet E.	Jan 3	6	1
Odena, C. T.	Apr 10	6	1
Padgett, Mrs. Carl	Jun 5	8	2
Pearson, Jeanie S.	Jun 5	8	1
Pickard, Matthew W. (Dr.)	Jan 3	5	1
Plant, Wesley	Mar 6	3	2
Pressler, Kurt	Apr 10	3	3
Price, William H. (Rev.)	Nov 6	8	1
Rabalais, Milton P.	Sep 11	1	1
Ransleben, Max	Aug 21	5	1
Rice, J. C.	May 1	2	2
Richards, Frank	Jan 17	1	1
Robertson, Mrs. T. H.	Jul 24	8	1
Rogers, Rose A.	Oct 22	8	1
Rose, Mary I.	Mar 27	8	1
Rosemund, Robert	Jan 3	5	1
Russell, Aldora O.	Feb 28	8	1
Schafner, Alice	Jun 26	7	1
Shafer, Mrs. E. C.	Jun 5	3	1
Shearn, Mrs. Charles P.	Jan 24	1	1
Shepherd, William B.	May 1	8	1
Skillin, Marjorie E.	Jul 31	7	1
Smith, Walter L.	Feb 21	8	1

1952
Film Roll #29

NAME	DATE	PG	SEC
Sparks, Herman	Apr 17	1	1
Stapp, Chester	May 8	8	1
Stevenson, Mrs. S. V.	Feb 14	8	1
Stoetzner, Mrs. W. U.	Jun 12	8	1
Sullivan, George	Apr 10	6	1
Sullivan, George C.	Apr 10	8	1
Tarum, Sever M.	Jan 31	6	1
Taylor, Joseph P.	Jun 26	1	1
Terry, Jay A.	Feb 7	8	1
Thompson, Henry G. (Thanks)	Apr 10	6	1
Trotter, Clinton P.	Sep 18	5	1
Tyner, David W.	May 8	8	1
Viles, Charles	Feb 7	8	2
Walker, Howard T.	May 29	4	1
Ward, Mrs. Benjamin Q.	Jul 17	6	2
Whetstone, Dee H.	Aug 21	5	1
White, Mrs. John S.	Sep 11	6	1
Wille, David C.	May 1	1	1
Williams, Henry E.	Apr 10	8	1
Williams, Mrs. H. E.	May 8	6	2
Williams, Mrs. Henry	Dec 25	8	1
Williams, Orillian	Nov 6	8	1
Wilson, Mrs. Jack	May 15	2	2
Withers, Lloyd L.	Nov 20	1	1
Wootton, Saleta	Dec 11	8	1
Yates, William H.	Sep 25	1	1
York, Mary J.	Jun 19	5	1

1953
Film Roll #30

Allen, J. T.	Jul 23	1	1
Allen, John E.	Mar 12	8	2
Anderson, Wayne C. (Ted)	Jan 8	6	2
Antoine, Mrs. Herbert J.	Sep 17	6	2
Ard, George	Jul 23	6	2
Baker, Allen Ray	Oct 8	1	1
Barrow, Annie Sterling	Dec 17	7	1
Basse, Mrs. F. C.	Jan 1	6	1

NAME	DATE	PG	SEC
Beaver, Leonard H.	Oct 15	4	1
Beaver, Leonard Harrison	Oct 22	4	1
Beaver, Mary Elizabeth	Apr 16	5	2
Bernar, Mrs. Eugene	Mar 5	8	1
Bingle, Roy Carter	Oct 8	4	1
Blankkolb, Jerry Le Roy	Oct 29	1	1
Blanks, Theodore,	Jan 22	5	2
Block, Herman (Dr.)	Jul 9	8	1
Blount, William Buck	Aug 6	8	1
Boatright, Floyd	Dec 3	4	1
Brasier, Frederick (Rev.)	Sep 24	6	2
Brink, Mehl Oran	Feb 26	5	1
Buchanan, Mrs. John Stark	Jul 16	8	1
Burney, Ivy H.	Jun 25	2	2
Butler, John R.	Oct 29	7	1
Campbell, J. W. (Rev.-picture)	Jan 22	8	1
Campbell, Jospeh W. (Rev.)	Jan 22	6	2
Carson, Allen	Jan 1	6	1
Childs, Mrs. W. B.	Aug 13	2	2
Clark, Cathy Kay	Oct 8	1	1
Cleveland, Mrs. R. S. (Della W.)	Feb 26	1	1
Coleman, Emily	Sep 17	4	1
Conn, Walter	Jul 2	8	1
Cooke, Mary Abigail	Sep 17	6	2
Council, twin son of E. A.	Dec 17	5	1
Cox, Claude Lano (Jr.)	Apr 30	5	1
Cross, Frank C.	Mar 19	2	2
Crotty, Charles	Jan 22	5	2
Crow, Eula Denman	Dec 24	8	1
Crow, Pascal C.	Dec 31	8	1
De Long, Maurine	Feb 5	8	1
Dobbs, Mollie Witt	Nov 12	4	1
Doss, Joe	Oct 15	7	1
Dowdy, Mrs. Lee Ella	Feb 19	1	1
Duberly, C. C.	Mar 5	8	1
Dubose, Mrs. E. M.	Dec 3	8	1
Edens, Hugh C.	May 21	3	2
Edens, Tabitha Jane	Sep 3	6	2
Eikel, Charles	Mar 5	6	2
Elkins, Frank R.	Jun 18	6	2

1953
Film Roll #30

NAME	DATE	PG	SEC
Ellisor, G. C.	May 28	7	1
Emsley, William Rosson	Aug 6	6	1
Ewing, Estelle	Oct 22	6	2
Fairchild, Ellis	May 14	1	1
Featherston, Billy Ray	Sep 3	6	2
Featherston, Mrs, Floyd	Sep 3	6	2
Fenton, Mrs. G. P.	Mar 5	8	1
Fisch, James Albert	Feb 19	7	1
Flores, Mrs. Gorgonio	Jan 8	7	1
Flowler, J. L. (Dr.)	Apr 16	6	2
Fowler, Nannie	Feb 12	4	1
Frederich, Louis T.	Mar 19	8	1
Gaddy, Margaret E.	Oct 22	6	2
Gammon, Ola B.	Dec 31	1	1
Garrett, George (Dr.)	Apr 16	8	1
Gerner, Frank William	Dec 24	8	1
Gilliam, Mrs. B. L.	Aug 13	6	1
Gold, Mrs. Adolph (nee Saenger)	Oct 22	6	2
Goodner, Alice	Mar 19	8	2
Gray, Jim	Dec 17	5	1
Gregorie, Effa E.	Jan 1	6	2
Griffin, John Henry	Apr 23	8	1
Haby, George	Oct 1	1	1
Hall, Dee Cory	Sep 3	1	1
Hall, Mrs. Kirk	Jun 11	6	2
Hall, William D (Jr.)	Jul 9	5	1
Heckler, C. E. (Sr.)	Jun 25	8	1
Henderson, Charles A.	Oct 15	1	1
Henke, Mrs. Otto	Dec 17	1	1
Higgins, Merydith A.	Feb 12	1	1
Hoffman, Mrs. Fred G.	Apr 16	8	1
Hyde, Mrs. Mack	Jul 30	1	1
Inscore, Mrs. R. D.	Jan 22	4	2
James, Grover Cleveland	Dec 17	1	1
Jung, Anna	Mar 26	4	2
Kaberkorn, Mrs. A. H.	Sep 24	8	1
Knight, Lee	May 7	8	1
Knight, Luther J. (Jr.)	Sep 17	8	1
Kowalski, Mrs. Sylvester	Jun 4	1	1
Kuenstler, John Albert	Dec 24	8	1

NAME	DATE	PG	SEC
Lackey, Levonne	Jan 15	8	1
Laney, L. K.	Nov 12	6	2
Latham, Fannie M.	May 28	4	1
Leaser, Solon Chase	Mar 26	7	1
Le Meilleur, Bonnie	Jan 15	8	1
Lewis, Mrs. Alonzo	Jun 11	8	1
Lewis, Samuel W.	Dec 10	8	1
Little, Willis B.	Sep 3	8	1
Lowery, John T.	Feb 5	8	1
Lowrance, Jim	Jul 23	1	1
Lowrance, Mrs. Joe	Oct 15	6	2
Maerchy, Mrs. P. G.	Apr 16	8	1
Mang, A. M.	Feb 19	8	1
Mangum, Jesse H.	Feb 19	5	1
Mangum, Mrs. Jesse H.	Feb 19	5	1
Marquardts, Kenneth Glen (Jr.)	May 28	8	1
Matthews, Mrs. Thomas Edgar	May 21	2	2
Mayeaux, Mrs. Isaac	Oct 22	7	1
Mc Bryde, Mrs. J. A. (Thanks)	Mar 5	4	1
Mc Gillivray, Winfield S.	May 28	4	1
Mc Lendon, William	Jan 1	6	1
Miller, Alfred	Apr 16	8	1
Mitchamore, son of Calvin Glenn	Oct 8	7	1
Morgan, Edward P.	Dec 31	4	2
Morris, Mrs. Charles	May 28	6	2
Morris, Charles Edward	Jan 15	1	1
Morriss, Carl Adam	Jan 31	1	1
Morrow, Mrs. Will	May 7	8	1
Mosby, Popie	Jan 8	5	1
Murphy, William (Pat)	Oct 8	8	1
Musgrave, Florence Cox	Sep 24	8	1
Neill, Mrs. Alexander	Mar 26	8	1
New, Liberty L. (Thanks)	Nov 26	5	1
Newberry, R. W.	Jan 22	6	1
Newman, Leathy Emeline	Feb 26	8	1
O'Connor, Mrs. S. W.	Jul 30	8	1
Oliver, J. R.	Jul 2	3	2
Osborne, Juanita	Apr 3	1	1
Page, Ruben Alvin	Nov 12	3	1
Parish, Ariel Robert	Oct 1	4	1

NAME	DATE	PG	SEC
Parsons, George W.	Feb 5	8	1
Pearson, Lourena	Nov 19	8	1
Pennick, Rosa	May 28	6	1
Perry, James L.	Sep 3	8	1
Peterson, Charles V.	Dec 31	1	1
Phillips, Nettie May	Jul 30	8	1
Phillips, Russell Albert	Sep 17	7	1
Phillips, Mrs. Stanley	Jun 18	7	1
Phillips, Mrs. Stanley	Jul 2	5	1
Plumb, Mrs. Lessie Richardson	Sep 17	4	1
Porche, Clement Douglas	Feb 12	6	2
Prade, Earl Thomas	Jun 4	6	2
Roach, Mrs. Lorraine Kott	Jul 9	6	2
Radeleff, Fritz	Mar 26	1	1
Ragsdale, Tolman (Rev.)	Feb 19	7	1
Reader, Mrs. T. E.	Oct 29	7	1
Rees, Mrs. Daniel Richard (Ellen)	Nov 19	8	1
Reves, Jewel	Apr 30	8	1
Rhea, Ada L.	Oct 29	6	2
Robertson, Salonia	Oct 8	4	1
Robinson, Henrietta	Jan 8	4	1
Rose, Ellen Sarah	Dec 24	8	1
Rowland, Cornelius T. (Dr.)	Jan 8	7	1
Russell, Ammons B.	Feb 12	1	1
Rylander, Mrs. W. E.	Feb 26	1	1
Saul, Mrs. J. H.	Apr 30	5	1
Schmidt, Erna Edna	Feb 12	1	1
Schwiening, Fred (Sr.)	Oct 22	6	2
Simpson, Frank Ford	Aug 20	1	1
Skaggs, Lee Andrew	Apr 3	1	1
Slater, Morris Thompson	Oct 15	8	1
Smith, George Word	Mar 5	6	2
Smith, Luke Payton	Oct 22	7	1
Snow, mother of Bob	Mar 12	7	1
Spangler, Magdalene	Jan 8	7	1
Spayton, son of Richard	May 7	6	2
Splawn, William Baxter	Apr 30	1	1
Stahl, Mary	Jun 25	7	1
Stapp, Dillard F.	Mar 12	8	1
Stehling, Mrs. Joseph	Oct 29	8	1

NAME	DATE	PG	SEC
Stevens, Mrs. Quill	Feb 19	1	1
Steves, Mrs. Allen	Sep 17	1	1
Stone, Mrs. Raymond C.	Jan 1	6	1
Stubeman, Alma	Dec 17	6	2
Surber, Mrs. Quincy	Jan 29	8	1
Swenson, Mrs. Wallace (Betty Davis)	Sep 24	1	1
Tanksly, Marshall E.	Jul 30	1	1
Taylor, Beal D.	Apr 23	4	2
Taylor, Pauline	Jan 22	8	1
Taylor, William Arthur	Sep 17	8	1
Tobin, Mrs. W. G.	Dee 31	4	2
Toler, Effie Dell	Dec 3	6	2
Tomlinson, Tina Patricia	Feb 19	6	2
Tompkins, Herbert A.	Oct 29	1	1
Wachter, Henry Emil	Jul 23	8	1
Walden, Donald Orford	Oct 29	4	1
Walker, Russell G.	Apr 23	8	1
Wall, Ora Belle	Nov 12	8	1
Wallace, Lee	Jul 9	1	1
Walters, Mrs. L. A.	Dec 3	8	1
Washburn, Shirley Jane	Oct 1	1	1
Weiss, Flora Dietert (Memorial)	May 21	3	1
Weiss, Mrs. Henry	Apr 23	1	1
Weir, Horace	Jun 25	8	2
Wheat, C. E. (Rev.)	Feb 5	6	2
White, Oscar A.	Feb 12	6	2
Whitley, Mrs. Edgar L.	Apr 16	4	2
Wilhelm, John Samuel	Feb 26	1	1
Wilson, Adam (3rd)	Jul 16	1	1
Wilson, Thomas C.	Jul 30	8	1
Woolsey, Samuel D.	Apr 9	5	1
Young, John Estle	May 21	1	1
Young, Wilber Y.	Jun 18	8	1
Young, Willis D.	Oct 15	4	1

1954
Film Roll #31

Adam, William Charles	Jul 1	6	2

NAME	DATE	PG	SEC
Allerkamp, Elsa	Sep 2	8	1
Anthony, Joe M.	Feb 18	5	2
Aubey, Victor	Jul 29	6	2
Barfield, mother of Mrs. Edwin	Dec 2	5	1
Barker, Andrew C.	Feb 11	6	2
Barnes, Nellie	Dec 9	1	1
Benedict, Bolton Osborn	Jul 29	5	2
Berryman, J. H.	Jul 29	6	2
Bierschwale, James Louis	Oct 28	7	1
Billnitzer, M. A.	Jun 10	8	2
Bird, Mattie	Nov 13	4	1
Black, Axel J. (Dr.)	Feb 18	1	1
Blaschke, Herman Rudolph	Nov 11	4	1
Bolt, Mrs. S. J.	Sep 9	8	1
Bonner, John Milford	Apr 22	1	1
Brailey, Lena	Jul 29	1	1
Brewer, Lafayette W.	Jan 21	6	1
Brigance, Charles L.	Oct 14	6	2
Brooks, Charles Spurgeon	Dec 23	8	1
Brown, Mason Cooper	Apr 22	5	1
Brown, Riley	Aug 5	6	2
Brown, Sarah Alice	Jul 8	5	1
Bundick, Louis	May 13	8	1
Burke, Nettie Jane	Nov 18	8	2
Burney, Mrs. D. (Ora Stone)	Dec 30	1	1
Burney, Mrs. Joel	Aug 26	8	1
Burney, John W.	Feb 18	1	1
Burney, Lee	Oct 28	1	1
Burrow, L. R.	Feb 18	4	1
Butcher, Sallie	Sep 2	8	1
Butt, Florence Thornton (Mrs. C. C.)	Mar 11	1	1
Caddell, Mrs. Ralph	Jul 8	1	1
Carr, Mrs. Jack (Jr) (Annabel P.)	Dec 23	1	1
Chamberlain, James Watt	Aug 12	7	1
Chambers, Herbert Lofton	Mar 11	6	2
Chism, Glen	Jan 14	7	1
Chisum, Mrs. Lee Della	Jul 15	3	2
Cleveland, brother of W. D.	Jan 14	7	1
Cocke, Frederick Frank	Jan 21	4	1
Colcord, Mrs. Vinson	Aug 5	8	1

1954
Film Roll #31

NAME	DATE	PG	SEC
Colbath, Mrs. Gus	Sep 23	6	2
Coleman, Walter C.	Dec 23	1	1
Cooke, Sidney	Jul 1	8	1
Cornett, Kate	Jul 22	8	1
Covert, Clarence Charles	Jan 28	6	2
Cravens, Thomas E.	May 13	7	1
Crider, Walter H.	Jun 24	1	1
Crider, William F.	Jun 10	4	1
Cruse, H. H.	Oct 28	5	1
Dale, Mrs. Goerge	Feb 4	6	2
Darby, Mrs. J. W.	Dec 2	1	1
Davis, Mrs. H. L.	Jan 28	3	2
Dent, J. J.	Jul 8	1	1
De Vogelee, Kate	Mar 23	6	2
Dollar, Tom Lamar	Apr 22	7	1
Domingues, Polycarp Joseph (Dr.)	Jun 3	5	2
Dommert, Amel Felix	Jun 17	8	1
Dorn, Victor R.	Oct 7	4	1
Doughty, Henry A.	May 13	7	1
Dowdy, Mary Arminata	May 20	4	1
Downard, Hiram	Feb 4	1	1
Duran, Mike Garcia	Aug 5	1	1
Edens, Lester L	Jun 3	8	1
Elliott, Andrew J.	Dec 30	6	1
Emmericks, George H.	Nov 25	8	2
Endress, Frank X.	Apr 15	6	2
Farr, Harold Kenneth	Apr 8	1	1
Font, Joseph Carl	Dec 16	1	1
Fruge, William Robert	Nov 13	1/8	1
Fuchs, Anna	Apr 15	6	2
Gill, Mrs. Ben H.	Oct 24	6	2
Gilmore, John	Nov 18	4	1
Glenn, William J.	Jul 22	6	2
Gold, Emil	Aug 26	1	1
Goss, Oliver William	Oct 24	8	1
Graham, Presley	Jul 1	8	1
Grasty, J. Milton	Dec 23	8	1
Green, Mrs. E. H.	May 6	1	1
Green, Mrs. Will (Thanks)	Feb 11	7	1
Griffin, John Edward	Sep 23	4	2

168

1954
Film Roll #31

NAME	DATE	PG	SEC
Griffith, Mrs. M. V	Jan 28	6	2
Guthrie, Rosa Jane	Feb 11	4	2
Haggerton, Mrs. Willie	May 20	8	1
Haines, Jane Louise	Aug 19	6	2
Hallmark, Addie	Dec 16	7	1
Hamilton, Hal Andrew	Sep 23	6	2
Hampson, John	Sep 16	6	2
Harmon, Mc Minn	Sep 30	8	1
Haney, Mrs. George A. (May Estes)	Nov 18	1/8	1
Harris, John Sidney	Jul 15	1	1
Harrison, Elizabeth Welborn	Aug 19	6	2
Harrison, Harry	Nov 25	8	2
Hawkins, Agnes	Nov 25	8	1
Hays, Robert S.	Jun 10	1	1
Henke, Otto	May 27	4	1
Hirsch, Mrs. Arthur	Jan 8	8	1
Holcomb, Afton Eli	May 13	8	1
Holcomb, Jeffery Lea	Jun 3	4	1
Holdsworth, Ernest	Dec 2	8	1
Hood, James O.	Jan 21	1/6	1
Horn, James Edwin	Dec 30	2	2
Horn, John	Dec 23	7	1
Hornbeck, Hallie	Nov 4	6	2
Howard, Alice	Dec 30	6	1
Humphries, Sam	Apr 22	6	2
Humphries, W. S.	Dec 30	1	1
Hyde, Theodore Marion (Mack)	Jun 24	1	1
Irving, Mrs. Richard	Apr 8	5	1
James, Grover C. (Bud)	Jan 8	2	1
Jetton, William Franklin	Jul 8	8	1
Joekel, Samuel (Dr.)	Nov 18	6	2
Johnson, Gary Lester	Mar 11	3	2
Jones, Edward Lake (Dr.)	Jul 15	1	1
Jones, Mrs. Harlan	Jul 29	6	2
Jones, Mrs. Millard E.	Sep 23	1	1
Jung, Mrs. C. D.	Jul 15	1/6	2
Keidel, Mrs. Victor	Mar 11	7	1
Keirsey, Parham J.	Jun 3	8	1
Kellam, Walter Lee	May 13	7	1
Kensing, Alvin	Aug 5	8	1

169

NAME	DATE	PG	SEC
Kime, Mrs. Leonard L.	Sep 16	7	1
Klenefelter, Mary	Oct 7	5	2
Koehler, Mrs. L. H. (George)	Jan 14	1/7	1
Kott, Albert	May 20	1	1
Lancaster, Mary Jane	Apr 8	1	1
Lane, Virgil	Jul 15	6	2
Langford, Bertha	Jun 3	2	2
Lee, John William	Sep 2	8	1
Linesetter, George F.	Nov 25	1	1
Lock, Lonnie L.	May 6	1	1
Madrid, Luisa	Nov 11	4	2
Mangold, Mrs. James (Mathilda S.)	Mar 23	2	2
Manning, John P.	Nov 4	6	2
Masters, John D.	Oct 28	1	1
Mc Caleb, Mrs. John	Sep 23	6	2
Mc Clister, William H.	Feb 11	8	1
Mc Donald, Mrs. C. C.	Jul 29	8	1
Mc Kenzie, Frank P.	May 6	7	1
Meek, Will V.	Jul 15	6	2
Meek, Mrs. Will V.	Mar 11	6	2
Meeker, Mrs. E. C.	May 6	8	1
Merritt, Burkett Foster	Feb 25	1	1
Meyers, Josephine Mary	Feb 25	6	2
Miers, George Henry	Apr 1	1	1
Miller, Mrs. Jess (Evelyn Brown)	Jun 24	5	1
Mitschke, Emma	Jan 28	4	2
Montgomery, Mrs. J. B.	Nov 11	3	1
Moore, Samuel Elmer	Mar 23	2	1
Morris, John S.	Mar 18	4	1
Mosel, William James	May 6	8	1
Moseley, John Garrison	Apr 1	1	1
Moseley, Willard R.	Jul 15	6	2
Mueller, Mrs. Eveanor Clifford	Feb 18	8	1
Nance, F. D. (Fats)	Feb 18	8	1
Nelson, Kitty	Aug 5	5	1
Nichols, Mrs. John Wesley (Annie)	Feb 11	1	1
Norman, James Lee	Oct 28	7	1
Norton, Clark W.	Sep 9	8	2
O'Bryant, Arlie Herbert	Nov 18	1/8	1
Oehler, Henry	May 20	4	1

1954
Film Roll #31

NAME	DATE	PG	SEC
Page, Aubrey Basil	Jun 24	5	1
Page, Mrs. Eli	Nov 25	5	1
Page, Mrs. J. E.	Sep 9	8	2
Parker, Clyde A. (Dr.)	Apr 22	7	1
Parker, Herbert Delbert	Aug 19	8	1
Parsons, Mrs. Bert C.	Jan 21	1	1
Paton, Mary	Oct 28	6	2
Perry, Mordello Stephen (Mott)	Feb 11	7	1
Peterson, Norris J.	Jul 29	7	1
Pickens, Thomas L.	Jul 22	1	1
Ponton, Mrs. Elmer	Dec 23	8	1
Powell, Harcourt Ormsby	Feb 4	6	1
Raiford, Rex	Sep 2	1	1
Raiford, Rex Aubrey	Sep 30	1	1
Raiford, Rex Aubrey	Oct 7	4	1
Ramsey, Orin Palmer	Nov 18	1	1
Ramsey, Mrs. Orin P.	Nov 18	1	1
Rankin, James	May 6	4	2
Ray, James	Apr 8	1	1
Ray, James	May 6	4	1
Raymond, William H.	Feb 11	6	2
Reeves, Delmore C.	May 6	6	2
Remschel, Jule	Aug 26	8	1
Retherford, Mrs. D. Jack	Mar 11	1	1
Robert, William C.	Mar 23	1	1
Roberts, L. B. (Col.)	Jan 21	5	1
Roberts, Leo B. (Col.)	Jan 28	8	1
Roberts, Lesley Wayne	Jun 10	8	2
Roe, William Robert	Apr 29	7	1
Rosenblatt, Joseph D.	Jul 29	7	1
Ruse, Edward Eugene	Dec 30	5	1
Schmidt, Charles	Jun 3	3	1
Schuh, John	Jul 1	4	2
Self, Alonzo E.	Mar 4	1	1
Shand, Robert F.	Jun 10	5	1
Shaw, Mrs. Vernon	Jun 10	3	2
Shudde, Mrs. Herbert George	Aug 12	6	2
Smith, Reed P.	Nov 11	8	1
Snelgrove, Mrs. George	Oct 28	6	2
Sparks, Oscar	May 13	1	1

NAME	DATE	PG	SEC
Spencer, Mrs. E. S.	Feb 18	3	2
Springall, Mrs. Herbert	Aug 26	6	2
Stark, Mrs. Irwin J.	Aug 26	6	2
Starkey, James J.	Oct 28	1	1
Starr, Harry Augustus	Jun 10	8	2
Sterling, Effie Bell	Jan 14	8	1
Stewart, Mrs. Jack A. (Pauline M.)	Jan 28	6	2
Stewart, James	May 13	8	1
Stone, Everett H.	May 6	8	1
Stone, Hazel	Nov 11	1	1
Stover, Mrs. J. A.	Feb 18	6	2
Strange, Walter Harris	Jan 14	8	1
Sullivan, Sallie	Feb 18	5	1
Surber, Maud Witt	Feb 4	5	1
Tanner, Mrs. J. R.	Jul 29	7	1
Tanner, Joseph Reed	Aug 19	8	1
Taylor, Johnny Thomas	May 20	5	1
Thompson, Ernest J.	Nov 25	8	1
Tilbury, Mrs. L. C.	Jun 10	8	1
Toups, William Joseph	Sep 30	8	1
Tracy, W. C. (Dick)	Feb 11	8	1
Trautschold, Carrie M.	Jul 8	1	1
Trautschold, F. B.	Mar 18	3	1
Traywick, Herbert	Jun 3	8	1
Trushel, Gus	Jun 24	8	1
Wachter, Mary	May 20	1	1
Walker, Ganahl	Apr 22	7	1
Walker, George P.	Nov 11	1	1
Walters, Eugene C.	Mar 4	8	1
Webener, B. H.	Feb 18	7	1
Wehmyer, Mrs. Alvin A. (Georgia)	Apr 15	8	1
Welch, Melvin E.	Jan 21	1	1
Wellborn, Mrs. Ernest	Oct 14	8	1
Wells, Mrs. Joe (Thanks)	Jun 10	7	1
Wells, Mrs. Monroe M.	May 27	8	1
Wemple, Mrs. J. D.	Aug 12	4	2
Whitehurst, Mrs. E. M.	Dec 2	8	1
Whittington, J. W.	Oct 24	8	1
Young, R. F.	Apr 8	6	1
Youngblood, Mrs. U. S.	Mar 4	6	2

1954
Film Roll #31

NAME	DATE	PG	SEC
Wheaton, Mrs. J. A.	Jan 14	8	1
White, Frank E.	Sep 23	1	1
Williams, Mrs. Norman	Apr 22	4	1
Wright, Eugene W.	Jan 21	6	1

1955
Film Roll #32

When photocopied, there are some papers where pages 1
through 4 of Section one were copied, then Section 2
pages 1 through 6/8, THEN page 5 through 8 of Section 1.
This will cause a lot of confusion in hunting the death
notice. They are listed here in the correct section of
each paper.

NAME	DATE	PG	SEC
Abbott, Morris Foster	Oct 13	8	1
Adams, Hearne Oliver	Oct 13	3	1
Allen, Lewis Raymond	Jan 6	6	1
Alley, James Thomas	Jan 27	6	2
Allsup, Mathilda	Feb 10	4	1
Anderson, Frank S.	Apr 28	1	1
Anderson, Lewis	Jan 6	1	1
Baker, Ivy Wright	Feb 10	8	1
Baldwin, William Howard	Oct 6	8	1
Ball, Roscoe C.	Dec 29	1	1
Bartley, J. T.	Mar 31	5	1
Bell, Willie Ella	Feb 17	6	2
Bellknap, Anna Pauline	Jun 23	4	1
Blackwood, David	Mar 24	1	1
Blackwood, Rose Nell	Apr 7	8	1
Bogle, James George	Jun 30	5	1
Boyer, Mrs. L. W.	Dec 22	4	3
Bradferd, Zella	Nov 17	8	2
Bratton, Mrs. J. C.	Jul 21	7	1
Brown, James W.	Dec 29	6	1
Bryant, J. L. (Rev.)	Oct 27	5	1
Buelow, Frank	Sep 29	1	1

NAME	DATE	PG	SEC
Burleson, Alfred Osborn	Dec 29	3	2
Butcher, Dona	Feb 24	6	2
Cade, Mrs. G. P.	Mar 10	8	1
Calcott, Mrs. Herbert H.	Aug 25	5	1
Camp, Ella	Feb 24	8	1
Campbell, John Craig (Rev.)	Dec 29	1	1
Cantwell, Mark Bean	Mar 24	1	1
Carey, James William	May 12	8	1
Cartwright, Mrs. Cecil Moore	Apr 21	4	1
Cartwright, Othea Elizabeth	May 19	6	2
Clarke, Bruce Tefft	Sep 15	8	2
Clayton, Emma	Dec 1	8	1
Cobb, William	Aug 18	8	1
Codrington, Thomas P.	Jan 13	2	2
Coldwell, Neal Vernon	Aug 25	6	2
Collins, Preston J. (Press)	Apr 7	7	1
Combs, Henry L.	Aug 25	4	1
Copple, Rachael Rosanna	Jun 16	6	2
Countre, Alois	Feb 24	8	1
Cowan, Mrs. M. W.	Jun 30	8	2
Craig, J. M.	Nov 24	8	1
Daniel, Walton	Aug 4	1	1
Davis, Lucy S.	Jan 20	6	2
Davey, Myrtle	Mar 24	8	1
De Coux, Mrs. Edward	Jan 27	5	2
Delaney, Mrs. J. J.	Sep 15	1	1
Dietert, Mrs. Emil	Dec 29	1	1
Dismukes, Mrs. C. M.	Feb 24	1	1
Doebbler, Mrs. Edgar	Mar 17	7	1
Dunks, Ira	Feb 3	5	1
Dunlap, Mrs. E. H.	Jul 7	6	1
Eakin, Ira Cleveland	Dec 1	8	2
Eckstein, Charles	Jun 30	1	1
Edwards, Charles	Jun 9	8	1
Ellison, Minnie Alma	Dec 1	8	1
Etie, William (Jr.)	Nov 3	5	1
Evers, Mrs. Otto	Aug 11	6	2
Fettro, Verner E.	Jan 20	7	1
Field, Mary	Dec 15	8	2
Furhmann, Felix	Dec 15	8	2

NAME	DATE	PG	SEC
Fussell, J. W. (Dr.)	Mar 10	1	1
Gabler, Arthur A.	Sep 1	1	1
Gardner, Georgia S.	Sep 15	1	1
Gerber, Anna Kallum	Feb 24	8	1
Gleason, Gretchen Gene	Jan 13	6	1
Glenn, Archie Le Roy	Sep 29	8	1
Gonzales, Mrs. Urbano	Dec 1	8	2
Graham, Elihu	Apr 7	8	1
Grantham, Mrs. Jesse	Dec 1	8	2
Granville, Chester W.	Jul 14	4	1
Guerrero, Pedro	Dec 8	6	2
Guidry, Russell J.	Nov 24	8	1
Guiterrez, Estaban	Nov 24	1	1
Guiterrez, Rosa Castillo	Nov 24	1	1
Guiterrez, Santos	Nov 24	1	1
Haby, Joseph Leo	Dec 15	8	2
Hamby, James W.	Jan 6	1	1
Hamer, Frank	Jul 14	2	2
Hamilton, Mauline (Thanks)	Mar 10	3	1
Hamilton, Mrs. Thomas C.	Feb 24	1	1
Happel, James (Dr.)	Nov 17	2	1
Hardin, Charles Thomas	Dec 29	3	2
Harper, Herman	Jul 28	1	1
Harris, Henry	May 12	1	1
Harris, Mrs. Newton	Aug 11	6	2
Hart, Mrs. Irving H.	Jul 14	8	1
Harter, William J.	Aug 25	6	1
Haynes, Mrs. M. D.	Jan 20	5	1
Heimann, Mrs. George	Apr 21	7	1
Henderson, Joseph E. (Ed)	Sep 22	1	1
Henke, Otto	Sep 29	8	1
Hill, Cleve C.	Sep 8	5	2
Hill, Thomas Watt	Sep 29	8	1
Hiller, D. A.	Jan 20	6	2
Holekamp, Moritz	Feb 10	1	1
Hubener, Peter Joseph	Nov 24	8	1
Huddle, Marion D.	Nov 24	8	1
Hyde, John Benjamin	Apr 28	7	1
James, Mrs. A. E.	Nov 3	8	1
James, Frank	Jun 9	6	2

NAME	DATE	PG	SEC
James, Helen	Dec 1	8	1
Jinnett, Mrs. Joseph	Nov 10	8	1
Johnston, Mary H.	Mar 10	8	1
Jones, Lee W.	May 26	8	1
Jones, W. D. C.	Aug 25	8	1
Jonon, Mrs. Frank	Jul 25	8	1
Jung, Sidney Lee	Aug 18	8	1
Kaiser, Mrs. Ed	Jul 21	7	2
Kalka, Zandy	Dec 1	8	1
Kent, Daisie	Dec 15	8	2
Kneip, Mrs. Roy	May 19	6	2
Koehler, Nancy	Nov 3	5	1
Klugman, Albert E.	Oct 13	6	2
Kramer, Albert	Nov 24	8	1
La Freniere, Joseph Norman	Oct 13	6	2
Lemmons, Walter	Dec 1	8	1
Lewis, Mrs. W. T.	Apr 28	8	1
Lich, Ernst	Feb 3	6	2
Little, J. C.	Oct 27	8	1
Looney, Mrs. Pressie O.	May 5	4	2
Mangum, Joe D.	Jan 6	5	1
Manny, Alfred	Dec 8	6	2
Matthews, W. A.	Oct 20	4	2
Mc Clellan, Clarence Lucien (Dr.)	Sep 22	1	1
Mc Clellan, Donal Meredith	Nov 10	1	1
Mc Elroy, Henry	Apr 21	8	1
Mc Farland, J. P.	Sep 29	4	1
Meadow, Garth Cecil	Apr 7	1	1
Meadow, Mildred Edith	Apr 7	1	1
Meyer, Emil A.	Mar 10	5	1
Meyers, Herman House	Apr 14	1	1
Miller, Frona	Feb 3	1	1
Miller, Frona A.	Feb 10	1	1
Morbly, Harry K.	Mar 24	1	1
Morris, Lewis	Feb 24	8	1
Moyer, Emmett	Feb 3	1	1
Moyer, Emmett E.	Feb 10	1	1
Mullins, Peter J.	Jun 2	8	1
Murphy, Benjamin Wesley	Mar 24	6	2
Neves, Thornton Pool	Nov 24	8	1

NAME	DATE	PG	SEC
Newman, Harris	Jun 2	8	1
Nichols, Rowland	Dec 22	1	1
Noble, Mrs. Clark	Dec 8	6	2
Norton, Maxwell M.	Dec 29	3	2
Nowlin, Oscar	Jan 13	1	1
Nunnally, M. A.	Aug 25	6	2
Oehler, Mrs. Henry	Jun 23	6	2
Orchard, Mrs. C. D.	Dec 1	8	2
Osborne, Paul C.	Jun 30	4	1
Oster, Kenneth E.	Dec 8	8	1
Packard, Mrs. Joe W.	Aug 4	1	1
Page, J. E. (Bud)	Nov 3	8	1
Pankratz, Bodo	Oct 27	8	1
Patton, Mrs. Edward	Oct 20	8	1
Payne, R. E.	Apr 7	8	1
Perkins, Charles Levi	Dec 22	1	1
Perry, Lela E.	Sep 8	6	1
Peterson, Tom G.	Sep 15	8	2
Pfeuffer, Louis George	May 5	6	2
Phelps, Eugene E.	Mar 10	2	2
Pierce, Amber Le	Dec 1	1	1
Pridgeon, Mamie	Aug 25	5	1
Pyron, Ray	Jan 13	1	1
Pyron, Ray	Jan 13	6	1
Raborn, Jesse James	Jan 13	8	2
Read, Mattie Bell	May 12	6	2
Reed, Mrs. William D.	Feb 17	1	1
Rees, Emil	Apr 21	1	1
Rees, James Casper (Tubba)	May 26	8	1
Rees, Nowlin F.	May 26	2	2
Reichenau, John Karl	Jan 13	8	2
Rentz, Mrs. C. W.	Oct 13	1	2
Reynolds, Otis Marion	Oct 13	8	1
Robertson, twins of W. A.	Nov 24	8	1
Robinson, Betty Grey	Sep 1	8	1
Roe, Osro	Mar 17	1	1
Ross, Truett	Aug 18	6	2
Ruse, Mrs. E. E.	Nov 3	8	1
Saenger, Emil Edmund	Jun 16	1	1
Savage, Mattie	Apr 21	7	1

NAME	DATE	PG	SEC
Scholl, Mrs. Henry	Mar 10	8	1
Scholl, Henry F.	Apr 28	7	1
Schupp, Charles H.	May 5	6	2
Schweitzer, Charles L.	Jan 13	1	1
Secrest, Burt	Apr 7	8	1
Shaeffer, Mrs. Miles	Jan 6	6	1
Simpson, George	Apr 14	6	2
Smith, James Henry	Mar 24	6	2
Smith, John Patrick	Jun 2	8	1
Smith, Jopie	Mar 17	8	1
Smith, R. L.	Jul 28	6	2
Smith, Mrs. S. J.	Dec 29	3	2
Sparkman, Claude	Sep 15	7	1
Sproul, Robert A.	Dec 15	1	1
Stapleton, Willie Ann	Jun 9	8	1
Stevens, James Oliver	Apr 21	8	1
Stone, Thelma Jean	Jun 16	1	1
Switzer, Charles Henry	Dec 1	8	2
Taylor, Mrs. Beal D.	Feb 3	6	2
Thalmann, Victor	Oct 27	8	1
Thompson, Benjamin F. (Rev.)	Jan 27	3	2
Townsend, Homer	Apr 28	8	1
Travis, John Preston	Jan 6	6	2
Vaughn, Fred Turley	Jul 14	5	1
Wade, Louis Ernest	Mar 31	3	1
Waid, Grover L.	Sep 8	6	2
Waite, Mrs. Horace	Oct 6	8	1
Walker, Ben Arthur	Dec 8	3	1
Watts, Annie L.	Feb 3	6	1
Weiss, Henry	Dec 29	1	1
West, Mrs. Charles H.	Oct 6	4	1
Wetterling, Mrs. Carl	Mar 24	6	2
Whetstone, Winona Lee	Oct 27	8	1
White, J. D.	Jun 23	4	1
White, John Sidney	Sep 1	8	1
Whitehead, James File	Jun 23	6	2
Whitehouse, John Leslie	Feb 10	1	1
Wickson, Lee Morgan	Jul 7	6	1
Wilkins, Mrs. Leroy (Wanda Lou)	Jan 27	1	1
Williford, Erna Caroline	Nov 24	8	1

1955
Film Roll #32

NAME	DATE	PG	SEC
Wilson, Paul	Jun 2	8	1
Wilson, William W.	Jan 20	1	1
Wood, John	Sep 29	4	1
Woodall, John (Dr.)	Sep 8	6	2
Worthington, Mrs. William H.	May 26	8	2
Wren, Walter	Dec 1	7	1
Yoast, Frank	Apr 7	8	1
Zander, Malcolm	Aug 11	8	1

1956
Film Roll #33

Abrahams, Mauda Virginia	Sep 13	3	1
Adkins, Mrs. Arthur	Jun 28	8	1
Ames, Frank Charles	Apr 5	8	1
Anglin, Walter B.	Jan 5	5	2
Arhelger, Mitchell Rolf	Oct 11	8	1
Arnecke, Valeri Ann	Aug 2	2	2
Auld, William	Jun 28	1	1
Averitt, John W.	Oct 11	8	1
Aydlett, Emma Shelby Thompson	Apr 19	8	1
Bailey, Roy	May 17	1	1
Baldwin, Easter Arizona	Jan 12	6	2
Bartlett, Mrs. W. R.	Nov 29	1	1
Bartlet, Mrs. W. R.	Nov 29	8	2
Barton, Mason A.	Feb 2	6	1
Barton, Mattie	Aug 23	8	1
Barton, Warren H.	Jan 19	6	2
Best, Fred Ernest	Jul 12	6	2
Black, Gena	Apr 26	2	5
Blackburn, John Arthur	Aug 9	8	1
Blacshe, Mrs. M.	Mar 15	4	2
Blakeny, George	Jul 5	3	2
Blevins, Mrs. Ceaman	Nov 29	1/3	1
Bowlin, Jackie Gene	Nov 22	1	1
Boyett, A. P. (Sr.)	Sep 20	8	1
Breen, Elizabeth A.	Sep 6	6	1
Brown, John Hood	Mar 29	4	1
Builta, Mrs. Samuel (Cassie J.)	Aug 16	8	1

NAME	DATE	PG	SEC
Butler, Camma Ida	Apr 19	8	2
Canafux, Bess Hammond	Mar 15	6	2
Cannon, Mrs. ----	Sep 13	8	1
Carson, Robert H.	Sep 13	8	1
Carson, Mrs. W. W.	May 17	4	1
Carpenter, Mrs. Fred	May 3	8	1
Cass, Theodore Roosevelt	Jan 5	4	2
Clarke, Mrs. H. K.	Mar 15	4	2
Collier, Mrs. Morris L.	Feb 23	6	2
Combs, Roy Roscoe	Aug 2	2	2
Cooper, Mrs. J. L.	Oct 11	8	1
Coward, James Burt	Nov 15	1	1
Cowart, Thomas J.	Jun 28	8	1
Cowen, Maggie Lee	Sep 6	1	1
Cowin, Mary	Dec 13	1	1
Cowin, Otto	Dec 13	1	1
Cozby, Harold (Dr.)	Sep 6	1	1
Creager, D. H. (Dr.)	Jan 12	8	1
Crider, Henrietta	Aug 2	2	2
Currie, Mrs. W. G.	Sep 20	2	2
Davis, Albert Eugene	Jul 12	1	1
Davis, Mrs. J. W.	Feb 2	3	1
Deering, Charles Albert	Sep 13	8	1
Deering, Charles Albert	Sep 20	1	1
De Vore, Leonard Lee (Thanks)	Aug 26	2	2
de la Gruz, Tules	Sep 27	1	1
Dietel, William	Aug 23	8	1
Diets, Clara	Dec 27	6	1
Doffing, John Louis	Sep 13	6	2
Drucker, Mrs. Harry	Oct 4	1	1
Edwards, Frank M.	Dec 20	1	1
Ferguson, Thomas P.	Dec 20	4	1
Flach, Mrs. Alfred	Jul 17	3	2
Fransen, Mays David	Nov 29	8	2
Fredspiel, John J.	Dec 13	4	1
Fulwood, Mrs. Edward H.	Oct 25	6	2
Furr, William Henry	Oct 11	1	1
Gaston, George Houston	Apr 5	5	2
Gilmore, Catherine Eva	Jul 12	4	2
Ginnachio, Gus	Jan 5	6	1

NAME	DATE	PG	SEC
Gotcher, Eula	Jul 12	1	1
Graham, Francis Isaac	Aug 16	8	1
Graham, Howard Hall	Dec 27	5	1
Gregg, W. T. D. (Dr.)	Jul 26	4	2
Griffin, Lydia Maulding	Aug 16	3	2
Harbour, Jerry (Dr.)	Nov 8	8	1
Hardy, Robert Lee	May 3	5	2
Harmon, Praze Flinell	Feb 16	6	1
Harris, Burton Bragg	Jan 19	8	1
Harris, Karen Jean	Feb 9	8	1
Harrison, Mrs. E. B.	Jan 12	5	1
Harrison, Harry	Jan 12	5	1
Hartshorn, James H.	Apr 26	3	1
Harwell, William O.	Feb 2	6	1
Hassmann, John	Jun 7	5	2
Haufler, William	May 3	1	1
Heiman, Mrs. Eddie	Mar 22	8	1
Heimann, Renatus G.	Jun 21	5	2
Heiser, Jesse W.	Dec 27	5	1
Herndon, James Robert	Dec 6	8	1
Hillman, Laura Ellen	Jul 5	6	1
Hodges, Mrs. Alfred	Sep 20	6	2
Holdsworth, Patricia	Mar 22	6	2
Holloman, Susie Isora	Nov 29	8	1
Honeycutt, Felicia	Apr 12	8	1
Huddle, William Edgar	May 24	6	1
Ivey, O. C.	Aug 9	2	2
Jacobs, Homer	Aug 23	6	2
Jefferson, John	Nov 29	1	1
Johnson, Frank Phillip	Apr 5	3	2
Johnson, T. I.	Oct 25	4	1
Johnson, Z. B.	Nov 15	8	1
Jordan, Jack	Nov 15	1	1
Kelly, Mrs. Joseph	Aug 2	5	2
Kelton, Samuel Morris	Feb 9	8	1
Kennedy, Albert Finley	May 10	5	2
Kime, Leonard L.	Apr 5	6	2
King, Bland	Mar 1	6	2
Kirkham, Judd H. (Dr.)	Sep 27	1	1
Kliner, Mrs. Harry	Aug 2	7	1

NAME	DATE	PG	SEC
Knopp, Mary L.	Jun 7	7	1
Knox, Mrs. Noah	Apr 19	8	1
Koerth, G. W.	Feb 23	2	1
Kothmann, Mrs. William	Feb 16	8	1
Kramer, Ernest	Apr 5	7	1
Lacey, Mrs. Robert E.	Nov 15	8	1
Lemmons, Ella Elizabeth	Feb 16	4	2
Leonard, Lesa Steel	Sep 20	1	1
Lindsey, Bob (Jr.)	Nov 1	8	1
Loftin, Jmaes O. (Dr.)	Jan 5	1/6	2
Loftin, Mrs. James O.	Jan 5	1/6	2
Long, Joe	May 3	8	1
Lott, Mrs. Gilbert H.	May 3	8	1
Love, P. O.	Sep 20	1	2
Low, Thomas	Dec 20	7	1
Lucas, Joseph D.	Aug 26	5	2
Luther, Doyle Sidney	Jan 5	6	1
Lutz, Emma S.	Mar 8	5	1
Mahaffey, H. O.	Mar 15	5	1
Matthews, Thomas Edgar	Jul 5	4	2
Mc Coy, George Caroll	Dec 6	1	1
Mc Coy, James W.	Sep 6	6	1
Mc Cullough, Mrs. S. L.	Feb 2	1	1
Mc Intosh, Annie	Feb 16	3	1
Mc Nees, Beatrice Young	Jun 28	4	1
Miller, Horace Kite	Nov 29	4	1
Mills, Mrs. Bob (Daisy)	Jul 17	4	2
Moore, John Wesley	Jun 21	6	2
Moore, M. H.	Dec 27	5	1
Moore, Mrs. N. J.	Aug 23	6	2
Morris, Mrs. Hal	Mar 1	4	1
Morris, Will A.	Oct 25	8	1
Morriss, Mrs. R. H.	Feb 23	1	1
Moulder, William M.	Oct 4	1	1
Neal, Robert (Jr.)	Feb 9	1	1
Neundorf, Mrs. F. M.	Feb 23	8	1
Nichols, Elvis	Jan 19	8	1
Noll, Henry	Feb 9	8	1
Norton, Jerry Max	Jun 28	8	1
Nowlin, Robert Crispin	Aug 16	8	1

NAME	DATE	PG	SEC
Nutter, Mrs. Paul M.	May 3	5	2
Pace, Perry (Sr.)	Sep 20	1	1
Pafford, Etta (Louetta)	Jan 5	3	2
Page, George Allen	Jul 17	5	1
Page, Margaret Hadden	Aug 23	6	2
Paine, Reuben Vernon	Mar 29	6	2
Palmer, Mack W.	Mar 15	6	2
Pape, W. O.	Jun 21	8	1
Pearson, Belle	Apr 12	5	2
Pfeister, Edwi;n	Aug 2	8	1
Pickens, Mrs. Stanley	Feb 2	3	1
Pipkin, Charles Grover	Jun 14	6	2
Prochnow, Vimter	Dec 27	1	1
Rogers, Joe J.	Nov 8	5	1
Rotge, Peter	Jul 17	6	2
Rothrock, Mrs. A. M.	Mar 22	8	1
Rusch, Mrs. Frank	Jun 7	6	2
St. Germain, Bert J. (Jr.)	Nov 22	6	2
Samuels, J. W.	Mar 22	8	1
Sandidge, Mrs. G. T.	Jun 7	8	1
Sattler, Adolph	Jul 17	5	2
Schilling, Ronald Royce	Aug 9	2	2
Schleifer, Lena Fannie	Mar 15	8	1
Sharp, Mrs. Daniel E.	Jul 17	6	1
Shaw, J. C.	Sep 13	1	1
Shaw, John C.	Sep 20	1	1
Shinault, Linda Hughes	Jun 21	7	1
Shotwell, Ann Ainsworth	Sep 20	8	1
Smith, A. Q.	Jan 5	6	2
Smith, Houston Newton	Feb 2	6	2
Smith, Richard T.	Nov 29	7	1
Snodgrass, Mary Georgiana	Sep 13	1	1
Solomon, Ralph W.	May 24	6	2
Stevens, Roy T.	Apr 26	5	5
Stone, William L.	Mar 22	1	1
Strange, Mary	Feb 16	7	1
Sublett, MRs. J. J. (Thanks)	Oct 4	5	1
Summers, Fredric (Dr.)	Oct 25	7	1
Surber, Mrs. Clata	Feb 23	4	1
Sutton, Richard Earl	Apr 26	7	5

1956
Film Roll #33

NAME	DATE	PG	SEC
Taylor, Ed C.	Apr 12	4	1
Taylor, Virginia Adeline	Mar 22	8	1
Thaxton, Clara	Jul 17	2	2
Thomas, William	May 17	5	1
Thompson, Sam E. (Dr.)	Jan 19	8	1
Thomas, Frank Neeland	Feb 16	6	2
Tucker, Eliza Ann	Sep 27	8	1
Turner, James Aaron	Apr 23	8	1
Upham, Charles	Aug 9	5	2
Vann, Baxter E.	Feb 23	8	1
Voss, Mary	Feb 16	4	1
Waller, Mrs. August	Mar 8	6	2
Warrener, Mrs. H. A.	Aug 9	3	2
Watson, Walter	Dec 27	3	2
Webster, Harvey Leon	Aug 23	8	1
Westfall, Edward V.	Dec 27	1	1
Wetterling, Carl Cavendish	Mar 22	1	1
Wilbanks, Emma	Jun 14	8	1
Williams, Laura	Sep 27	2	2
Williams, Michael Ray	Jun 14	8	1
Worrell, Lonnie Lee	Sep 20	1	1
Yarborough, Mrs. Ira B.	Feb 2	6	1
Yeager, Ruby	Jul 12	4	2
Young, Paris Sherman	Nov 15	1	1

1957
Film Roll #34

Adams, Lester	Sep 5	6	1
Albaugh, Edward R.	Nov 21	1	1
Alsey, T. A.	Dec 12	3	2
Anderson, H. R.	May 16	6	2
Andrews, Henrietta Lamar	Oct 31	8	1
Annis, Mrs. J. B	Sep 12	5	2
Aven, Mrs. J. M.	Sep 19	2	2
Babb, Louie	Jan 24	8	1
Baethge, Mrs. Hnery (Sr.)	Sep 5	6	1
Baker, Mrs. Marvin	Aug 8	3	2
Balliet, Donald	Jun 27	1	1

184

NAME	DATE	PG	SEC
Balliet, Flavius J.	Jun 27	1	1
Balliet, Robert	Jun 27	1	1
Barton, Nancy Gail	Jan 3	6	1
Beard, John E.	Jan 24	8	1
Beddingfield, James Claude	Oct 17	1	1
Bennett, Karl M.	Dec 12	8	1
Benson, George M.	Apr 4	4	1
Bernhard, William	Sep 26	1	1
Besse, Annette B. (Thanks)	Apr 25	2	2
Boerkoel, John D.	Jun 20	8	1
Brener, Bobbie Jack	Apr 4	1	1
Brandt, Phillip L.	Aug 22	1	1
Brigance, Sarah B.	May 2	6	2
Briscoe, Virgil Lee	May 9	6	2
Brittain, James M.	Oct 31	2	2
Brock, Mrs. Arthur	Sep 26	6	2
Brooks, Nellie C.	Sep 19	6	2
Brown, Charles A.	Aug 8	6	1
Burgess, C. R. (Bob)	Dec 19	2	2
Burney, Mrs. John	Apr 4	1	1
Byrd, Sular W.	Dec 19	6	2
Callison, Clarence P.	Sep 26	1	1
Campbell, Lucien J.	Jan 31	6	1
Canfield, Arthur R.	Oct 17	6	2
Cheney, Russell Sterling	May 2	5	2
Cherry, Edmond W.	Jan 24	8	1
Choats, Emma V.	Aug 29	1	1
Coleman, Lula	Mar 21	8	1
Coller, Wayne Robert	Mar 28	5	2
Cunningham, Mrs. G. C.	Dec 19	4	2
Custer, Mrs. Jim	May 23	5	1
Curtis, Mrs. W. A.	Jul 11	1	1
Cutsinger, John	Nov 7	4	1
Davis, James J.	Oct 17	2	2
Davis, Nelson	Mar 7	1	1
Day, William E.	Oct 24	1	1
Denton, Annie Norwood	Dec 5	6	2
Derby, Susannah Cooper	Jul 4	8	1
De Vore, Charles	Aug 29	4	1
Dietert, Theodore F. W.	Oct 3	1	1

1957
Film Roll #34

NAME	DATE	PG	SEC
Dorn, Amelia	Feb 28	8	1
Duderstadt, Elizabwth H.	Dec 19	8	2
Dunn, Ellwood M (Jr.)	Jun 6	6	2
Eakin, James Lee Michael	Aug 1	8	1
Eaton, Mrs. Courtlandt	Mar 21	3	2
Eaton, William Isaac	Jan 10	8	1
Edwards, Arthur	Sep 12	1	1
Evans, Newton	Mar 28	3	2
Farr, Zannie	Mar 28	6	2
Fears, Robert Howard	Apr 4	1	1
Ferris, Aaron A.	Sep 5	6	1
Fisk, Raymond O.	May 23	8	1
Flora, Debra Jean	Nov 7	3	1
Forrester, Ray	Nov 21	5	2
Fowler, Mrs. James L.	Nov 28	1	1
Franklin, Barney	Apr 25	1	1
Fritz, Myrtle Blanche	Oct 3	1	1
Furr, Mrs. W. H. (Nancy)	Nov 28	1	1
Gaines, Mrs. J. E.	Mar 28	1	1
Gaines, Scott	Aug 1	3	1
Ganz, George Washington	Apr 13	5	2
Gault, Mrs. John	Aug 1	4	1
Gibbens, Mary Louise	Jan 24	6	2
Gifford, Eva Mae	Nov 27	3	1
Griffin, Mrs. David	Mar 28	5	2
Grounds, Mrs. Scott	Aug 1	8	1
Hanna, James D.	Jan 3	3	1
Harbecker, Edward	Jan 4	4	2
Hardin, H. W. (Dr.)	Jul 18	8	1
Hardy, Marvin	Aug 1	8	1
Harris, Jesse Bryan	Apr 25	8	1
Hart, William L. (Sr.)	Dec 26	1	1
Hauschild, Henry J.	Mar 21	3	1
Haynes, Arthur Burney (Rev.)	Oct 31	4	1
Henke, Chester William	Feb 7	1	1
Henderson, Bennie	Aug 22	1	1
Henderson, Bessie Elizabeth	Jul 18	8	1
Hoffman, F. C.	Nov 7	4	1
Huber, George W. (Ike)	Mar 14	1	1
Hunter, J. Marvin	Jul 4	6	2

1957
Film Roll #34

NAME	DATE	PG	SEC
Hunter, J. R.	Jul 11	5	5
Johnson, Eula	Feb 21	6	2
Johnson, Jesse M.	Nov 21	4	1
Jones, Laura	Sep 26	2	2
Jones, Martha E.	Aug 29	6	2
Karger, Edwin	Sep 19	8	1
Kelly, Joseph T (Jr.)	Feb 14	1	1
Kemper, Henry Michael (Rev.)	Oct 17	6	2
Kennedy, Mrs. MArvin	Aug 22	1	1
Key, James Floyd	Apr 11	8	1
King, Claude	Feb 21	6	2
King, Martin M.	Mar 14	6	1
Koehler, George L. H.	Apr 18	5/8	1
Kott, Mrs. Hilmer	Jan 31	6	1
Landgrebe, Carla Marie	Dec 5	1	1
Lane, Sara	Oct 17	6	2
Lane, Oma Weston	Oct 24	4	2
Laney, Mrs. L. K.	Sep 19	3	2
Lange, Minnie	Jan 31	5	1
Larendon, Mrs. George H. (Sr.)	Jan 24	4	2
Leinweber, Mrs. Charles (Corilla)	Dec 12	1	1
Leisering, Julius F.	Apr 25	1	1
Littler, Roy W.	Mar 28	6	2
Long, Mrs. W. B.	Nov 28	8	1
Love, Mrs. R. C. (Ica Ruth)	Jul 18	8	1
Low, Tom Byrnes	Mar 21	1	1
Lowrie, Mrs. A. M.	May 30	6	1
Massey, Green Henry	Mar 28	4	2
Massey, Robert Pruell	Jul 11	5	2
Marshall, Oris Q.	Dec 19	8	2
Matthews, John Lindsey	Jan 17	5	1
Mc Broom, Mary Melissa	May 16	8	1
Mc Bryde, William Andrew	Dec 19	3	2
Mc Cown, Jesse Sidney	Feb 14	1	1
Mc Lean, Buford Franklin	Jul 18	8	1
Mc Murtrey, Elisha Lali	Jul 11	6	2
Mc Rae, Alexander	Aug 29	5	2
Merritt, Mrs. J. W.	Sep 5	6	1
Middleton, Isabel P.	Feb 21	6	2
Miller, Rudolph	Jul 11	4	2

NAME	DATE	PG	SEC
Mitanck, Ervin A.	Dec 5	5	2
Moas, Clara Bell Crowell	Aug 1	8	1
Moas, Henry Leroy	Aug 1	8	1
Moas, Leslie Elaine	Aug 1	8	1
Moas, Shari Elizabeth	Aug 1	8	1
Moore, Ed C.	Dec 26	4	1
Moore, Emmett Clarence	Feb 21	6	2
Morgan, Elizabeth Agnes	May 2	5	2
Morgan, Nancy	Nov 14	1	2
Morriss, Annie Mae	Mar 7	1	1
Moss, M. M.	Jan 10	4	2
Neidert, Charles	Jul 25	1	1
Nelms, Frank Llewellen	Aug 15	8	1
Nittler, Mrs. F. J.	Jul 25	5	2
Norris, Joe C.	Nov 14	7	2
Osborne, Wayne (Thanks)	Feb 21	4	1
Overstreet, Mrs. Frank	Nov 7	3	1
Owens, Burwell Henry	Jan 31	6	1
Packer, Sarah	Jan 24	2	2
Parks, Mrs. Calvin R.	Nov 7	4	1
Parks, William Barkley	Oct 10	6	1
Peter, Mrs. Willie	Dec 19	1	1
Phillips, Stanley	Jul 25	1	1
Pickett, Olga	Apr 18	2	2
Pimlott, James T. (Rev.)	Mar 28	8	1
Poirier, Archie	Dec 26	2	1
Raymond, William Apfel	Jun 27	8	1
Retherford, David J.	Feb 7	4	2
Rice, William Berry	Jan 17	8	1
Roane, Ellen J.	Aug 1	2	2
Rogers, Charles Arthur	Mar 14	1	1
Rotge, Ernest	May 16	2	2
Schmidt, Edgar	Oct 24	8	1
Scogin, Gabriel Newton	May 9	4	1
Scott, Earl	Sep 12	1	1
Scott, Russell	Jul 11	6	2
Seffell, Elmer	Jan 24	6	2
Shepherd, Bertha E.	Dec 19	5	2
Siffor, Gladys A.	Sep 26	6	2
Sifford, Maggie W.	Jul 4	5	1

1957
Film Roll #34

NAME	DATE	PG	SEC
Simmon, Mrs. W. A.	Aug 15	1	1
Sing, James Clarence	May 23	8	1
Skaggs, Eugene	Feb 14	6	1
Sloan, Mrs. A. D.	Feb 14	6	1
Smith, Mrs. Claude	Jun 27	4	1
Smith, Donald A.	Dec 26	1	1
Smith, Hayden Alton	May 2	1	1
Sniady, Meiteck	May 23	8	1
Snow, Braden	Jun 6	5	2
Sonnen, Mrs. Louis	Nov 21	4	2
Spence, E. L. (Cap)	Mar 21	1	1
Spencer, Eber Edwin	Jan 17	8	1
Spenrath, Anna	Aug 1	2	2
Spenrath, Mrs. Max	Jul 25	6	1
Spriggs, Burt	Mar 7	8	1
Stehling, Oscar	Sep 19	4	1
Stewart, Andy H.	Dec 26	1	1
Stewart, Jack Heron	Mar 7	8	1
Stokes, J. W.	Jun 13	1	1
Strohacker, Mrs. Oscar	Apr 11	7	2
Strohacker, Oscar	Feb 7	1	1
Stubblefield, James Edward	Nov 7	3	1
Summer, John M.	Aug 1	4	1
Surber, Louis Harrison	Apr 25	2	2
Talley, A. T. (Dr., Sr.)	May 16	6	2
Taylor, Guy L.	Nov 21	1	1
Taylor, Magdalene Violet	Sep 19	8	1
Thomason, Mrs. John	Jun 20	2	2
Thorp, William T.	Aug 15	4	1
Tillman, C. M.	Oct 3	8	1
Traeger, Mrs. A. E.	Jun 27	5	1
Tredul, Harry	Oct 10	6	1
Trevino, girl child	Jun 13	1	1
Trevino, Ziola (Thanks)	Jun 20	5	2
Tucker, Herbert V.	Dec 5	6	2
Turner, Walter C. (Ike)	Feb 28	6	2
Vanham, Joe	Mar 28	2	2
Vargas, Mrs. Telesfora	Sep 26	1	1
Vaughn, Mrs. Fred T.	Nov 21	2	2
Wahlers, Mrs. Clarence	Nov 21	6	2

189

NAME	DATE	PG	SEC
Washer, Charles	May 30	6	2
Wayne, Elizabeth Anne	Sep 12	3	2
Wharton, Eleanora Love	Jul 18	8	1
Wheless, Mrs. J. S.	Feb 28	8	1
Whetstone, Fred G.	May 9	8	1
Whitworth, Mrs. W. H.	Jul 25	5	2
Williams, Floyd Clinton	Aug 22	6	2
Williams, Leonard W.	Aug 15	6	2
Willson, Mrs. T. M. (Jr.)	Oct 3	1	1
Wilson, John Henry	Feb 14	1	1
Wood, A. D.	Jun 20	6	2
Wray, Mrs. Joy	Dec 12	2	2
Zenz, Kay	Oct 17	5	2

NAME	DATE	PG	SEC
Albrecht, Mrs. William	Feb 20	5	1
Alcott, Mrs. Donald	Jan 23	6	2
Anderson, Mrs. S. E.	Aug 7	3	2
Atkins, Mrs. W. B.	Jun 5	7	1
Ault, Jackie	Jun 12	1	1
Ball, Agnes	Dec 18	5	2
Ballard, Mrs. Loman	Feb 6	3	2
Baker, Mattie C.	Jan 23	2/4	2
Barlow, Mrs.W. B.	Apr 24	8	2
Barton, Mrs. Warren	Mar 13	8	1
Baylis, Henery Eugene (Dr.)	Dec 4	2	2
Beard, Mrs. J. E.	Apr 3	8	1
Bell, Vida Stella	Jan 9	7	1
Bernhard, Otto Henry	May 22	8	1
Blakely, Elva Lynn	May 29	7	1
Blakeney, Mrs. Joe	Apr 10	3	1
Bogle, Mrs. J. G.	Sep 11	8	1
Bouldin, Jesse J.	Nov 6	8	1
Bowers, Hortense	Jul 10	5	1
Brewer, Mrs. L. W.	Jan 16	5	2
Brown, Mrs. A. P.	Apr 24	8	1
Brown, W. E. (Rev.)	Jun 5	1	1

NAME	DATE	PG	SEC
Burnett, Lynn	Oct 2	6	2
Burrier, Robert (Sr.)	Jul 3	5	2
Burton, Fred	May 1	5	1
Buswell, Mrs. C. E.	Nov 20	7	1
Cage, James B.	Apr 10	8	1
Callahan, Charles E.	Jan 23	5	2
Carlisle, Aletha Elizabeth	Mar 13	4	1
Carlton, James S.	Dec 18	3	2
Carpenter, James W.	Jun 26	2	2
Carroll, Mary	Nov 6	8	1
Carson, Annie	Dec 11	6	2
Carson, Edward Perry (Thanks)	Jun 26	6	2
Chalk, J. D.	Dec 4	1	1
Chalk, Mrs. J. D.	Dec 4	1	1
Chamberlain, Myrtle	Jan 2	8	1
Clark, Mrs. Harry J.	Jan 2	8	1
Cobb, Emma	Dec 4	8	1
Coffey, Charles R.	Jun 19	2	2
Colbath, Alfred Lafayette	Oct 2	1	1
Conway, Maude Chumley	Mar 27	2	2
Cook, Henry Allen	Jul 17	4	2
Cooke, Harold G. (Dr.)	Mar 29	5	1
Copple, Ira Edward	Jun 19	8	1
Couch, E. C. (Sr.)	Jan 23	8	1
Crick, Walter Awalt	Dec 18	8	1
Davis, Mrs. Stewart	Jan 30	2	2
Davis, John Edward	Apr 24	8	2
Deere, Mrs. I. C.	Mar 27	3	2
Delrai, Jack Delequist	Apr 10	4	1
De Masters, Roxie Alice	Dec 4	8	1
De Tue, Margaret Fitzgerald	Jan 2	3	1
Dibrell, John L.	Jul 3	6	2
Dickey, William P (Dr.)	Mar 13	8	2
Dietert, Otto	Aug 7	8	1
Dimitre, Nicholas	Oct 2	4	2
Dixon, Bertha L.	May 22	4	1
Dixon, Robert Marshall	Mar 20	6	2
Doebbler, Agnes	Feb 20	3	1
Doss, Joe	Dec 18	5	1
Doughty, Emma	Feb 27	3	2

NAME	DATE	PG	SEC
Edward, Milton	Apr 17	2	2
Erwin, A. C. (Ace)	Mar 6	2	2
Ervin, Mrs. A. C. (Ace)	Sep 25	8	1
Ethridge, Mrs. Travis	Jun 19	8	1
Evans, Lemuel Nelson	Jan 23	8	1
Fenton, Ed R.	May 29	7	1
Fenlon, Tom	Mar 13	8	2
Ferguson, Annette Bittel	Nov 13	2	2
Fine, Mrs. Charles D.	Nov 13	8	1
Fishback, Louis F.	Dec 25	8	1
Fletcher, Mrs. Pierce (Geraldine)	Jul 31	8	1
Frazer, Paul	May 15	8	1
Friedrich, Abbie A.	Nov 13	6	2
Fuller, Mrs. Taylor	Jan 23	5	2
Galbraith, Florence Mary	Jan 23	1	1
Gallatin, Herbert Hayes (Dr.)	Nov 6	1	1
Garrett, Mrs. Frank	Nov 13	3	2
Gillentine, Sam	Nov 20	5	2
Glenn, Thomas D.	Jul 17	6	2
Goodwyn, Mrs. Lennie	Aug 28	7	1
Green, John Albert	May 1	3	2
Grimes, Mrs. Goerge	Feb 6	6	2
Gross, A. L. (Doc)	Jul 3	3	2
Hamlyn, Mrs. Thomas Bean	Jul 3	6	2
Hanna, Mrs. James D.	May 15	1	1
Hare, John Samuel	Nov 20	8	1
Harrison, Sarah Lou	Feb 16	8	1
Hart, J. Rufus	Dec 25	1	1
Hauser, William Frank	Jan 9	5	2
Heard, Tom	Mar 13	5/8	2
Henry, Bertha	May 8	1	1
Hill, Pierre Bernard (Dr.)	Jan 23	6	2
Hill, Mrs. P. B.	Jun 12	1	1
Holcomb, Mrs. Oliver	Apr 17	4	1
Hollacker, Jean	Jan 30	5	1
Horsman, Mrs. Russell	Aug 14	3	2
Howard, Lulu	Feb 20	5	1
Howse, Walter H.	Jul 3	5	2
Hunt, Ellis J.	May 15	8	1
Ingenhuett, Mrs. Martin	Apr 17	6	2

1958
Film Roll #35

NAME	DATE	PG	SEC
Jackson, Mrs. John Dee	Sep 4	1	1
James, Samuel Newberry	Oct 16	1	1
Jeter, Linda Gale	Mar 13	8	2
Jeter, Samuel Leonard	May 15	8	1
Johnson, J. O.	Feb 27	3	2
Johnson, Mary E.	Dec 25	8	1
Jones, Mrs. Prentice W.	Mar 20	6	2
Jordan, Mrs. W. L. (Bess Grinstead)	Jan 30	5	2
Karger, Harry	Jun 12	8	1
Kelley, Mrs. E. T.	Apr 3	2	2
Kent, Jack	Mar 6	1	1
King, Ben F.	Nov 13	6	2
King, James L.	Jan 16	8	1
King, J. T. (Rev.)	Jan 23	5	2
Kirkpatrick, William R.	Jul 24	2	2
Klepple, H. L.	May 15	8	2
Knight, Bessie	Oct 2	6	2
Kunsch, Ralph Albert	Feb 6	6	2
Leazar, Mrs. W. G.	May 22	8	1
Lehmann, Gus Eugene	Mar 27	1	1
Lindsey, Mrs. Ross	Feb 20	1	1
Lochte, Erna	Dec 18	7	2
Lomnes, Gurie Thoen	Sep 18	5	1
Lotta, James D.	Sep 25	8	1
Luglin, Mrs. Henry	Jun 5	7	1
Mares, Charles (Dr.)	Jun 5	1	1
Master, Mrs. B. S.	Jul 24	8	1
Matthieson, August	Jul 10	8	1
May, Albert L.	Nov 20	8	1
Mayeaux Mrs. Isaac	Oct 9	3	1
Mc Caleb, Mrs. Walter	Oct 2	8	1
Mc Connahachie, James	Jan 30	1	2
Mc Cullough, G. L.	Jun 26	8	1
Mc Donald, William E.	Jul 17	5	2
Mc Kenzie, Mrs. Frank	Jan 30	5	2
Mc Mahon, John Thomas	Feb 16	8	1
Mc Nealy, Mrs. O. L.	Jan 2	8	1
Mc Pherson, J. O.	Oct 16	1	1
Meadow, William W.	May 8	7	2
Meeker, Ernest B.	May 29	7	1

NAME	DATE	PG	SEC
Miller, Nelson, Arthur	Jun 19	8	1
Miller, Otto	Oct 16	1	1
Moody, F. A.	Jun 5	1	1
Mooney, Mrs. Art	Jan 30	6	2
Moore, Mrs., Edward	Oct 30	6	1
Moore, Mrs. Jim	Mar 20	8	1
Moss, C. C.	Feb 6	8	1
Moss, Mrs. M. M.	Jul 17	6	2
Mosty, Harvey	Aug 22	1	1
Motte, James Newton	Mar 6	8	1
Munch, Delia	Aug 14	4	1
Murphy, Oscar Lee	Jul 31	4	2
Nabors, Cora B.	Oct 30	1	1
Nagel, Eva	Jun 12	8	1
Nelson, Pleny L.	Jul 10	1	1
Neuschafer, George	Aug 7	6	2
Noble, Clark D.	Oct 9	5	2
Noble, Larry	Sep 4	1	1
North, Mrs. T. C.	Sep 4	1	1
Nowlin, Le Roy	Nov 20	8	1
Oatman, harles Sheppard	Sep 18	2	2
O'Connor, Samuel W.	Sep 25	5	2
Oliver, Effie Gertrude	Nov 6	7	1
Onderdonk, Mrs. R. T.	Feb 27	6	2
Page, Mrs. Willie	Dec 25	7	1
Pampell, John Lee	Nov 20	1	1
Parsons, James L.	Feb 6	1	2
Partridge, Susie De Lee	May 1	3	2
Perkins, Edith Williams,	Apr 10	8	1
Perry, John W.	Oct 30	7	1
Peterson, Joe Sid	Jan 16	1	1
Petri, Mrs. Alfred	Nov 27	2	2
Phillips, Dennis Eugene	Feb 16	6	2
Piper, Mrs. Madison C.	Decr 18	5	1
Price, Mrs. E. M.a Mata	Aug 14	8	1
Ralston, Mrs. J. F.	Jan 9	8	1
Raymond, O. L.	Nov 6	8	1
Rees, Herman Clarence	Mar 20	6	2
Ridgaway, William Pitt	Nov 20	8	1
Ridgeway, Robert S.	Dec 18	6	2

NAME	DATE	PG	SEC
Ritcheson, Mary E.	Jul 31	4	2
Roberts, J. D.	Sep 4	6	2
Rotge, Raymond	Feb 16	4	2
Sabins, Sheila	Sep 4	1	1
Saenger, William Fred	Dec 4	1	1
Scheele, Rudolph H.	Feb 16	2	2
Scholl, Hermina	Mar 20	5	2
Schulze, Mrs. G.	Dee 18	6	2
Schwarz, A. M.	Oct 16	1	1
Schweining, Mrs. Fred	Jan 2	7	1
Schwethelm, Mrs. Arno	Mar 13	3	2
Serrano, Angel R.	Jul 10	8	1
Shanklin, James Logan	Jul 10	8	1
Shannon, Mrs. Morris	May 1	4	2
Shaw, Mrs. John	Apr 17	4	1
Shelburne, Mrs. R. A.	Jul 17	8	1
Shofer, William R.	Jan 23	3	2
Slane, Lefonse	Oct 16	1	1
Smith, Albert	Jul 10	4	1
Smith, A. S.	Dec 18	4	2
Smith, Bertha Wise	Apr 10	6	2
Smith, Judith Lynn	Jan 16	1	1
Smith, Lawrence Baker (Skeeter)	Aug 28	4	1
Smith, Lawrence (Skeeter)	Sep 4	6	1
Spence, Mrs. E. L.	Jan 23	1	1
Spenrath, Eric	Mar 6	8	1
Spohn, Bonnie Jean	Apr 17	2	2
Stafford, Mrs. Charles	Aug 28	7	1
Stapleton, William Z.	Dec 18	7	1
Stevens, Alvin James	Mar 20	5	2
Stewart, Andy (Thanks)	Jan 9	5	2
Stieler, Fritz	Sep 25	1	1
Stone, John E.	Oct 9	6	2
Stotts, Mrs. J. L.	Jan 16	2	2
Sullivan, Della	Feb 6	1	2
Swenson, Paul Oliver	Feb 20	6	2
Swisher, Mrs. Warren C.	Mar 13	8	2
Terry, Sarah James	Apr 24	5	1
Thacker, William M.	Dec 11	5	2
Thomas, Connie	Aug 28	8	1

NAME	DATE	PG	SEC
Torres, Kathryn	Nov 27	8	1
Travis, Oliver W.	Jan 23	4	2
Trevino, Espirion A.	Oct 2	6	2
Trotter, Leona	Mar 27	4	2
Tucker, Silas	Jul 10	1	1
Tyre, Walter Albert	Feb 6	6	2
Vallier, Jessie Wellborn	Nov 27	5	1
Von Roeder, Richard O.	Feb 27	3	1
Walker, Charlotte	Mar 27	6	2
Walsh, Mrs. F. C.	Mar 6	3	2
Wemple, J. D.	Jan 30	6	1
West, Mrs. Milton	Apr 3	6	2
White, John Edward (Dr.)	Sep 11	1	1
Wickson, Mrs. Delbert	Jun 12	7	1
Wiedenfeld, Louis	May 22	8	1
Williams, Samuel John	Jan 30	1	1
Willis, James Francis	Mar 27	1	1
Willson, Mrs. T. Morris	Oct 9	1	1
Wilmoth, Robert Leslie	Nov 27	7	1
Wootton, Thomas Jefferson	May 1	4	2
Worley, Mrs. E. E.	Apr 3	6	2
Wyatt, William	Apr 24	8	2
Young, Ethel	Apr 17	8	1
Zastera, Adolph	Jan 16	4	1
Zumwalt, Susie	Nov 20	8	1

Adams, Mrs. Hearne	Oct 8	5	1
Alexander, Albert	Aug 20	6	1
Alliger, William Thomas	Jun 18	1	1
Anderson, Stewart R. (Dr.)	Aug 6	1	1
Andrews, Samuel Sylvester	Jul 16	8	1
Ashby, Ambers B.	Jul 16	7	1
Baker, Mrs. A. B.	Jul 2	4	2
Baker, Yancy	Jan 29	8	1
Barton, Winston	May 21	3	2
Beal, Bruce A.	May 28	8	1

1959
Film Roll #36

NAME	DATE	PG	SEC
Benner, Mrs. Earl	Aug 15	6	2
Bierschwale, Earle	Sep 3	8	1
Bill, Reyes	Jul 23	2	1
Bowlin, Mrs. Roy (Thanks)	Dec 24	2	1
Bottimer, Mrs. L. J.	Jan 8	6	2
Brown, Evalina Winnie	Aug 27	6	2
Brown, Everett E.	Oct 8	5	1
Brown, Herman Naward	Apr 30	8	1
Bryden, Raymond Starr	Jan 8	4	1
Buckler, David W.	Nov 19	8	1
Bundick, Doarveal	May 7	5	1
Burkhart, Frank	May 28	6	2
Butler, Mamie	Oct 29	8	1
Cabbiness, Julia Etta	Dec 3	6	2
Cade, Marioin F.	Jul 30	8	1
Carpenter, A. R.	Apr 2	8	1
Carruth, Edward Bennett	Jul 23	1	1
Chenault, John H.	Jul 23	8	1
Chipman, Emmett	Apr 30	8	1
Clark, Mrs. James J.	Dec 24	1	1
Clingon, Cecil E.	Dec 31	3	2
Copeland, Charles W.	Aug 27	3	2
Chopelas, Mrs. George	Jul 16	8	1
Clark, Harry J.	Feb 5	7	1
Clark, Willis Alton	Mar 19	1	1
Clements, William D.	Jun 11	8	1
Cocke, Mrs. Brownie Rees	Jun 4	7	1
Coker, William Henry	Oct 29	8	1
Cole, Evelyn Marie	Nov 26	1	1
Collins, Mrs. E. R.	Feb 12	7	1
Cone, George S.	Apr 16	6	2
Cook, John Francis	Jan 1	6	1
Corkill, Lee J.	Sep 3	6	2
Coulter, Eddie	Apr 23	8	1
Covan, H. J.	Jul 18	6	2
Cox, James G.	Jun 4	1	1
Cox, Robert Earl	Jan 15	1	1
Cox, Robert Sheldon	Apr 30	1	1
Crawford, Joe S.	Oct 8	6	1
Currier, Pearl	Nov 12	8	2

197

NAME	DATE	PG	SEC
Dade, Harry T.	Jun 11	8	1
Dale, Milam L.	Jun 25	6	2
Daniels, Mrs. George	Oct 8	7	1
Daniels, Ralph E.	Jul 23	1	1
Daughtery, Johnson	Apr 16	8	1
Davidson, Mrs. W. R.	Mar 19	1	1
Davis, Mrs. Ambrose J.	Aug 20	1	1
Davis, Robert C.	Nov 19	7	1
Deal, Weldon Bailey	Jan 15	8	1
Dean, Mrs. Henry	Feb 26	5	2
Deike, Mrs. Edward	May 14	1	1
Delany, J. J. (Dr.)	Jul 2	1	1
Delavan, Willian Walter	Feb 19	2	2
Dietch, Harry A.	May 7	8	2
Dietert, Edward	Oct 1	1	1
Dietert, Mrs. Henry	Feb 26	8	1
Duncan, Cecil W.	Jun 11	8	1
Eberhart, Floyd L.	Nov 19	8	1
Eckloff, Wallis Herman	Apr 30	1	1
Eckstein, Simon	Nov 26	8	1
Edmonds, Mrs. Kenneth	Nov 12	1	1
Engleking, Mrs. Martin	Aug 27	6	2
Epps, W. O.	Feb 5	1	1
Ersch, Emil	Mar 12	6	2
Espinosa, Juanita	Jun 11	6	2
Everett, Mrs. Joseph W.	Dec 31	5	1
Faltin, Mrs. August	Jan 22	4	2
Fauver, Dorotha	Sep 3	1	1
Fisher, Mrs. A.	Aug 27	6	2
Flores, Mrs. Carauna	Nov 12	8	1
Foreman, Wendell Lee	Apr 30	1	1
Foquette, Frederick D.	Oct 29	8	1
Fryer, Jesse James	Sep 3	2	1
Furr, Louisa	Jun 18	8	1
Galloway, Edna	Apr 23	6	2
Garza, Jesse	Oct 8	5	1
Gerdes, Mrs. W. A.	Jun 4	8	1
Gerloff, Alan	May 7	4	2
Gilbert, Gertrude	May 14	8	1
Gipe, Rubin C.	Oct 22	8	1

NAME	DATE	PG	SEC
Gold, Mrs. Emil	Dec 10	8	2
Gonzales, Alma Lydia	Jul 30	8	2
Goodman, Louis L.	May 14	5	1
Gouger, Mrs. Bryan	Oct 8	1	1
Green, Mrs. Z. A.	Aug 15	3	2
Griffith, Robert G.	Feb 5	1	1
Hackbusch, Mrs. K. A.	Nov 19	6	2
Hahn, Otto	Jun 11	8	1
Hammett, Arthur J.	Dec 31	5	1
Harbin, Mary Dudly	Jun 11	4	2
Hardin, Mrs. Myrel	Mar 26	8	2
Harrison, D. F.	Feb 26	8	1
Hartman, Alois Alfred (Abie)	Jan 15	2	2
Heckathorne, C. E.	Sep 24	8	1
Heide, Charles	Sep 17	8	2
Heidemann, William	Aug 15	6	2
Heimann, Nora	Dec 17	1	1
Hitt, Harvey	Feb 5	1	1
Hodges, Robert E.	Nov 19	6	2
Holcomb, Mrs. W. W.	Dec 3	8	1
Holdsworth, Thomas Kirk	Jan 1	1	1
Hopkins, Marshall L.	Jun 18	6	2
Hughes, D. H.	Feb 12	1	1
Hutson, W. C.	Oct 15	8	2
James, Mrs. Sam	Mar 12	6	2
Johnson, William	Mar 5	4	2
Jonas, Mrs. W. J.	Feb 26	4	2
Jones, George	Apr 2	5	2
Jones, L. W.	Feb 5	3	2
Jones, W. W.	Dec 24	1	1
Joret, Earl	Jun 4	6	2
Joy, Alva Curtis	Aug 6	8	1
Kapplemann, Elva E.	Oct 8	8	1
Karnes, Mrs. J. F.	Apr 2	8	1
Kayser, Robert R.	Oct 15	8	1
Kennedy, Mrs. R. J.	Oct 22	7	1
Kensing, Edward H.	Oct 29	8	2
Ketchum, Abner R.	Aug 6	4	2
Kihlberg, Mrs. Fred E.	Nov 5	1	1
Kilborn, Ray	Jun 18	4	2

NAME	DATE	PG	SEC
King, Austin	Aug 6	8	1
Kolter, Jennie	Sep 17	8	1
Kunz, Mrs. Theo (Louise Maurer)	Aug 6	6	2
Landrum, Calley	Dec 3	8	1
Ledbetter, Carl Bryan	Mar 12	8	1
Lee, James Abe	Jul 9	8	2
Leinweber, Florence E.	Jul 16	8	1
Lemmon, Theodore W.	Mar 5	3	2
Lenhart, Charles C.	Feb 12	6	1
Livingston, William D.	Jun 25	8	1
Locke, Ranson Lee	Mar 12	6	2
Longnecker, Etta G.	Jul 23	6	2
Loop, Kenneth	Feb 12	1	1
Love, Roscoe Tot	Dec 3	6	2
Lowery, R. J. (Pinky)	Jun 11	2	1
Lyon, Mrs. Thomas F.	Apr 23	6	2
Manning, Mrs. J. C.	Feb 19	6	2
Markwordt, Henry Frank	May 14	5	2
Mc Cutchen, Mrs. Leighton B.	Apr 9	8	1
Mc Dermott, Mrs. Charles M.	Mar 12	8	1
Mc Dougal, D. G. (Rev.)	Jun 18	6	2
Mc Elroy, George	Oct 8	1	1
Mc Jimsey, Albertus	Jul 23	1	1
Meehan, Sadie	Jul 23	8	1
Merchant, Dave Henry	Mar 12	6	2
Miles, Margaret	Apr 16	8	1
Mills, Jay C.	Apr 16	8	1
Mitchell, Crawford	Apr 16	5	1
Mitchell, Mrs. Loyd	Oct 15	1	1
Morgan, Bessie L.	Jan 22	8	1
Morin, Raymon Bill	Jul 9	1	1
Morris, Mrs. Thomas E.	Mar 19	3	2
Morrow, George F.	May 21	4	2
Morrow, Leonard A.	Dec 10	8	2
Moseley, Benjamin Elisha	Dec 31	5	1
Mosty, Mrs. Harvey	Oct 22	8	2
Nagel, August F.	Jun 11	8	1
Nelson, Mattie (Mrs. Rankin)	Feb 12	7	1
Newberry, J. H.	Nov 26	1	1
Newcomer, Jonathon	Apr 2	8	1

1959
Film Roll #36

NAME	DATE	PG	SEC
Newton, Elizabeth	Jan 1	1	1
Novak, Joe	Dec 3	7	1
Nowlin, Charles	Sep 10	6	2
Nowlin, Mrs. Roy	Dec 17	6	2
Oakley, Edna	Jul 99	5	2
Oatman, Julius F.	Mar 26	8	2
Oelfke, George	Feb 26	7	1
Orsack, Frank	Aug 27	8	1
Pack, Harold W.	Aug 20	6	1
Partain, Graham	Sep 3	1	1
Pent, Iris Harrison	May 21	7	1
Phillips, Henry	Jan 8	5	2
Price, Charles Robinson	Jan 8	6	2
Pullen, Mrs. G. W.	Apr 9	1	1
Pullin, George Washington	Sep 17	1	1
Purvis, L. Hardy	Jul 23	6	2
Ragland, Colis S.	Jul 23	6	2
Ransleben, Mrs. R. A.	Oct 29	8	1
Rauch, Wayne C.	Apr 9	8	1
Rees, Georgette	Oct 15	1	1
Rees, Mrs., Sid	Dec 31	1	1
Reynolds, Hilton H.	Aug 20	1	1
Rhoden, Emmett W.	Aug 6	6	2
Riley, Emil H.	Oct 1	8	2
Ritchie, George A.	Apr 9	2	2
Ritchie, Lura Lee	Dec 10	8	1
Robinson, Susan	Apr 23	1	1
Ross, John L.	Apr 30	8	1
Sandlin, Elmer Lee	Nov 26	6	2
Sansom, Ernest E. (Rev.)	Nov 12	2	2
Satterwhite, D. S.	Jun 25	2	2
Schuett, Harry Carl	Nov 5	6	2
Schumacher, Willie F.	Apr 16	1	1
Schwethelm, Mrs. Ernst	Jan 29	1	1
Sears, George Du Bose	Apr 30	1	1
Seffel, Olga	Sep 17	8	1
Setzer, Lily Pearl	Apr 23	1	1
Shaw, Oma Humphries	Nov 5	1	2
Sherm, Mrs. Charles (Jr.)	Nov 19	1	1
Shell, Jack	Jul 23	4	2

1959
Film Roll #36

NAME	DATE	PG	SEC
Shortt, James Franklin	Jul 9	2	1
Smart, Mrs. Earl	Jan 1	1	1
Smith, Arthur T.	Jan 1	6	1
Smith, Mrs. P. W.	Feb 12	5	2
Sneed, Will	Jan 15	1	2
Sonnen, Louis	Jun 25	6	2
Stewart, Leonard Lafayette	Feb 19	7	1
Stout, Martin A.	May 28	6	2
Stutte, Mrs. John H.	Nov 5	6	2
Sutherland, George C.	Nov 5	8	1
Switzer, Mrs. Elmer H.	May 7	8	2
Tackett, George C.	Mar 26	7	2
Tally, Jacob C.	Apr 16	6	2
Taylor, James M.	Jun 4	8	1
Thompson, A. L.	Aug 6	8	1
Tomlin, W. T.	Jul 16	6	2
Travis, Arthur L.	Sep 17	8	2
Travis, George Guy	Jul 9	1	1
Valderaz, Esther	Sep 3	7	1
Valdez, Victoria	Dec 10	8	1
Vanderford, Mrs. William	Sep 17	8	1
Vann, Henry J.	Apr 23	1	1
Vinning, Mrs. Belle	Dec 31	5	1
Waddell, Tommie Neil	Jun 11	1	1
Wakefield, Thomas N.	Jan 29	5	2
Walker, Mrs. Fred	Jun 11	5	1
Wallace, Henry Frank	Jul 2	1	1
Wallace, Mrs. Lee	Dec 17	8	2
Warren, Gordon Murray	Jan 1	1	1
Watkins, Frederick (Ted)	Jan 15	4	2
Weston, Alice	Jun 25	6	2
Wheeler, Houston	Mar 26	8	1
Wheeler, Mrs. Houston	Mar 26	8	1
White, Frank E. (Thanks)	Mar 12	6	2
Whitworth, Howard	Nov 26	1	1
Wilcox, Mrs. John Gordon	Apr 2	1	1
Wilks, Deborah Celeste	Jun 25	8	1
Williamson, Mrs. A. B.	Dec 24	1	1
Willis, Harry F.	Dec 31	5	1
Wilson, Mrs. Walter W.	Apr 16	5	1

```
                      1959
                  Film Roll #36

NAME                      DATE          PG  SEC

Windsor, Anna             Aug 6         6    2
Yarbrough, Mattie         Dec 3         6    2
Young, Thomas             Sep 3         8    1
York, Mrs. L. W.          Jul 23        6    2


                      1960
                  Film Roll # 37

Adair, Lloyd              Nov 10        8    1
Adams, Elsie F.           Apr 14        4    2
Adams, Mrs. W. F. (Sr.)   May 19        1    3
Aleala, Cristoval         Dec 29        6    2
Anderson, Mrs. Guy        May 19        4    2
Andrew, E. V.             Oct 20        1    1
Armstrong, R. E.          Mar 10        6    2
Aubey, Mrs. Horace        Feb 4         1    1
Ayala, Mrs. Louis         Aug 11        6    2
Bailey, Mrs. Randolph E.  Jan 8         6    1
Barrett, son of Ray R.    Jun 30        3    1
Bartel, Fritz             Oct 27        8    1
Bauer, Paul               Nov 24        8    2
Bauer, Mrs. Paul          Mar 31        1    1
Beagle, L. E.             Jan 14        7    1
Beakley. R. W. (Bobby)    Oct 13        1    1
Beard, Forrest Allen      Aug 25        1    1
Berry, H. B.              May 26        2    1
Blake, William G.         Jul 14        6    2
Blessing, Della           May 26        5    2
Boeckmann, Ernest N.      Jan 14        8    2
Boyd, Mrs. John H.        Apr 7         3    2
Bradley, Hugh M.          Mar 17        8    1
Brehmer, Margaret Frances May 5         8    1
Brigham, Leonard N.       Mar 17        8    1
Brooks, Meryl Mc Call     Nov 17        8    1
Brown, George P. (Jr.)    Jun 2         1    1
Buelow, Mrs. Frank        May 5         6    2
Burke, Nina               Apr 28        4    2
Burney, Joel W.           Nov 24        8    1
Bushong, Edgar E.         Feb 18        7    1
```

NAME	DATE	PG	SEC
Cagle, Mrs. O. Lorell (Virginia)	Jun 30	3	3
Callahan, John	Mar 31	6	2
Campbell, Emma	Apr 14	6	1
Carnes, John T.	Jan 14	8	1
Carroll, Walter L.	Aug 11	8	1
Carson, Nugent C.	Jan 21	2	1
Cervantes, Apolonio	Sep 15	7	1
Chaffee, Donald Dean	Jun 16	8	1
Chandler, Bertha	Mar 2	6	1
Cofer, Roy C. (Jr.)	Jan 21	1	1
Cole, Earl	Oct 13	8	1
Coleman, Alfred	Jan 14	8	2
Collins, Eula	Apr 7	1	1
Cone, Mrs. George Sealy	Nov 3	6	2
Conn, Kelton	Apr 28	4	2
Cooper, J. L.	Apr 28	8	1
Corey, Obed I.	Sep 8	1	1
Cox, Robert Payne	Aug 11	7	1
Cragg, Leonard E.	Aug 18	6	2
Crawford, Kelly Ann	Nov 3	2	2
Crotty, John T.	Dec 8	1	1
Cunningham, Charles	Dec 22	6	1
Curtis, Luther H.	Dec 29	6	1
Danner, Roy D.	Oct 20	1	1
Davenport, Mrs. Joe	Jun 2	6	2
Davis, Ambrose J.	Jan 28	8	1
Dietert, Mrs. Edward	Apr 21	8	2
Dismukes, Mrs. C. M.	Nov 24	8	2
Donahue, J. N.	May 12	8	1
Dowdy, Mrs. George E.	Sep 22	6	1
Doyle, Frank	Feb 4	6	2
Drane, Joseph Lamar	Sep 1	1	1
Dreeves, Mrs. Harry	Jun 2	8	1
Dudgeon, Minnie	Oct 20	8	1
Durrin, Charles S.	Mar 10	1	1
Echols, Florence	Mar 2	6	2
Edens, Haskell T.	Dec 8	1	1
Edens, Mrs. Hugh	Apr 21	1	1
Edwards, Milton	Apr 21	8	2
Ellebracht, Alfred	Jun 16	1	1

NAME	DATE	PG	SEC
Ellebracht, Alfred L.	Jun 23	8	1
Emanski, Stanley J.	Feb 25	7	2
Epinosa, (Espinosa) Seferino	May 12	1	1
Evans, Alda	Nov 17	8	2
Evans, Claud F.	Sep 22	5	2
Evans, Joel Wiley	May 12	8	1
Evans, Walter Jackson	Feb 18	6	2
Everett, Mary	Jan 8	5	1
Ferguson, Mrs. R. C.	Jan 21	5	2
Fisher, Leslie James	Apr 28	3	2
Fly, Joseph Dalton	Mar 17	2	2
Flynn, Charles Bartlett	Jan 14	1	1
Flynn, Joseph	Feb 11	1	1
Folmar, Monroe	Nov 17	1	1
Fortenberry, T. L.	Nov 17	8	1
Fouty, Mrs. Grant	Sep 1	8	1
Forgy, Theodore Leslie	Jun 9	8	2
Fouty, Dora Olivia	Mar 2	6	2
Franklin, N. O. (Jr.)	Apr 12	5	2
French, Minnie	Apr 21	4	1
Frisch, Mrs. Luther	Jun 2	6	2
Galbraeth, Charles	Oct 13	8	1
Garrett, James L.	May 26	3	2
Gillaudeau, Mrs. T. L.	Jan 14	8	2
Glenn, Kate M.	Aug 11	8	1
Greebon, Arnold E.	Dec 8	8	1
Green, Etna	Dec 29	6	2
Hendricks, Bobby Davis	Apr 28	6	1
Henley, Harrison	Dec 15	1	1
Henley, Mrs. George	Apr 7	3	2
Herndon, Mrs. J. R.	Sep 1	1	1
Hines, Mrs. Jack	Jan 21	8	1
Hobbs, Mrs. L. L.	Sep 29	1	1
Holekamp, Mrs. Alex	Mar 31	1	1
Holmes, Walter E.	Feb 4	6	2
Holekamp, Richard	Sep 22	1	1
Hopkins, Mrs. M. L.	Jun 30	3	1
Horton, Johnny	Nov 10	4	2
Hotcher, W. Gregory	Dec 8	5	2
Howell, James E.	Dec 22	8	2

1960
Film Roll #37

NAME	DATE	PG	SEC
Hudson, Mrs. John Black	Sep 29	6	2
Hughes, Mrs. Dee H.	Sep 1	1	1
Huitt, Arthur W.	Sep 1	6	2
Johnson, daughter of Robert	Jul 14	6	2
Jones, John L.	Aug 25	3	1
Kamens, Mrs. Adolph A.	Aug 25	6	1
Kellogg, Mrs. W. B.	Jan 8	1	1
Klein, Henry	Apr 14	8	2
Lackey, James R.	Jul 14	8	1
Lang, Mrs. Garland	Jul 21	1	1
Lebus, Mrs. George	Oct 13	8	2
Lee, Walter	Apr 7	1	1
Leonard, Joseph F.	May 5	1	1
Lewis, William Thomas	Sep 22	8	1
Leyendecker, Mrs. Thomas	Oct 13	8	1
Linesetter, Addie	Jul 21	8	1
Long, Thurman	Sep 15	7	2
Lotspiech, William L.	Mar 10	1	1
Love, John C.	Mar 17	3	2
Lueders, Otto	Feb 18	5	1
Luska, Zofie	Mar 24	8	1
Luther, Horace Norman	Feb 4	8	1
Mahon, Mrs. L. F.	Jun 30	6	1
Mayfield, Mrs.	Dec 29	1	1
Mc Carver, Mrs. James	Jan 21	6	2
Mc Cormick, Mrs. H. C. (Thanks)	Jun 9	2	2
Mc Curdy, J. H.	Sep 29	6	2
Mc Donald, B. O.	Mar 2	6	2
Mc Gill, James C. (Jr.)	Oct 13	4	2
Mc Kee, Guy	Nov 24	1	1
Mc Laughlin, George W.	Feb 4	1	1
Mc Nair, D. G.	Aug 11	8	1
Meeker, Elijah C.	Jun 9	8	1
Meinecke, Debra Lou	Jun 9	3	2
Milam, Mrs. J. A.	Oct 20	6	2
Miller, Callie Dora	Feb 11	8	1
Millice, Bill	Jul 7	8	1
Morris, Reginald	Apr 7	8	1
Moseley, Ben (Thanks)	Jan 14	7	1
Muir, Ian (Dr.)	Feb 11	6	2

NAME	DATE	PG	SEC
Neal, Frances	Mar 2	6	2
Nelms, A. L.	Jul 7	6	2
Neuschafer, Mrs. Goerge	Feb 18	8	1
Nimitz, Otto	Feb 11	1	1
Oatman, Charles C.	May 12	8	1
Oatman, Mrs. C. S.	Mar 17	2	2
Overly, Leon David	Feb 11	1	1
Parfit, Edward	Aug 18	6	2
Payne, Mrs. Alexandeer	Feb 18	6	2
Pettigrew, Ruth	Nov 24	8	2
Phillips, Mrs. Henry	Dec 1	8	2
Pickett, John Stanley	Nov 10	6	1
Pitcher, Eunice	Jun 30	6	3
Powell, Guy M.	Oct 27	8	2
Priour, Thomas F.	Jul 21	1	1
Raines, Renard T.	Jan 21	6	2
Read, R. L.	Jan 14	8	2
Reagan, Minerva Jane	Mar 10	3	2
Reicherd, Charles R.	Mar 31	6	2
Renault, Mrs. Ramon	Jun 2	8	1
Reutzel, Mrs. Frank	Mar 2	6	2
Reynolds, Mrs. M. W.	Apr 21	3	2
Roberts, James Mc Cord	Jun 23	6	2
Robertson, Robert Lee	Jun 30	3	3
Robles, Matias (Shorty)	Nov 10	8	1
Roe, Daniel Thomas	Jun 9	8	2
Rogers, Mrs. John F.	Sep 15	8	1
Rush, Alfred O.	Jul 7	8	1
Russell, V. C.	Aug 4	5	3
Ryan, Mrs. J. J.	Aug 25	3	1
Ryan, John J.	May 26	8	1
Sample, Mrs. J. F.	Sep 22	8	1
Sandefer, Angelina	May 12	8	1
Sanford, William L.	Mar 17	2	2
Schultz, Fred	Jan 8	4	2
Scoggins, Mrs. S. O.	Sep 8	1	1
Scott, Nannie	Jun 23	8	1
Seeger, Gordon L.	Sep 29	6	2
Shaw, Mabel Gertrude	Apr 14	8	1
Shearn, Charles P.	Nov 3	6	2

NAME	DATE	PG	SEC
Sheffield, Frank D.	Dec 1	1	1
Sheffield, Julius O.	Nov 24	8	2
Sherwood, Joseph	Mar 17	3	2
Smith, Albert L.	Nov 10	8	2
Smith, Mrs. James G.	Jun 9	3	2
Spell, Mrs. Radie	Jul 7	5	2
Spriggs, Mrs. Bert	Apr 28	8	1
Springer, Laura Field	Dec 22	8	1
Springer, Roy	Dec 15	6	1
Sprott, Felix	Oct 20	8	2
Stallings, Allen	Jul 21	3	1
Stanley, Thomas	May 5	8	1
Staudt, W. A.	Mar 31	1	1
Stevens, James O.	Feb 11	7	1
Stevens, Mary Wood	Dec 22	8	1
Stehling, Rudolph	Sep 15	1	1
Stolle, Francis M.	Mar 10	1	1
Stringham, Emerson A.	Dec 8	1	1
Swayze, George A.	Nov 3	8	1
Tarr, Robert R.	Jun 23	1	1
Thomas, Otha	Jul 21	2	2
Thompson, Mrs. J. M.	Mar 24	8	1
Thompson, Ollie Hartwell	Jun 30	5	2
Townsend, Raymond N.	Sep 29	4	3
Turner, Helen	Sep 29	5	1
Walker, Mrs. John	Jun 2	1	1
Warren, Hattie	Oct 27	6	1
Watson, Alvin Floyd	Nov 3	8	1
Watson, W. A.	Aug 11	3	1
Watson, Mrs. W. A.	Mar 24	2	1
Webb, Clarence	Feb 4	6	2
Webb, Dan S.	Sep 8	8	2
Welch, Leonard W.	Sep 29	6	2
Wharton, Hays	Feb 11	6	2
Williams, Paul R.	Mar 10	1	1
Williamson, James A.	Nov 10	7	1
Wilson, Mrs. Leonard	Dec 8	8	1
Witt, Woodrow W.	Jul 7	5	2
Worthington, Ambrose	Oct 13	8	1
Wren, Mrs. Ross	Nov 24	1	1

NAME	DATE	PG	SEC
Young, George	Jun 30	3	1
Zastera, Mrs. Adolph	Jun 16	8	1

1961
Film Roll #38

Adams, Mary Ollie	Nov 9	8	1
Alderdice, James A.	Aug 24	1	1
Alsup, G. W.	Dec 14	5	1
Andrews, L. A.	Jan 19	1	1
Archer, G. T.	Jul 27	4	2
Bader, Leslie	Mar 9	6	2
Baker, Mrs. Y. W.	Feb 9	1	1
Barret, Eula Lacy	Mar 2	7	1
Barron, Mrs. T. W.	Mar 2	6	2
Barton, Juanita Louise	Jul 27	8	1
Bates, Ehrment P.	Jul 13	5	2
Beakley, F. C.	Oct 19	8	1
Beasley, Emory	May 25	8	2
Beasley, Roland	Oct 14	7	1
Bergmann, Henry	Dec 14	6	1
Black, A. J. (Jr.) (Dr.)	Mar 16	8	1
Blackmore, Bertha	May 11	5	2
Dlanks, Jenny Mae	Oct 14	8	1
Boerner, Mrs. Eddie	Mar 23	5	2
Boldt, Albert	Jul 6	7	2
Bonner, Edward	Dec 28	6	2
Boren, Lemuel Evans	Mar 30	8	2
Brebham, Thomas (Dr.)	Apr 20	6	2
Brock, Arthur W.	Sep 21	8	1
Brooks, Mrs. W. F.	Dec 21	3	4
Broughton, Mrs. J. T.	May 25	7	1
Brown, Arthur A.	Jun 22	8	2
Burow, Fritz	Jun 22	4	2
Burney, Mrs. Lee	Jun 15	8	2
Burton, Floyde Hancy	Sep 21	6	2
Butt, Kearney	Apr 6	1	1
Byas, W. O. (Thanks)	Nov 9	6	1
Cantwell, George	Aug 10	1	1

1961
Film Roll #38

NAME	DATE	PG	SEC
Carruthers, John	Oct 26	8	1
Carson, Herman	Aug 31	1	1
Chapman, Mrs. George	Apr 27	8	2
Chauvin, Maud	Nov 23	8	1
Clark, Melvin Ray	Aug 2	1	1
Colbath, Moulton L.	Apr 20	6	2
Coleman, Mrs. Frank	Jan 19	8	2
Coleman, Lester (Leslie)	Jul 20	1	1
Cooper, Mrs. C. E.	Mar 9	6	2
Cooper, Norman A.	Jul 13	6	1
Copeland, Byron E.	Nov 30	8	1
Corbett, Pauline Helen	Jun 22	8	2
Cosper, William J.	Sep 21	7	1
Crawford, Philip E.	Sep 28	7	1
Creager, Beth M. (Dr.)	Sep 14	8	2
Crider, Mrs. J. Austin	Mar 23	8	1
Cross, Dan D.	Jun 15	8	2
Crow, Mrs. Jim	Feb 9	1	1
Cuno, Robert E.	Oct 12	8	1
Du Bose, Mrs. J. E.	Nov 23	8	2
Duncan, Annie W.	Nov 30	8	2
Dunks, Mrs. Ira James	Feb 16	8	1
Dunlap, Edwin H.	May 4	8	1
Duvall, Thomas C.	May 11	8	2
Dyas, James H.	Jan 19	1	1
Dyer, Alice	Nov 16	8	2
Edwards, William K.	Dec 7	6	1
Ehlers, Bertha	Jun 1	6	2
Elliott, Lura	Aug 31	8	2
Evans, Mrs. L. E.	Aug 31	1	1
Flato, Minnie Oliver	Apr 6	3	2
Fluitt, Pervis William	Feb 9	1	1
Galliher, Mrs. Edwin	Aug 24	6	2
Gatyhings, Ruby Booth	Oct 19	1	1
Gerdes, William A.	Jun 8	8	1
Gerst, George C. (Dr.)	Apr 27	8	1
Gibson, Mrs. John R.	Aug 31	4	2
Gillett, Mrs. J. T.	Mar 2	8	1
Gloeckner, Alma	Jul 6	7	2
Gnade, Richard Edward	Feb 23	7	1

NAME	DATE	PG	SEC
Gorrell, Mrs. W. E. (Vera Hine)	Jul 6	1	1
Grantham, Benjamin F.	Sep 21	6	2
Greenlee, Kate Mahoney	Jul 20	6	2
Greenwood, E. A.	Mar 9	3	1
Grider, Narcissa	Mar 23	8	1
Grona, Walter	Aug 17	1	1
Grounds, Joe	Jan 19	8	2
Grounds, Joe W.	Apr 27	8	1
Haggerton, Willie	Mar 30	8	2
Hamil, Mrs. Curtis	Feb 9	1	1
Hansen, Charles H.	Aug 10	8	2
Hargett, Beulah	Sep 28	7	1
Harless, Edna	Oct 5	6	2
Harless, Lee D.	Aug 10	1	1
Harless, Mrs. Lee D.	Oct 5	6	2
Harper, Mrs. Gordon J.	Jun 15	6	2
Harper, Mrs. Herman	Jan 5	6	2
Hatch, Amos Frank	Oct 19	8	1
Herring, John	Feb 23	8	1
Hey, Mrs. Gus	Sep 21	8	1
Hodge, Mary O.	Sep 28	7	1
Hofemeister, Elmer	Apr 13	6	2
Holekamp, Mrs. Moritz	Sep 7	6	2
Holland, Mrs. W. O.	Dec 7	5	1
Holst, Alice M.	Apr 27	8	1
Honse, Frank	Jun 29	6	1
Horlacher, Theresa N.	Feb 16	6	2
Howze, Mrs. J. E.	Feb 9	8	2
Hughs, Mary E.	Nov 23	6	2
Hull, John	Aug 24	8	1
Hull, Maude	Jun 8	8	2
Hunt, Robert Allen	May 4	1	1
Hyde, Walter	Mar 23	7	2
Jackson, Barney H.	Aug 2	8	1
Jackson, Mabel Hardin	Sep 7	1	1
Jackson, W. P.	Dec 7	6	2
James, Mrs. Paul F.	Apr 20	2	2
Jarmon, Ella	Feb 9	1	1
Johnson, Mrs. James Lee	Apr 6	7	1
Johnston, Mrs. Tom	Feb 2	1	1

NAME	DATE	PG	SEC
Jones, Mrs. Frank	Nov 2	8	1
Joseph, Fritz	Nov 3	8	1
Juenke, Mrs. Emelie J.	Mar 23	8	1
Kaiser, Albert H.	Apr 6	7	1
Kasey, Emmett H.	Jun 29	4	2
Kelly, Sarah Emma	Mar 16	6	1
Kenley, Cora Ada	Mar 16	6	2
Kennedy, R. J.	Feb 2	1	1
Key, Mrs. Roy	May 18	1	1
Key, Mrs. Roy	May 25	8	2
Klein, Edgar C.	Jun 15	8	2
Klingmann, Sidney	Apr 13	8	1
Knapp, Mrs. Dwight R.	May 18	1	1
Kneese, Mrs. Otto	Jul 13	6	2
Kott, Hilmer A.	Mar 9	6	2
Kremer, Martha A.	Apr 27	7	1
Lawrance, J. H.	Oct 12	8	1
Leavell, Alomon M. (Pete)	Aug 10	1	1
Le Beff, Tom	Dec 14	6	1
Le Blanc, Mrs. Joseph	Nov 2	8	2
Lemos, Pedro S.	Mar 23	8	1
Lewis, Bob W.	Mar 2	6	1
Lipps, Mrs. Walter	Oct 19	7	1
Lorenz, Annie	Jul 13	6	2
Love, Mitt	May 11	8	2
Loveland, Howard G.	May 4	3	1
Marsden, Edward Johnston	Jan 26	6	1
Marshall, Stephen Craig	Aug 17	1	1
Mc Angus, Hugh	Apr 13	1	1
Mc Caleb, C. C.	Oct 12	8	1
Mc Caleb, Minor M.	Sep 28	1	1
Mc Calip, H. E. L. (Dr.)	Aug 17	1	1
Mc Chesney, Ira David	Jun 15	1	1
Mc Clung, Paul	Apr 6	7	1
Mc Clung, Mrs. Paul	Jan 26	6	1
Mc Cullough, Troy	Jun 8	8	2
Mc Cully, Emil F.	Jan 5	1	1
Mc Daniel, Mrs. Harold	Feb 2	6	2
Mc Donald, Lizzie Cordelia	Nov 23	1	1
Mc Kean, Henry S.	Apr 27	8	1

1961
Film Roll #38

NAME	DATE	PG	SEC
Mc Kinley, Mrs. Leona	Feb 16	6	1
Mc Maninee, Vern	Feb 16	6	2
Mc Neill, Alexander	Apr 20	6	2
Medina, Paulina	Mar 2	2	2
Meredith, J. H. (Rev.)	May 11	8	1
Meredith, Roderick Allen	Jan 5	1	1
Merritt, Goerge H. (Dr.)	Sep 21	6	1
Meyer, Arthur E. (Dr.)	Jan 19	1	1
Meyer, Otto	Aug 31	6	2
Middleton, Charles P.	Jun 8	3	1
Mills, Jim Henry	Jan 12	1	1
Mills, Mrs. Roger Q.	Oct 5	4	2
Moore, Mrs. C. L.	Jan 26	6	2
Moore, William Joseph	Feb 9	1	1
Morgan, Mack	Oct 5	4	2
Morquecho, Arturo R.	Apr 13	8	2
Morris, Mrs. John	Apr 20	2	2
Morriss, Ernest Edward	Nov 2	1	1
Muenker, Lena Real	Jul 20	1	1
Muennink, Charles B.	Jun 1	8	1
Mulcahy, James Murray	Jul 20	4	2
Murray, John M.	Mar 9	6	2
Neidert, Dora Myrtle	Nov 2	1	1
Neill, Alexander	Apr 20	6	2
Nichols, Bruce	Aug 17	8	1
Nichols, Airs W.	Oct 26	6	2
Nowlin, Walter	Mar 16	5	2
O'Neal, Percy	Feb 16	5	2
Ozuna, Salvador	Jul 20	1	1
Pearson, Vernon	Mar 2	6	2
Pettit, Roy B.	Jun 8	8	1
Pfeuffer, Virginia L.	Dec 28	5	1
Pickle, L. C.	Feb 23	6	2
Phelps, Duval	Jun 8	8	2
Pond, William M.	Nov 30	8	2
Pope, F. M. (Dr.)	May 25	7	1
Powell, Clyde A.	Apr 6	3	2
Price, Helen	Sep 28	2	1
Queen, Johnson	Jun 22	8	1
Quist, Alvin O.	Feb 23	6	2

NAME	DATE	PG	SEC
Ragsdale, Frank G.	Jan 26	1	1
Ramsey, Mary Ida	Jun 22	8	1
Randolph, Earl C.	Oct 12	8	1
Rawls, Littleton N.	Jun 29	6	1
Reagan, Joe Glynn	Jul 20	6	2
Real, Mrs. Arthur	Sep 21	1	1
Real, Fred F.	Jan 19	8	2
Reeves, John Elmer	Jun 8	8	2
Remschel, Alfred	Dec 14	3	2
Reynolds, Elizabeth Ann	Jul 13	6	1
Richardson, Danny	Dec 7	6	1
Riesel, Karl	Jul 27	8	1
Riesel, Mrs. Karl	Jul 27	8	1
Roberts, Mrs. A.A.	May 18	8	1
Roberts, Mrs. James Mc Cord	Sep 7	1	1
Roberts, Mrs. Leo Bond	May 11	8	1
Robertson, George F.	Jul 13	4	2
Robinson, Ira L.	Jun 1	8	2
Robinson, J. B.	Sep 21	8	1
Rodgers, Mrs. Charles	Oct 5	8	2
Roe, Billy Jack	Sep 7	6	2
Rogers, Mrs. C. L.	Apr 20	6	2
Roper, Aden C. (Rev.)	Jun 1	8	1
Ruff, George	Oct 19	8	1
St. John, Mrs. Herbert L.	Jan 26	6	2
Samuelson, Cathy	Jun 8	8	1
Sanders, Ernest Lee	Jan 19	1	1
Sanders, Mrs. L. J. (Dusty)	Aug 31	8	2
Sanders, Wayburn L.	Nov 23	8	2
Saucier, Mrs. John	Nov 9	8	1
Schneider, Sam	Apr 13	8	1
Schulze, W. O. (Rev.)	Mar 30	8	2
Schulze, W. W.	Mar 30	8	2
Scott, Maude	Feb 23	4	2
Scott, Sarah Elizabeth	Mar 2	6	2
Seide, Victor E.	Feb 9	1	1
Seidensticker, Daniel	Jan 5	2	1
Shelton, Sam C.	Jan 5	1	1
Short, Jacob Lindsey	Sep 14	8	2
Silvas, Mrs. John E.	Jun 15	8	1

NAME	DATE	PG	SEC
Silvery, Estella Jane	Jul 20	6	1
Smith, Timothy (Jack)	Sep 7	8	1
Sommer, Mrs. Kenneth	Jun 15	3	2
Spell, Ed	Jul 6	7	2
Spence, Margaret	May 11	8	1
Stafford, Mrs. Earl (Kitty Spears)	Jul 27	6	1
Starkey, G. Rankin	Sep 28	1	1
Steen, James P.	Sep 28	8	1
Steiner, Matt	Nov 23	6	2
Steves, Edgar	Mar 2	1	1
Stieler, Mrs. Walter	Nov 30	6	2
Stimson, Cornelia Vaughn	Apr 13	5	2
Stone, Mrs. Everett H. (Thanks)	Jul 6	8	2
Stone, Mrs. Willie (Thanks)	May 11	6	2
Storey, Mrs. E. M.	May 11	1	1
Storey, Mary	Mar 2	8	1
Stovall, Joe Wood	Fen 9	8	1
Stowe, Adney	Jul 20	5	3
Strege, Mrs. Fred	Sep 14	4	2
Strombeck, Lois	Oct 5	8	2
Stroud, Harold H.	Aug 17	8	1
Swayze, Mrs. H. Y.	Mar 23	1	1
Taylor, Mrs. W. E.	Sep 28	1	1
Taylor, R. A.	Jul 13	6	1
Thaker, Robert S.	Apr 6	8	2
Thompson, C. H.	Apr 6	7	1
Tomlinson, Thomas T.	Jan 26	1	1
Tomlinson, Waller W.	Mar 16	8	1
Trushel, Alfred	Jun 22	8	1
Wachter, Mrs. I. J.	Nov 2	1	1
Wallace, Frank	Jul 6	1	1
Warren, Mrs. Henry	Mar 30	7	2
Warren, Leah	May 18	1	1
Webster, Mrs. Noah	Mar 23	8	2
Weeks, Matt	Aug 24	6	1
Wells, Samuel	Jul 20	6	2
Wesch, Charles	Apr 6	8	1
Whitfield, Mrs. W. C.	Mar 9	7	1
Wildenstien, Mrs. Herbert	Jan 12	6	2
Wilkins, Joe S.	Oct 26	8	1

NAME	DATE	PG	SEC
Williams, Noah W.	Feb 23	4	2
Woerner, Henry	Nov 9	8	1
Woody, Louis W.	Dec 14	6	2
Wright, Mrs. Clarence	Nov 16	1	1
Wyatt, Charles E.	Dec 7	6	1
Yariger, Elgin H.	Jun 22	8	2
Young, James B.	Aug 24	1	1
Young, Mattie	Aug 31	8	2
Zimmermann, Paul D. (Jr.)	Jul 20	1	1
Zwanzig, Charles J.	Sep 7	5	2

NAME	DATE	PG	SEC
Abbott, Sidney	Jun 20	3	1
Acklen, Lottie	Sep 5	4	1
Adams, Earl D.	Dec 19	1	1
Adcock, Sarah	May 9	6	3
Allen, Lucille Thurman	Jan 31	8	2
Andrews, Beulah	Jun 27	6	2
Armstrong, Cecil Maurice	May 23	1	1
Armstrong, Quinton S.	Jan 17	8	2
Arredondo, Morris	Mar 28	4	1
Arreola, George B.	Jul 25	8	1
Auld, Mrs. Dan	Jun 13	1	1
Avant, Lee H.	Jul 25	8	1
Avern, James M.	Dec 12	6	3
Bacon, Delbert	Nov 7	8	1
Baker, Mrs. W. C.	Nov 21	8	1
Baldwin, Johnnie Lynn	Feb 14	3	2
Baldwin, Mrs. W. H.	Dec 12	6	3
Beaver, Mary Elvira	Apr 11	6	3
Blackwell, Mrs. William R.	Sep 19	8	2
Blondeau, Eugene P.	Jul 25	1	1
Boerkel, Josephine	Dec 19	1	1
Boerkoel, Josie D.	Dec 26	1	1
Brehmer, Mrs. Richard	Jul 4	8	2
Brown, Elmo H.	Jul 4	1	1
Brown, Jennie Cooper	May 9	6	1

1962
Film Roll #39

NAME	DATE	PG	SEC
Brundrett, Mrs. Arnold	Feb 14	4	2
Bugg, Allen C.	Nov 14	1	1
Burkett, Joseph Washington	Mar 14	4	2
Burleson, Byron L.	Sep 5	8	1
Burnett, Reba	Nov 21	4	2
Caffall, Emma	Jun 13	7	2
Callcott, Herbert	May 9	6	3
Campbell, Mary	May 2	6	2
Carney, Lisa Dell	Feb 14	8	2
Carr, Thomas K.	Jan 17	8	2
Carr, Thomas K.	Feb 7	8	2
Carr, Mrs. Thomas K.	Mar 14	1	1
Cartwright, Wade	Feb 7	8	2
Chamberlain, Earl S.	Jul 11	6	2
Chambers, Troy Francis	May 23	6	2
Colbath, Mrs. M. L.	Feb 7	8	1
Coleman, Teresa Gay	Sep 19	1	1
Crenshaw, William H.	Nov 7	8	1
Crum, R. L.	Jan 3	1	1
Culver, Mrs. C. F.	Mar 28	8	2
D'Abini, Mrs. Gus	Jan 31	4	2
Davenport, Joseph E.	Nov 21	1	1
Davis, Minnie Ann	Oct 10	8	1
Dawson, Dan	Feb 7	8	2
Deaton, Jesse Carl	Nov 7	8	1
Deering, Harvey H.	Dec 19	1	1
Denton, Mrs. Howard	Jun 27	8	1
Dicken, Mrs. George D.	Aug 22	1	1
Diehl, Charles William	Feb 28	8	2
Dilley, Mrs. M. F.	Jan 10	5	2
Doran, William H.	Jul 25	6	2
Dowdy, Charlie	May 9	2	2
Dowdy, Mrs. Frank	Aug 15	1	1
Dowling, E. J.	Apr 11	6	1
Duderstadt, George	Mar 21	8	1
Duderstadt, George W.	Mar 28	8	2
Duke, Eddie Gene	Aug 29	8	1
Eason, James	Apr 4	8	1
Epperson, Woodrow	Jul 25	6	2
Ernst, George W.	Sep 5	4	1

217

NAME	DATE	PG	SEC
Evertson, Fred	Mar 21	1	1
Faulk, Henry L.	Apr 11	6	2
Fessenden, Mrs. Leroy (Thanks)	Feb 21	7	2
Finch, Laird Boyd	Jan 17	2	2
Floyd, Ed J.	Aug 8	8	2
Fuglaar, J. V. (Pete)	Sep 5	8	1
Fuller, Nell	Sep 26	2	3
Fuller, Nell Hodges	Sep 12	1	1
Gallatin, Mrs. H. H.	Jun 20	1	1
Garrett, Bill	Mar 28	5	1
Gigandet, James	Feb 14	8	2
Gilbert, P. S.	Dec 19	1	1
Goerner, Dorothy	Jan 17	8	2
Goss, J. B. (Jack)	Aug 8	8	2
Graham, Elwyn A.	Jul 25	1	1
Greene, E. A. (Andy)	Jul 4	1	1
Greene, E, A, (Andy)	Jul 11	6	2
Greeson, C. E.	Nov 21	4	2
Gregg, Mrs. Estelle M.	Apr 11	4	2
Griffith, Benjamin M.	Nov 14	6	1
Grosslicht, Ethel May	Feb 14	4	2
Gydeson, Mrs. C. F.	Aug 29	8	2
Habermann, William	Feb 28	8	2
Hall, Ralph C.	Mar 21	8	1
Hart, Mrs. Sam	Aug 15	1	1
Hartshorn, Mrs. James (Lessie)	May 23	6	3
Hay, Gus Henry	Dec 12	6	1
Hazelett, M. D.	Jun 6	6	2
Heck, William Howard (Jr. Dr.)	Sep 26	1	1
Heckler, Mrs. Charles E.	Oct 31	4	2
Heffernan, Hattie M.	Jan 17	6	2
Henzes, Maude F.	Jan 17	8	2
Herbst, Mrs. Charles	May 2	1	1
Herbst, Theresa Pfeiffer	May 16	3	2
Holcombe, Lizzie Irene	Mar 14	5	1
Holdsworth, Thomas Kirk	Jan 10	1	1
Hollomon, George Guy	Jan 3	5	1
Horne, James	Sep 26	6	2
Hoskins, Clara F.	Aug 15	8	1
Howell, Jewell	Jan 17	8	1

NAME	DATE	PG	SEC
Hull, Jack L.	Nov 7	7	1
Hull, Pearl	Jun 6	1	1
Jackson, Arthur Z.	Jul 25	1	1
James, Thomas	Mar 21	8	2
Jensen, Thomas C.	Jun 27	6	2
Johnson, Norman W.	Jan 31	1	1
Johnson, W. E.	Oct 31	8	2
Johnston, Tommie W.	May 30	8	2
Jolly, Joseph A.	Aug 8	7	2
Jonas, R. L.	Aug 29	8	1
Jones, Gordon,	Aug 1	8	1
Jones, Herman	May 2	3	3
Jones, Lue B.	Jul 4	8	2
Jorns, Mrs. Albert C.	Jul 4	1	1
Jones, R. W.	Jun 27	6	2
Karger, Alex	Oct 17	2	2
Kenley, Wilson	Apr 4	1	1
Kennedy, Roy D.	Oct 10	8	1
King, Olive Wells	Dec 12	6	1
Kinsey, Rhoda B.	Jun 13	7	2
Kipp, Mrs. E. J.	Nov 21	8	1
Kirkland, Fannie	Aug 15	8	1
Kleekamp, Bertha	Jul 25	6	2
Klein, Mrs. Billy Fred	Dec 19	1	1
Knopf, Libbie	May 2	6	1
Knox, J. C.	Aug 22	8	1
Lackey, Elmer F.	Aug 22	1	1
Lainhart, John	Oct 31	5	1
Leatherman, Ella	Jan 3	1	1
Le Blanc, Joseph	Oct 17	7	2
Lee, Mrs. Bruner S.	Dec 12	1	1
Lee, Mrs. John	Nov 7	8	1
Lee, Robert	Aug 1	1	1
Lewis, E. C.	Jun 13	8	2
Little, Lena B.	Sep 5	4	1
Loeffler, Emil A.	Jun 20	8	2
Lovewell, Mary	Jul 25	4	2
Lott, William A.	Mar 28	8	1
Luckett, M. M.	Oct 10	8	2
Luckie, Albert	Feb 28	8	1

NAME	DATE	PG	SEC
Lutz, H. Carl	Sep 26	3	2
Martin, Stokley B.	Apr 4	8	1
Martinez, Jesse A.	Oct 24	1	1
Massey, Ben	Sep 26	1	1
Mateer, Laura	Feb 21	1	1
Matthews, John C.	May 30	8	1
Mauldin, Homer J. (Gene)	Jun 13	3	2
Mayor, Mary Frances	Oct 3	1	1
Mc Cullough, Ethel C.	May 16	8	1
Mc Donald, E. M.	Aug 22	1	1
Mc Elrath, George D.	Sep 19	1	1
Mc Ginnis, Sam H.	Jan 10	1	1
Mc Leod, David (Jr.)	Aug 29	8	1
Mc Kinney, Clyde	Jul 11	1	1
Mc Mains, Mrs. L. A.	Dec 26	3	2
Mc Mullen, Jim G.	Mar 14	8	1
Mc Murtrey, Albert H.	Jun 13	7	2
Mc Pherson, Herbert	Nov 14	1	1
Mell, Carrie Louise	Aug 15	8	1
Miller, Mrs. Robert S.	Sep 19	1	1
Miller, William T.	Mar 28	8	2
Moellendorf, Donna	Apr 25	1	1
Moellendorf, Hugo Henry	Apr 25	1	1
Moellendorf, Margie	Apr 25	1	1
Moellendorf, Theodore	Apr 25	1	1
Moore, Mrs. Charles W.	Feb 14	8	1
Moore, Edwin E.	Jan 3	1	1
Moore, Jennings Talbert	Apr 11	6	3
Moose, Chester	Mar 21	8	1
Morriss, Charles Edward	Feb 28	8	1
Morriss, Robert H.	Oct 3	6	2
Mussaelwhite, Clarence E.	Jan 10	6	2
Nees, Mrs. L. R.	Aug 29	8	2
O'Brien, Annie L.	Sep 5	8	1
Page, Seth Ernest	Feb 14	8	1
Palmer, Jesse E.	Jun 20	1	1
Paris, Tom R.	Feb 14	8	2
Park, Calvin R.	Apr 18	1	1
Park, Calvin R	Apr 25	7	2
Parker, Kelley Coy	May 16	3	2

NAME	DATE	PG	SEC
Patton, Oscar	Feb 14	8	2
Peterson, Hal	Mar 14	1	1
Phillips, Mrs. John	Mar 14	8	2
Pistol, Glenda May	Sep 26	1	1
Poag, Isa Wray	Aug 15	7	2
Prade, Mrs. Earl T.	Jan 31	8	1
Real, Amanda	Oct 31	1	1
Remschel, Roger	Nov 14	1	1
Richardson, Mrs. Walter D.	Jul 4	1	1
Rickerts, Dolores	Aug 1	8	1
Rickerts, John Curtis	Aug 1	8	1
Rickerts, Mrs. John Curtis	Aug 1	8	1
Rinker, Robert	Oct 17	1	1
Rhodes, Sherri Ann	Oct 3	1	1
Robinson, Mary O.	Jul 18	5	1
Ross, Prentice	Jan 10	6	2
Rouse, Mrs. J. M.	Jun 13	3	2
Russell, William C.	Nov 7	4	1
St. Germain, Mrs. Bert J.	Jan 3	6	2
St. Germain, Rasymond J.	Aug 1	1	1
Sandefer, George B.	Mar 21	1	1
Sandersd, Luther B.	Sep 5	8	1
Saucier, John Randolph	Feb 21	6	2
Scheele, Clarence (Thanks)	Jul 11	2	2
Schmidt, Annie	Aug 22	6	2
Schreiner, Gustav F.	Jun 6	1	1
Secrest, Frank H. (Bee)	Aug 22	1	1
Shellhase, Mrs. Henry	Aug 1	2	2
Smith, Alvin E.	Feb 7	8	2
Smith, Mrs. G. Word	Apr 11	1	1
Smith, George W.	Feb 7	1	1
Smith, Gertrude	Jan 31	8	2
Smith, Jesse Lee	Jul 4	8	2
Smith, Percival Martin	Jul 18	7	1
Smith, Mrs. Randolph P.	Jan 17	1	1
Sommer, Albinus P.	Jul 25	1	1
Specht, Rudolph C.	Oct 31	6	2
Spencer, Mrs. C. A.	Mar 28	1	1
Sprague, Lloyd A.	Mar 7	1	1
Sprott, Mrs. Felix	Jul 18	1	1

NAME	DATE	PG	SEC
Stalder, Mrs. Marvin (Dorothy)	Mar 21	8	2
Staudt, Mrs. Rudolph	Aug 22	6	2
Storms, Daisy	May 9	3	2
Stubblefield, James Marion	Feb 21	1	1
Stucky, Clifton C.	Mar 28	8	1
Surber, Bertha	Jul 11	6	2
Swires, Teddie	Oct 31	1	1
Taylor, Lee C.	Jan 17	8	2
Teague, Ella	Jul 4	4	2
Thompson, Stephen H.	Jun 6	1	1
Thornton, Mrs. Prudence F.	Mar 14	5	2
Tobin, Teresa	May 23	3	2
Trevino, Espirion	Aug 15	8	1
Vinz, Louis	Apr 25	1	1
Vogt, William	Dec 19	1	1
Vogt, William	Dec 26	1	1
Wager, Charles Reed	Jul 11	6	2
Walker, Mrs. Roger C.	Jul 18	7	1
Washington, Sussie Victoria	May 23	6	2
Wehmeyer, Arnold	Apr 18	3	2
Weinheimer, A.	Mar 7	1	1
Wellborn, Claude	May 9	1	1
Wells, Roscoe W.	Apr 25	1	1
Weston, M. F. (Mac)	Jan 3	1	1
Whetstone, Mrs. J. F.	Oct 10	8	2
Wiedenfeld, Mrs. Louis	Apr 4	1	1
Willard, Walter W.	Jun 6	1	1
Williams, Albert C.	Mar 14	8	2
Williams, Cecil E.	Aug 8	6	2
Williams, R. D. (Rev.)	Oct 10	8	1
Williamson, Payne Lee	Aug 15	8	1
Wilson, J. N.	Apr 18	2	1
Woodruff, Sanford	Feb 28	8	2
Worrell, L. C.	Dec 12	1	1
Young, James M.	May 30	8	2

NAME	DATE	PG	SEC
Alexander, Alicia Elizabeth	Apr 16	1	1
Anderson, Kenneth Lee	Dec 4	1	1
Anderson, Luther T. (Jr.)	Dec 11	8	1
Andrews, Mary D.	Sep 11	8	1
Attaway, Mrs. E. F.	Nov 13	2	3
Auld, Ayleen Aydeen	Jul 31	1	1
Ayala, Sarita	Jan 30	8	1
Badger, Austin H.	Jun 12	2	3
Baethge, Alvin	Apr 16	1	1
Baker, Charlie A.	Jul 17	1	1
Baker, Virgie	Apr 24	3	2
Baldwin, Clyde	Nov 13	6	3
Baron, Mrs. A.	Nov 13	1	1
Baskin, Ben F.	Mar 20	1	3
Batchelor, Mrs. Sloan	Apr 24	4	2
Baxter, Mrs. George B.	Apr 10	6	3
Beach, Mrs. R. E.	May 15	8	2
Benson, E. J.	Feb 27	4	2
Bertch, Mrs. Charles	Feb 20	8	2
Bessier, Bertha	Jan 30	8	2
Bickham, Mrs. L. B.	Sep 25	6	2
Blackburn, Bessie	Feb 13	8	1
Blume, A. F.	Aug 21	8	1
Bratton, Roy	May 22	6	1
Britt, Elmer	Jul 24	8	2
Brown, George N.	Nov 13	1	1
Broyles, George M.	Feb 13	8	2
Bruff, Mrs. John Harper	Jan 30	5	2
Bugbee, Harold	Apr 3	6	2
Burge, Addison	Aug 21	2	2
Burnett, Mc Collum	Jan 9	7	1
Burney, Mrs. Milton	Aug 28	8	1
Burrough, Earl H.	May 22	6	2
Burrow, Fred	Dec 11	4	1
Buss, Earl Howard	Jan 16	5	1
Butler, Fred R.	Sep 18	8	1
Byrd, Mrs. Robert W.	Nov 13	5	2
Canine, Charles V.	Jun 5	2	2
Carr, Mrs. Wayne	Aug 7	1	1
Carson, Fritz H.	Oct 16	1	1

NAME	DATE	PG	SEC
Carter, A. W. (Jack)	Jan 2	6	2
Carter, Mrs. L. L.	Mar 20	8	1
Cassity, David	Jul 10	8	2
Castleberry, John M.	Jun 12	1	1
Chamberlain, Mrs. Earl S.	Mar 27	6	2
Christley, Paul M.	Aug 21	8	2
Cissell, Glen R.	May 15	8	2
Colbath, Mrs. Rumor	Jan 23	8	2
Coleman, Edward H.	Jul 31	1	1
Coleman, Edward H.	Aug 7	8	3
Coombs, Mrs. Harold G.	Feb 27	8	2
Coose, Oscar W.	Oct 30	5	2
Coots, Sherman M.	Apr 16	6	2
Council, E. A. (Buster)	May 8	6	2
Cowden, Geroge	May 8	5	3
Cozby, Mrs. A. C.	May 1	8	1
Cray, Robert	Oct 30	8	1
Crenshaw, Leonard	Mar 6	5	2
Crow, Alice	Jul 31	6	2
Cunningham, W.	Jan 30	2	2
Davidson, Sam	Aug 14	2	2
Davis, L. T.	Oct 23	6	3
Davis, Lewis T.	Oct 16	1	1
Dennison, Andrew	Dec 11	8	1
Dickey, Mrs. Brooks I.	Sep 26	6	2
Dinwiddie, Mrs. Worth	Apr 24	1	1
Drury, Cooper C.	Oct 30	1	1
Duderstadt, Dena	Nov 6	8	2
Dugosh, Casper	Aug 28	8	2
Edmunds, E. B.	Mar 20	8	1
Edwards, M. M.	Aug 7	7	3
Ellington, Willian Q.	Nov 20	6	3
Emerson, Ralph W. (Sr.)	Nov 6	8	1
Erfurt, Adolph	Jan 30	8	2
Estes, Ned B. (Jr.)	Apr 10	1	1
Fawcett, William C.	Jan 9	1	1
Fifer, Lester G.	Oct 2	6	2
Fish, Katherine	Aug 28	8	1
Flores, Isais G.	Jan 9	8	2
Floyd, Helen	Oct 30	8	2

NAME	DATE	PG	SEC
Fritz, Henry Anton	Mar 13	8	2
Fultz, Mrs. Billie	Jul 31	4	3
Garza, Tobias	Jun 19	4	2
Geddie, Laura Maude	Jul 3	8	1
Gilstrap, Harry	Oct 30	8	1
Goode, Crawford	Jul 10	8	2
Goodman, Lewis P.	Apr 24	4	2
Gotthard, Alvin T.	Jan 2	6	1
Grafa, Julian	Oct 30	8	1
Graham, Mrs. Elihu	Feb 27	8	3
Graham, John	Apr 3	6	3
Graham, O. H.	Dec 4	8	2
Graham, Orville W.	Mar 27	5	2
Grosenbacher, Mrs. Arthur	Sep 11	6	3
Hagerty, William J.	Oct 16	8	1
Haifmaister, Mrs. Elmer	Aug 7	8	3
Hall, Edward (Jr.)	Aug 28	1	1
Hall, Jessie (Thanks)	Oct 23	5	3
Hammock, Billie Joe	Oct 16	2	2
Hardy, Mary R.	Oct 2	4	1
Harrell, S. B.	Aug 21	3	2
Harris, William Temple	May 22	6	2
Harrison, Stella	Jul 24	1	
Harwood, James R.	May 8	5	3
Heinen, Hugo	Dec 25	8	4
Helman, Marie	May 29	8	1
Hendricks, Sam M.	Jan 30	8	1
Henley, Mrs. Jennie Elizabeth	Dec 11	4	2
Hill, Kay Pollen (Thanks)	Feb 27	5	2
Hill, Pearl	Apr 3	1	1
Hill, Mrs. W. W.	Feb 13	8	1
Hine, Fred R.	Jan 16	8	2
Hirch, Minna	Jan 9	3	2
Hixon, B. M.	Sep 18	1	1
Hohenberger, Walter	Dec 11	8	1
Holbrook, Freeman C.	Feb 20	1	1
Holmes, Mrs. E. W.	Mar 27	6	2
Hopkins, Frank Ernest	Sep 11	2	2
Horn, Bessie	Sep 25	8	1
Horn, Fred Nash	Jun 5	8	2

NAME	DATE	PG	SEC
Hornsby, J. L.	Sep 11	6	3
Hulett, Walter K.	May 29	5	2
Hull, Elsie May	Feb 6	4	1
Hunt, Gregory Lance	Jun 12	1	1
Irby, Charles C. (Thanks)	Jan 9	7	2
Jackson, Dannette	Jul 3	1	1
Jackson, James W.	Jul 3	1	1
Jacobs, Kate Jackson	May 1	2	2
James, Leslie	Nov 27	6	2
Jenschke, Angelius	Dec 11	8	1
Jenschke, Otto George	Jul 24	6	2
Jones, Charles C. (Dr.)	Sep 18	1	1
Jones, Cora	Jun 19	5	3
Jones, Emory Louis	Feb 27	7	1
Jones, Pink (Thanks)	Apr 16	6	3
Keith, Otto	Feb 20	1	1
Kendall, Walter	Jul 24	1	1
Kelley, James T.	Oct 2	6	3
Klein, Yolanda	May 22	1	1
Kneese, Walter Otto	Jan 2	6	1
Koerth, Mrs. C. J.	Mar 13	1	1
Koerth, J. C. (Dr.)	Mar 20	6	2
Lacey, John Phelps	Feb 6	4	1
Lackey, Mrs. H. D.	Nov 20	5	3
Lee, Bruner S.	May 29	6	2
Lee, S. M. (Mitt)	Jun 12	1	1
Leinweber, John A.	Apr 3	1	1
Leinweber, Ray G.	Jul 10	1	1
Leinweber, S. G. (Gerd)	Jul 3	1	1
Limbert, Louis Edward	Oct 30	8	1
Lloyd, A. J.	Oct 30	8	1
Lock, Mrs. Albert	Jan 9	1	1
Lopez, Camilo	Jun 12	1	1
Lowrance, Maggie	Jan 16	1	1
Magee, Mrs. Phil	Feb 27	1	1
Mann, Susan	Jan 9	1	1
Martin, Emma	Jul 24	1	1
Mc Clellan, Mrs. C. L.	Sep 18	1	1
Mc Coy, Debra	Oct 9	4	1
Mc Coy, Edward D.	Jul 3	1	1

NAME	DATE	PG	SEC
Mc Donald, Maggie A.	Apr 16	1	1
Mc Donald, Paul C.	Apr 16	1	1
Mc Grew, John A.	Feb 20	7	2
Mc Murtrey, Mrs. E.L.	Nov 6	2	1
Meitzen, Richard W.	Nov 20	6	1
Miltbaler, Royce	Apr 16	6	3
Mitchell, Mrs. L. B.	Nov 20	6	3
Mitchell, Loyd	Oct 23	1	1
Mitchell, M. W.	Feb 6	8	1
Mollendorf, Otto	Aug 28	8	1
Monroe, M. L. (Dr.)	Sep 4	8	1
Monroe, Myrick L. (Dr.)	Sep 11	6	2
Moore, Mrs. Claude	Feb 20	5	2
Moore, Mrs. Wilton W.	May 8	5	3
Morgan, Mary	Nov 20	3	3
Morgan, Yolanda Klein	May 29	8	1
Morris, Mrs. Martin W.	Nov 27	1	1
Mosel, H. Ben	Jul 24	8	2
Motley, J. D. (Doug)	Nov 20	6	3
Mullins, Ben Arthur	Mar 27	6	2
Mund, Benjamin Franklin	Jun 12	1	1
Mundhenke, Elizabeth	Sep 4	8	2
Nash, Phillip Eugene	Feb 27	8	1
Nelson, Frank Clark (Jr.)	Sep 11	1	1
Nichols, Mrs. A. Newton	Dec 11	4	1
Nichols, Mrs. Bruce	Feb 13	8	1
Noble, Margaret	Jun 19	3	3
Nowlin, Radford	Feb 13	5	2
Orr, Nancy Payne (Thanks)	Nov 13	6	2
Osborne, Mrs. Hayden	Nov 20	6	3
Owens, Lon D.	May 15	1	1
Paak, Herman	Aug 14	1	1
Palmerton, James O.	Oct 30	5	2
Parker, Mrs. Sam H.	May 29	3	2
Paterson, William Ed	May 1	6	2
Patterson, William (Jr.)	Nov 27	8	2
Pawloski, Mrs. Herbert G.	Jun 12	5	3
Pearson, Mrs. Dan	Oct 16	8	2
Perez, Olivia (Dr.)	Jul 31	1	1
Peters, Mrs. Ross (Georgia)	Nov 27	1	1

1963
Film Roll #40

NAME	DATE	PG	SEC
Pfeuffer, Mrs. Howard	Nov 27	8	2
Phelps, Mrs. E. E.	Aug 14	5	3
Pickle, Mrs. L. C.	Mar 20	6	2
Piper, Edith M.	Oct 23	2	1
Pool, John C.	Jan 16	1	1
Powell, Vernon	Jul 31	1	1
Powell, Vernon	Aug 7	8	3
Ramsay, Fred	Jun 26	1	1
Rasberry, Gary Ray	Apr 3	6	2
Raymond, Mrs. W. H.	Sep 18	1	1
Rees, D. A. (Dolph)	Jul 17	8	2
Rees, Ivy	Mar 20	6	2
Rees, Louis Luke	May 15	1	1
Rees, Sidney A.	Mar 27	1	1
Rehberger, Ferdinand	Feb 6	1	1
Reid, W. W.	Apr 3	1	3
Richardson, Benjamin	Aug 21	1	1
Richardson, Mrs. Dwight	Dec 11	8	1
Richardson, W. A. (Bill)	Jun 26	1	1
Rios, Raul B.	Nov 13	1	1
Rippy, W. F.	Oct 16	6	2
Roberts, Mrs. William C.	Jul 3	1	1
Robertson, Luther	Nov 27	1	1
Rocke, Nancy Belle	Mar 13	4	1
Rogers, James F.	Apr 16	6	3
Rolfson, Ollie R.	Jun 15	4	2
Ruse, Eugene (Jr.)	Aug 28	5	1
Rust, Herman	Jan 23	7	1
Russell, C. M.	Jan 30	8	1
Russell, J. W. (Jr.)	Mar 13	1	1
Sanchez, Mrs. Florencio	Dec 25	1	1
Sanders, J. A.	Aug 7	1	1
Schofield, Mrs. C. A.	Jul 24	5	1
Scholes, Alma	Sep 11	1	1
Scott, Howard	Nov 27	5	2
Seegers, Thomas Grady	Jun 19	3	3
Shubert, Mrs. Raymond H.	Dec 4	8	2
Simpson, R. Keith	Dec 25	1	1
Singleton, C. L.	Jan 9	5	2
Smalley, Ray W.	Jun 5	1	1

228

NAME	DATE	PG	SEC
Smith, Hazel Stowers	Jan 16	8	2
Snow, Barker	Jul 17	1	1
Spiller, Mrs. R. A.	Aug 7	8	3
Sprott, Mrs. Benno	Jun 19	4	2
Spurgin, Mrs. G. H.	Mar 6	6	2
Stevens, William H.	Mar 20	6	2
Storms, Virgil	May 8	1	1
Stone, Mrs. Austin B.	Nov 27	1	1
Stout, John Oron	Aug 14	1	1
Strohacker, Emilia	Feb 13	5	1
Sullivan, John C,	Apr 3	6	2
Swayze, Mrs. Fannie L.	Feb 6	1	1
Syers, Edward L.	Mar 13	8	2
Taylor, Mrs. E. J.	Jul 3	1	1
Taylor, Mrs, Earl J.	Jul 3	8	2
Taylor, Jo Ann	May 8	6	3
Teague, L. A.	Apr 29	1	1
Terrell, Mrs. E.D.	May 22	2	3
Thomas, Jay W.	Jan 9	1	1
Thomas, Mrs. Johanna Meckel	May 22	6	1
Thompson, Emory	Jun 5	2	2
Thompson, John S.	Feb 13	1	1
Thompson, Mrs. Sam	Feb 20	1	1
Thurman, Andrew J.	Oct 30	8	1
Toler, Richard	Dec 11	4	2
Tom, Walter C.	Jun 19	6	1
Travis, Eugene P.	Dec 18	8	1
Tuttle, Fitzhue M.	May 1	8	1
Vann, Walter W.	Dec 11	1	1
Wade, James S.	Feb 20	8	2
Warden, J. L.	Jan 2	6	2
Warneck, Adolph A.	Jan 23	7	1
Weatherby, W. E.	Sep 4	8	1
Whipkek, Joseph	Jun 12	5	2
Whitehead, Len Alston	Oct 16	8	1
Whittleman, James Robert	May 15	8	1
Whitton, W. A.	Feb 13	5	2
Williams, Roy David	Jan 23	8	2
Willmann, Mrs. A. J.	Mar 6	6	1
Wilson, Leslie Geraldine	Feb 6	8	1

NAME	DATE	PG	SEC
Windom, W. L.	Apr 3	1	3
Womack, Thomas R.	Mar 6	1	1
Wyse, Isabel Bond	Feb 27	8	1
York, Luther Wiley	Feb 13	8	2
Yoss, Fred E.	Dec 11	8	1
Young, Andrew F.	Dec 25	8	4
Young, Mrs. G. W.	Jun 5	8	2
Young, Mrs. James B.	Jun 19	1	1

1964
Film Roll #41

Abbott, Columbus Garve	Jan 15	2	1
Abbott, Oran B.	Mar 11	6	1
Anderson, Anna	Sep 2	5	1
Armstrong, John (Jr.)	Feb 26	6	2
Aubrey, Debra Ann	Mar 18	1	2
Ayala, Natividad G.	Apr 22	2	3
Baethge, Emma	Feb 26	1	1
Baker, Albert	Jun 17	6	1
Baker, Dudley	Jun 17	6	1
Baker, Mrs. Hugh	Feb 12	8	1
Barrett, Byrtie	Apr 22	6	3
Bazan, Davis Castro	Oct 7	2	2
Bean, Elizabeth	Mar 11	2	1
Beaver, H. H.	Nov 4	8	2
Beeman, Mrs. E.A.	Sep 23	6	3
Benson, Robert S.	Nov 4	8	2
Bergman, Arthur	Aug 19	1	1
Bettencourt, Edward J.	Dec 30	1	1
Biermann, Mrs. Louis	Apr 1	8	2
Bigger, Mrs. J. C.	Dec 9	4	1
Billeiter, John	Jul 3	1	1
Black, Q. P.	Jan 29	6	3
Blake, Mrs. J. R.	Dec 23	8	2
Blakeley, James	May 6	1	1
Blevins, John Seaman	Jan 29	6	2
Boulware, Ernest	Jul 3	1	1
Bowles, Percy C.	Jan 22	2	1

230

NAME	DATE	PG	SEC
Brewer, Joseph A.	Jan 15	6	2
Brinkman, Barbara Ann	Jul 3	6	3
Brown, Alonzo Potter	Mar 4	8	2
Brown, Billy Ray	Feb 5	8	2
Brown, Mrs. Everett	Jan 8	8	1
Brown, Goerge T.	Oct 14	1	1
Bruton, Mrs. D. H.	Apr 22	6	2
Bunn, Martin Luther	Aug 26	1	1
Bunn, Mrs. Martin Luther	Aug 26	1	1
Burney, Mrs. Delma (Naomi)	Jul 8	8	2
Burney, William	Mar 18	1	1
Burney, Mrs. William	Jun 10	8	1
Burney, Mrs. William	Jun 17	3	2
Burrer, Milton C.	Dec 2	6	2
Burrer, Milton Charles	Nov 25	8	1
Burris, Clarence	Feb 12	4	2
Butler, Edward W.	Jan 22	8	2
Calentine, Carrie L.	Dec 2	6	1
Canfield, Mrs. P. G.	May 20	8	1
Carden, Laura Doree	Feb 19	8	1
Carmichael, Jesse D.	Sep 23	6	3
Carruthers, Mrs. H. D.	Nov 25	5	2
Case, J. C.	Feb 19	7	2
Castillo, Ramon J.	Nov 25	1	1
Chance, Cornelia Williams	Dec 9	1	2
Chapman, Charles M.	Feb 19	8	1
Clark, Mrs. Ewing	Jun 17	2	3
Cloudt, Frank Monroe	Jan 29	6	1
Colbath, Guy Eric	Dec 16	1	1
Colbath, Rumor	Mar 11	6	1
Coton, Bessie	Dec 22	8	2
Coward, Mrs. D. E.	Feb 12	6	2
Cox, Juliette Grace	Mar 25	3	3
Cox, Thomas L. (Pat)	Mar 4	8	2
Crawford, T. H.	Apr 8	2	1
Crawford, William C.	Aug 12	1	1
Crick, A. D.	Sep 30	1	1
Cummings, Edith Frances	Aug 5	8	2
Cummings, Irene	Jan 29	6	1
Cummings, Pearl May	Dec 30	6	2

NAME	DATE	PG	SEC
Daniels, Morgan	Jan 8	8	1
Davis, Leroy T.	Jan 8	5	2
Davis, Lula B.	Jul 8	8	1
Dibala, Joseph Hubert	Jul 15	1	1
Dionne, Thomas Anthony	Sep 30	8	1
Dismukes, Samuel Walker	May 13	6	3
Doebbler, Reuben (Thanks)	Apr 15	2	2
Dowdy, Frank Gibson	Dec 16	5	1
Dowdy, Carleton Leo	Nov 4	8	2
Dowdy, Mrs. J. A.	Jun 3	5	2
Drewer, Donald	Nov 4	8	2
Duderstadt, Mrs. John	Oct 21	6	1
Dunbar, Mrs. Percy	Apr 15	6	1
Duncan, Jefferson J.	Jun 24	1	1
Durant, Anna Dixon	Sep 30	1	1
Dyson, Jeff Arnold	Jan 8	1	1
Edwards, Dee	Jul 8	1	1
Ehler, Ferdenand E.	Jul 8	8	2
Engleman, Hugh B.	Jul 22	8	1
Fleming, Lamar (Jr.)	Jul 8	8	1
Ford, Mrs. Elton	Jan 29	4	3
Fordtran, Myrtle	Dec 2	6	1
Ernst, William Henry	Sep 2	1	1
Eylicio, Joe	Nov 25	8	1
Eylicio, Mary	Nov 25	8	1
Eylicio, Pat	Nov 25	8	1
Faifer, Mathilda	Nov 4	8	2
Fellay, Gus F.	Oct 14	2	1
Fine, Charles David	Oct 28	5	1
Gamble, John Francis	Sep 2	1	1
Garcia, Arthur	Nov 25	8	1
Garza, Mrs. Ramiro	Dec 30	1	1
Gibson, John H.	Oct 21	6	2
Gideon, Joe	May 20	2	2
Goins, James Harold	Jul 15	6	2
Goodson, W. J.	May 6	5	2
Graves, Hugh Sidney	Jul 22	1	1
Grayson, Mrs. J. M.	Jan 29	1	1
Griffin, Mrs. David	Jun 17	4	2
Habecker, Emil	Jan 29	2	2

NAME	DATE	PG	SEC
Hadden, Will A.	Dec 2	6	2
Hardie, James F. (Dr.)	Jan 22	8	2
Harrell, Frank C. (Rev.)	Dec 9	6	3
Harrison, Archie L.	Oct 28	1	1
Harrison, Mrs. Archie L.	Oct 28	1	1
Harrison, Benjamin Franklin	Jul 15	8	1
Hart, Mrs. James R.	Jun 17	1	1
Hartman, Henry	Jul 29	7	2
Hatch, Enoch	Mar 18	1	1
Haufler, Mrs. Ernst	Jun 3	5	2
Hedrick, Lewis Everett (Rev.)	Feb 19	8	2
Heide, Mrs. Charles S.	Nov 11	8	2
Heimann, Mrs. Clarence	Jan 1	6	4
Heimann, Eddie	Sep 30	8	1
Helm, Gettie Baker	Dec 16	4	1
Henke, August W.	Mar 25	1	1
Hensly, A. A.	Jan 8	4	2
Herzog, Mrs. Oswald	May 20	8	1
Holland, Clara A.	Mar 4	5	2
Holtz, John Wesley	Jan 8	1	1
Hornbuckle, John	May 6	8	1
Hyde, Mrs. H. P.	Jul 29	1	1
Ingram, Marion O.	Aug 26	2	2
Irving, William R.	Nov 4	8	2
Isensee, Mrs. John	Jun 17	4	2
Jackson, Ella Lee	Jan 15	8	1
James, Martha Annie	Jun 10	5	1
Jameson, Almus D.	Sep 30	5	1
Jaschke, Edward	Jan 8	8	1
Jeffers, J. Martin	Feb 19	2	2
Jefferson, Luther J. (Hoss)	Dec 9	1	1
Johnson, Price K.	Jan 1	6	4
Johnson, Mrs. W. E.	Apr 1	3	1
Jones, Mrs. Oakley	Oct 14	1	1
Jones, Mrs. Willie Victoria	Dec 9	6	3
Karger, William	Aug 12	1	1
Kendall, Lourine	Dec 23	6	2
Kennedy, Charles A.	Aug 26	8	2
Kennedy, E. A.	Oct 28	5	1
Kennedy, Fannie Ruth	Feb 19	8	2

NAME	DATE	PG	SEC
Kenisell, Mrs. W. C.	Jun 3	1	3
King, Mrs. A. Arleigh	Nov 18	6	3
King, Tom	Jul 8	8	1
Kirsopp, Doris Elizabeth	Oct 7	4	2
Kleschnick, Samuel	Jun 3	1	1
Kothmann, Mrs. Marvin	Aug 12	6	1
Kuhlmann, Joseph V.	Nov 25	8	1
Kunz, Herman	Jun 24	8	1
Kurtz, Herman F.	Oct 14	6	2
Lackle, Raymond	Jul 22	8	1
Lamb, George Arthur	Jul 22	8	2
Leach, John Sayles	Mar 25	5	2
Leyeendecker, Arthur A.	May 13	4	2
Light, Harvey	Feb 26	6	3
Limberger, Charles F.	Dec 23	8	1
Lockel, Mrs. J. L.	Oct 21	1	1
Lowrance, Robert Shelby	Mar 11	6	1
Maddox, Mrs. E. F.	Apr 22	6	2
Mahon, Edward L.	Nov 25	1	1
Mallett, Mrs. C. J.	Sep 23	1	1
Mandola, Juan	Jan 1	2	1
Manly, Ronald E.	Feb 15	6	1
Mann, Alex	Feb 26	6	3
Marshall, W. C.	Sep 23	6	2
Mather, George	Mar 11	1	1
Matthews, Johnnie T.	Oct 14	6	2
Maxwell, Grace	Sep 30	4	1
Mayfield, William Holly	Mar 11	6	2
Mc Clish, Claude L.	Dec 30	1	1
Mc Cord, Francis	May 27	6	1
Mc Cormick, Albert J.	Jan 8	1	1
Mc Coun, Mrs. Jim B.	Sep 2	8	2
Mc Creight, Mrs. James	Aug 12	6	2
Mc Gee, Mrs. Rendy	Jan 15	8	1
Mc Neil, Mrs. Jobe	May 27	6	1
Meyer, Mrs. Armond	Oct 7	5	2
Miller, Alvin B.	Oct 7	6	3
Miller, Henry	May 27	6	2
Miller, Otto	Jun 3	2	1
Modgling, Henry M.	Oct 21	6	2

1964
Film Roll #41

NAME	DATE	PG	SEC
Moore, Effie	Jan 8	8	1
Moore, Jennie Lou	Dec 2	6	1
Morris, Ben	Apr 15	5	2
Morriss, Hadda Sproul	Oct 28	5	2
Morrow, Mrs. Leonard A.	Mar 11	6	3
Mosty, Karl	Dec 16	1	1
Mosty, Lee A.	Mar 18	1	1
Mosty, Mrs. Lee	May 20	1	1
Negley, Mary S.	Jan 22	3	2
Nelson, Mrs. Frank	Feb 5	2	2
Neunhoffer, William	Dec 2	6	1
Nichols, Flora A.	Feb 12	8	2
Nichols, Mrs. John F.	Oct 14	1	1
Nielson, Mrs. T.V.	Oct 14	6	2
Northrup, Mrs. John	Mar 25	6	2
Oehler, Mrs. Edmund	Mar 18	8	1
Oldham, Mrs. Evan	Apr 15	6	1
Oldham, Raymond	Oct 7	2	1
Pacheck, Mrs. Alois	Jan 1	2	1
Parke, Thomas Jefferson	Nov 18	6	3
Parker, Bart N.	Oct 7	5	2
Paul, Robert E.	Jun 24	1	1
Peril, Robert O.	Feb 26	6	1
Phillips, Mrs. Aaron	Apr 22	2	3
Polson, Glenn L.	Nov 4	8	1
Poore, Homer H.	Mar 4	8	2
Powell, Jennie	Dec 23	8	1
Priddy, Arthur Benton	Nov 18	6	3
Reader, T. E.	Jan 15	6	2
Rhoden, E. F.	Jun 3	6	3
Riley, Mrs. Emil H.	Jun 17	4	2
Robb, Edgar Alfred	Feb 12	6	2
Robinson, Joseph T.	Mar 4	7	1
Robinson, Lily	Nov 25	8	2
Rodriguez, Erasmo G.	May 6	6	1
Roney, John R.	Mar 25	6	2
Rose, Billy Joe	Oct 28	4	1
Russell, Wesley Edward	Mar 4	7	1
Salter, Ray	Oct 28	4	3
Samora, Lucas	May 27	4	3

235

1964
Film Roll #41

NAME	DATE	PG	SEC
Schad, Joseph F.	Sep 9	8	2
Schreiner, A. C. (Jr.)	Jan 1	1	1
Schumacher, Mrs. Will (Alice Clark)	Oct 7	2	2
Schultz, Irene Ottilie	Oct 7	6	3
Scoggins, Serenia M.	Dec 9	5	2
Scott, Mrs. John	Mar 11	6	3
Shanklin, Mrs. J. L.	Nov 11	8	1
Shelby, Carl H.	Feb 15	8	1
Sherman, Nathan	Feb 12	8	2
Shipman, William E.	Jan 8	8	1
Shippy, W. M.	Aug 5	5	2
Skeen, Prentiss (Matt)	Feb 15	7	1
Skinner, Mrs. Willie	Nov 11	6	2
Smith, Mrs. Charles	Jan 8	1	1
Smith, Ethel (Susie)	Apr 22	2	3
Smith, H. Marshall (Rev.)	Dec 9	3	3
Smith, J. R. (Thanks)	Jul 15	7	2
Spears, Miles B.	Sep 2	2	2
Sterling, Albert A.	Aug 19	1	1
Sterne, C. G.	Apr 29	7	1
Stewart, Roscoe E.	Jan 15	6	2
Stone, Cecil (Bud)	Jan 22	2	2
Storey, Mrs. Henry L.	Jan 1	1	1
Storms, George B.	Sep 9	8	2
Streentz, Mrs. F. J.	Sep 9	8	2
Surber, Quincy Clay	Aug 5	3	2
Sutton, Mrs. Harry D.	Aug 19	1	1
Swisher, Warren	Feb 5	8	2
Switzer, Dora	Feb 19	8	1
Switzer, Julius J.	Jun 10	8	2
Taylor, Mrs, Marion L.	Jul 15	8	2
Telford, Edward John (Thanks)	Nov 25	5	2
Thompson, Jim M.	Oct 14	2	1
Thorson, Swan C.	Dec 9	6	2
Torres, Johnny	Nov 25	8	1
Toscano, Ross	Oct 7	6	3
Trimble, Aileen	Nov 11	4	1
Tucker, Levi R.	Nov 11	8	1
Tullos, Hannah Edith	Dec 9	6	2
Turley, John Marshall	Jun 10	8	1

236

NAME	DATE	PG	SEC
Tuttle, Alvin Elmor	Apr 15	3	2
Val Verde, Esteban	Sep 16	6	1
Vonderan, George	Feb 12	8	1
Wallace, Mrs. Henry	Mar 25	1	1
Walters, Vada	Nov 25	8	2
Ward, William	Apr 15	1	1
Warren, James Peyton	Apr 15	3	3
Washan, Mrs. Hayn (Lucille Welder)	Sep 9	1	1
Webb, Grover C.	Jun 24	8	2
Webre, C. J.	Aug 5	8	1
Wehmeyer, Emil G.	Mar 18	3	3
Wehmeyer, Emil Gustav	Mar 11	3	2
Wells, Rufus Le Roy	Dec 2	6	2
Whalen, James	Jun 10	8	2
Wharton, Mrs. Hays	Jul 29	8	1
Wharton, Mrs. N. C.	May 27	5	3
Whatley, Mrs. Howard	Jan 22	8	2
Whilhelm, Charles L.	Feb 5	6	1
White, Etta	Oct 28	6	3
White, Joe Frank	Apl 22	6	3
White, Mrs. John E.	May 6	1	1
White, Viola	Aug 5	4	1
Whorton, J. T.	Jun 10	4	2
Williams, Henry O.	Dec 9	2	1
Willis, William W.	Jul 29	1	1
Wilson, Ruth Tighe	May 6	8	2
Witt, Prentice	Dec 9	1	1
Wolfmueller, Carl H.	Dec 23	1	1
Wood, ----- (Thanks)	Nov 25	2	2

1965
Film Roll #42

Alcala, Rita L.	Jan 13	8	1
Anderson, Merriweather L.	Mar 17	8	2
Appleby, A. D.	Aug 18	6	2
Archer, N. D.	Mar 10	2	1
Ashton, Sidney	Apr 21	8	2
Atkinson, James L. (Jr.)	Jun 16	6	2

NAME	DATE	PG	SEC
Ayala, Gabriel	Sep 29	8	1
Ayala, Jesus	Dec 8	1	1
Baker, Darlene Kenny	May 19	1	1
Bauman, Hazel Jones	Jan 6	1	1
Beaver, Mrs. J. E.	May 26	8	2
Beck, Mrs. C. E.	Feb 3	8	2
Bell, Ernest Hal	Feb 24	2	1
Best, William D.	Jan 13	8	2
Betty, Lemuel P.	Feb 3	2	2
Bierschwale, Frederick	Jun 23	3	3
Blanks, Milton	Sep 15	8	1
Blount, Eula Lee	Nov 24	8	2
Blount, Hubert F.	Aug 25	8	1
Ayala, Gabriel	Sep 29	8	1
Ayala, Jesus	Dec 8	1	1
Baker, Darlene Kenny	May 19	1	1
Bauman, Hazel Jones	Jan 6	1	1
Beaver, Mrs. J. E.	May 26	8	2
Beck, Mrs. C. E.	Feb 3	8	2
Bell, Ernest Hal	Feb 24	2	1
Best, William D.	Jan 13	8	2
Betty, Lemuel P.	Feb 3	2	2
Bierschwale, Frederick	Jun 23	3	3
Blanks, Milton	Sep 15	8	1
Blount, Eula Lee	Nov 24	8	2
Blount, Hubert F.	Aug 25	8	1
Boals, Mrs. Miles A.	Dec 1	6	1
Bocock, Nell	Nov 10	6	1
Boles, Della (Thanks)	Dec 8	6	2
Briggs, Fred S.	Jan 27	6	2
Brown, Mrs. F. E.	Dec 15	6	3
Brown, Lorna C.	Jun 2	8	1
Brown, Mrs. W. E.	Feb 10	8	1
Burns, David L.	Jan 27	1	1
Burt, Mynard	Jan 6	1	1
Bynum, Mrs. Meddie Trimble	Jun 2	1	1
Cade, Gilford	Sep 29	8	2
Campagna, Mrs. Angelo	Mar 17	8	1
Carter, Oscar James	Sep 8	1	1
Cavell, Henry	Dec 1	1	1

1965
Film Roll #42

NAME	DATE	PG	SEC
Childers, M. A.	Dec 29	4	1
Clark, Leonard A.	Jul 28	6	1
Clark, Mrs. Walter S.	Nov 3	1	1
Clarke, Mrs. L. A.	Aug 18	6	1
Clower, Mrs. B. B.	Apr 14	2	2
Colbath, Trudie	May 19	1	1
Collins, Mrs. Preston	Nov 10	6	2
Cooper, Jennie Hill	Jun 30	6	2
Cooper, Manly W. (Sr.)	Mar 24	1	1
Copenhaven, Charles Wayne	Dec 29	5	1
Cottle, Roy	Jul 7	8	1
Couch, Christopher Robert	Oct 20	3	2
Cowden, Mrs. G. E. (Thanks)	Jun 2	3	2
Crawford, Timmy Ray	Nov 24	8	1
Crider, Donna A.	Feb 3	5	2
Cronk, Mrs. Walter	Dec 1	6	3
Crow, Annie Walker	Oct 20	4	3
Crow, R. N.	Jun 1	1	1
Dakin, Charles A.	Mar 17	3	2
Daniels, Al	Mar 31	5	2
Delaney, Joe Curtis	Apr 14	1	1
Delory, Mrs. Pearl	Dec 22	2	1
De Masters, F. L.	Mar 3	8	2
De Vore, Sue Carol (Thanks)	Jan 20	8	1
Dietert, Randolph L.	Apr 14	8	1
Dinsmoor, Mrs. L. E.	Sep 8	1	1
Dowding, Eva	Oct 6	1	1
Doyle, Mrs. George M.	Mar 17	1	1
Durden, J. M. (Thanks)	Jan 27	3	2
Eads, Alice	Jun 16	6	2
Eckler, Eugene B.	Oct 20	2	1
Eikel, Mrs. Charles	Jul 21	1	1
Elam, Kelley L.	Aug 11	6	2
Espinosa, Juan	Oct 6	1	1
Evans, John E.	Nov 24	8	1
Fahrenthold, Jonelle	Oct 13	6	1
Fahrenthold, Mrs. Robert	Oct 6	6	1
Fairis, Percy	Dec 22	1	1
Fanning, Richard	Aug 4	1	1
Faribault, Clara	Mar 24	8	1

NAME	DATE	PG	SEC
Fellows, Ada R.	Mar 10	8	2
Fernandez, Antonio	Sep 8	1	1
Fernandez, Michael	Sep 8	1	1
Fernandez, Peter Anthony	Sep 8	1	1
Findlater, Frank	Nov 24	8	2
Fischer, Mrs. John	Apr 21	4	2
Forman, E. M.	Aug 18	1	1
Foster, Thomas E.	Feb 3	5	2
Fox, Neal B.	Dec 29	4	1
Fry, Mrs. Morris	Feb 10	6	2
Garrett, Blanche	Apr 14	5	2
Garrett, William Gray (Jr.)	Oct 6	1	1
Garza, Mrs. Logina A.	Mar 3	3	2
Garza, Kirk Allen	Apr 28	6	2
Gillespie, Hubert Eugene	Sep 8	1	1
Goff, Mamie	Sep 29	1	1
Granholm, Mrs. John	Nov 24	8	1
Graybill, M. H.	Dec 15	1	1
Greene, Magnolia Neighbors	Sep 15	8	2
Grona, Herman	Nov 17	6	3
Gumbert, Herman Henry	Sep 22	6	2
Haire, Annie	Mar 3	8	2
Hallenberger, Virgil Lee	Dec 1	6	2
Hamm, Amy M.	Dec 22	1	1
Hansen, Helga	Jun 23	6	2
Harrell, Mrs. Willie Ethel	Jul 14	8	1
Harris, Joseph A.	Dec 15	1	1
Hart, I. H. (Jack)	Apr 28	8	2
Haufler, Erhard	Mar 10	2	2
Heidel, C. W.	Sep 22	8	2
Heimann, Theresa	Dec 22	1	1
Heinen, Hubert	Feb 24	6	3
Henderson, Howard Bailey	Sep 1	8	2
Hessler, Carl A.	Jan 20	8	1
Hilburn, Harry H.	Jan 13	8	1
Hobbs, Lee L.	Sep 15	8	2
Holekamp, Mrs. Dan T.	Nov 10	6	3
Holloway, William R.	May 5	3	2
Holmes, Mrs. James D.	Sep 22	2	2
Hood, Marcus M.	Sep 8	1	1

NAME	DATE	PG	SEC
Hood, William Newton (Thanks)	Jun 2	6	2
Howell, Carol R.	Oct 27	1	1
Hubble, Robert D.	Jun 9	1	1
Hutchinson, Guy	Apr 7	5	2
Inman, Mrs. Ike	Jan 20	8	2
James, Frank	Sep 22	8	2
Jennings, William H.	Mar 10	8	1
Jetton, Terry L.	Apr 7	6	1
Jobes, Sam Shelby	May 12	6	1
Johnson, Emma D.	Jan 27	1	1
Jorda, Anna Julia	Dec 1	6	3
Jordon, William W.	Apr 21	8	2
Joseph, Mrs. August	Sep 22	8	2
Joseph, Mrs. Fritz	Mar 31	4	1
Junkin, Mrs. E. D.	Aug 4	6	1
Justice, Mrs. J. E.	Sep 8	8	1
Kane, Herbert	Mar 17	3	2
Karger, Mrs. Harry	Jan 20	1	1
Karnes, Henry	Aug 25	5	1
Kelley, Earl (Thanks)	Dec 1	6	3
Kennedy, May L.	Feb 3	1	1
Kihlberg, Fred	Sep 15	1	1
Kitchum, Floyd A.	Jan 20	8	1
Klugman, Mrs. A. (Margaret)	Nov 10	6	3
Klugman, Kenneth	May 26	8	1
Kneese, Harry E.	Mar 17	4	1
Kovar, John	Oct 13	1	1
Kovar, Mrs. John	Oct 13	1	1
Kramer, Walter	Sep 22	8	2
Kunz, William Ernst	Mar 31	5	1
Lackey, Ann Elizabeth	Oct 13	1	1
Lackey, Mrs. Lamar	Oct 13	1	1
Lawson, Marion S. (Bud)	Apr 28	5	1
Layton, Chester P.	Jul 28	6	1
Leavell, Ruby	Dec 8	6	1
Lee, Mrs. Josie	Feb 3	8	1
Leinweber, Mrs. Roy	Jul 14	8	2
Lindhart, Walter	Jul 28	6	3
Lloyd, Connally	Feb 3	4	2
Lochte, Mrs. Werner A.	Jan 13	8	2

1965
Film Roll #42

NAME	DATE	PG	SEC
Lohmann, Minnie	Apr 28	4	2
Ludeke, Leonard H.	Mar 31	4	1
Mann, R. J.	Mar 17	8	1
Mc Conley, Eugene C.	Nov 10	6	2
Mc Kim, Mrs. Ray	Aug 25	1	1
Mc Vey, Ada	Jan 6	8	2
Meador, Illa	Feb 10	8	1
Meikel, Edward	Feb 3	3	2
Merritt, Mrs. W. H. (Pop)	Jun 2	8	2
Michon, Regina	Jul 7	1	1
Miesch, Jack	Dec 1	6	3
Mitchell, Alice Swearingen	Jun 23	1	1
Moellendorf, Edward A.	Sep 1	5	1
Moore, Charles W.	Sep 22	1	1
Moore, Harry	Dec 29	4	2
Moore, Mrs. Tom J.	Sep 29	1	1
Moore, Willie B.	Jan 27	8	2
Morrow, Mrs. Carl C.	Mar 3	7	2
Morrow, George	Jan 6	8	2
Moston, Harry	Dec 15	6	3
Muse, Richard Howard	May 12	5	1
Neuhaus, Henry Joseph	Dec 22	1	1
Newton, Hosea K.	Oct 27	2	1
Nichols, Robert R.	May 12	4	1
O'Bryant, Anna	Nov 3	6	1
Oehler, Theo	Dee 1	6	3
Oestreich, Terry Wayne	Aug 18	1	1
Orgain, William	Nov 24	2	1
Orr, James	Aug 13	6	2
Page, Cleve	Feb 3	8	1
Parker, William R.	Oct 20	6	1
Pennybacker, Mrs. John	Nov 24	8	1
Pettit, Mabel	Dec 15	1	1
Pickett, Mrs. Guy	Oct 6	5	3
Pulliam, Roy	Jun 2	8	1
Rader, Frank	Dec 1	6	3
Rader, Mrs. Frank	Dec 1	6	3
Ray, Ben Clarence	Sep 8	1	1
Reeh, Bruno	Jan 27	8	2
Remschel, Robert H.	Jun 16	1	1

242

NAME	DATE	PG	SEC
Richards, Mrs L. S.	Feb 3	4	2
Rippy, Mrs. Ollie Powell	Dec 8	3	3
Roberts, Ella Baldwin	Mar 10	8	2
Roberts, T. C.	Mar 24	6	2
Robinson, Ruby R.	Aug 4	6	1
Rogers, Proctor W.	Oct 6	6	1
Rutledge, May B.	May 12	6	1
St. Germain, Bert J.	Mar 10	4	1
Sanchez, Maria	Jun 22	8	1
Sanders, Mrs. Dewitt	Sep 22	7	2
Sanders, Douglas R.	Oct 27	6	1
Sandidge, George T.	Oct 27	6	3
Saunders, Dewitt	Apr 14	5	1
Schleuter, Edwin	Apr 14	6	3
Schumacher, Henry	Feb 10	8	1
Scott, Fannie	Nov 17	6	3
Shand, Meta	Jan 6	8	2
Shepherd, Mary Virginia	Nov 17	8	1
Simpson, Mrs. R. K.	Jul 28	6	3
Smith, Arthur	Feb 24	6	3
Smith, Charles	Mar 17	3	2
Smith, James B.	Jan 13	1	1
Smith, Mrs. M. E.	Dec 22	1	1
Smith, Mae	Aug 25	1	1
Spann, Albert	Jun 16	8	1
Spenrath, Fritz	Nov 24	8	1
Spenrath, Martin	Aug 11	6	1
Startzman, Ervin Lynn	Dec 15	4	2
Staudt, Lawrence E.	Aug 18	6	3
Staudt, Tlitha Mae	Oct 6	6	1
Stevens, Marion	Sep 22	5	2
Stewart, George	Dec 8	6	1
Stieler, De Wayne	Dec 22	1	1
Stockton, Frances Iola	Nov 24	4	1
Stone, Luare	Sep 8	8	2
Stratton, Bess	Jun 16	1	1
Streetman, Mary M.	Apr 21	5	1
Swayze, Mrs. Thomas	Jul 7	8	2
Sykes, Rachael	Mar 24	8	1
Tatsch, Ferdinand	Apr 7	5	2

NAME	DATE	PG	SEC
Taylor, Marion L.	May 5	3	2
Teague, Thomas B.	Mar 10	8	2
Thacker, Mrs. R. B.	Nov 3	1	1
Thomas, Nancy Witt	Oct 6	6	1
Thompson, Mrs. Grady	Sep 1	1	1
Thompson, Herbert L.	Apr 28	8	1
Thompson, Mrs. Hoxie	Dec 22	1	1
Torres, Mrs. Pete (Delphina Gomez)	Jun 2	1	1
Travis, Mrs. Eugene P.	Aug 25	8	2
Villaneuva, Aurelia S.	May 5	4	1
Wahrmund, Mrs. Alfred	Apr 21	5	1
Walton, Orel P.	Oct 13	6	3
Watkins, Armanda (Mrs. Ted Sr.)	Sep 8	1	1
Watkins, Mary Eleanor	Feb 24	6	3
Watters, Alice T.	Jan 20	8	1
Weatherby, Dan	Dec 15	1	1
Weatherby, Mrs. Dan	Dec 15	1	1
Webb, J. Coates	Apr 21	1	1
Wedekind, Mrs. Fred	Sep 1	8	2
Weinman, Mrs. Wilhelm	Jun 9	4	2
Wells, Sherman T.	Sep 22	6	2
Werkstein, Mrs. Frank	Dec 15	6	3
Whalen, Katie C.	Nov 17	6	3
Wheatley, Kahler	May 12	6	1
White, Lillian Akers (Thanks)	Oct 13	6	3
Whitley, Ada Garland	Jun 16	5	2
Whitley, Claude M.	Sep 22	1	1
Wilke, Mrs. Eugene	May 19	6	3
Williams, Mrs. Donald (Bertha Wood)	Dec 8	6	3
Williams, Mrs. Mathew	Apr 28	8	1
Williams, Mrs. Sam J.	Mar 10	1	1
Williams, Roxie	Jan 6	1	1
Wilson, Adam (Jr.)	Feb 3	1	1
Wingfield, W. W.	Jan 20	8	2
Wiseman, Mrs. Sinton	May 12	2	1
Wood, Ruby	May 26	7	2
Woodin, Percy Thad	Dec 22	1	1
Wray, Bruce	Apr 7	5	1
Yarbrough, Nelson	Dec 8	1	1
Yarbrough, Mrs. T. W.	Jul 7	1	1

1965
Film Roll #42

NAME	DATE	PG	SEC
Yokley, Otto D.	Dec 8	1	1
Young, Annie Katie	Mar 3	8	2
Young, Ara Dee	Dec 29	1	1
Zumwalt, Isaac W.	Oct 13	1	1
Zumwalt, William T.	Jul 28	3	1

245

www.ingramcontent.com/pod-product-compliance
Lightning Source LLC
Chambersburg PA
CBHW071349280326
41927CB00040B/2417